Litigation Nation

THE AMERICAN WAYS SERIES

General Editor: John David Smith
Charles H. Stone Distinguished Professor of American History
University of North Carolina at Charlotte

From the long arcs of America's history, to the short timeframes that convey larger stories, American Ways provides concise, accessible topical histories informed by the latest scholarship and written by scholars who are both leading experts in their fields and polished writers.

Books in the series provide general readers and students with compelling introductions to America's social, cultural, political and economic history, underscoring questions of class, gender, racial, and sectional diversity and inclusivity. The titles suggest the multiple ways that the past informs the present and shapes the future in often unforeseen ways.

CURRENT TITLES IN THE SERIES

LITIGATION NATION

A Cultural History of Lawsuits in America

Peter Charles Hoffer

ROWMAN & LITTLEFIELD
Lanham • Boulder • New York • London

Published by Rowman & Littlefield
An imprint of The Rowman & Littlefield Publishing Group, Inc.
4501 Forbes Boulevard, Suite 200, Lanham, Maryland 20706
www.rowman.com

6 Tinworth Street, London SE11 5AL, United Kingdom

British Library Cataloguing in Publication Information Available

Library of Congress Cataloging-in-Publication Data

Names: Hoffer, Peter Charles, 1944–, author.
Title: Litigation nation : a cultural history of lawsuits in America / Peter Charles
    Hoffer.
Description: Lanham, Md. : Rowman & Littlefield, 2019. | Series: American ways |
    Includes bibliographical references and index. |
Identifiers: LCCN 2019015617 (print) | LCCN 2019018352 (ebook) | ISBN
    9781538116586 (electronic) | ISBN 9781538116579 (cloth : alk. paper)
Subjects: LCSH: Torts—United States—History. | Actions and defenses—United
    States—History.
Classification: LCC KF1250 (ebook) | LCC KF1250 .H64 2019 (print) | DDC
    346.7303—dc23
LC record available at https://lccn.loc.gov/2019015617

Contents

Preface

EVERY BOOK HAS A HISTORY. This one began many years ago with a paper read to the McNeil Center for Early American Studies in Philadelphia. That paper explored a sudden and puzzling increase in the volume of civil litigation (one person suing another) in the early eighteenth-century British North American colonies. What I found was both striking and simple. A significant shift had occurred in the way people expected to do business with one another. Some sellers and buyers of goods with interests in transatlantic trade had adopted a more formal way of paying for transactions involving British North American colonists, while other colonists, more traditional in their outlook, wanted to retain customary face-to-face methods of doing business. When disputes between these two groups erupted, the result was litigation.

I folded those findings into a little book on law in the American colonial world. Over time, after extending my exploration of litigation to the nineteenth and twentieth centuries, I came to believe that litigation and cultural expectations were linked throughout our legal history. When one party's sense of honor, based on cultural beliefs, is offended, they sue the offending party. When that party, clinging to another set of cultural values, feels his honor is slighted, he refuses to settle. The result is litigation. That is the project I present here.

The book is topical; that is, each chapter addresses a different type of litigation. The book is also chronological, in that each topic reflects a particular time and place, and the chapters as a whole move from the seventeenth-century origins of our law and courts to the present day. More on the organization of the book appears at the end of the introduction.

I am grateful to N. E. H. Hull for her reading of the manuscript; to John David Smith, consulting editor of the American Ways series, for his edits and his extraordinary patience with the author; and Jon Sisk at Rowman & Littlefield for sticking with the project. My colleagues Cindy

Hahamovitch and Scott Nelson read and greatly improved chapters 4 and 5, respectively.

One final thought: when one looks at the law in America, one usually focuses on constitutions and famous cases. This book is chock full of cases, but few of them are famous. Instead, they are typical of the sorts of cases that ordinary Americans find themselves litigating. That is intentional on my part. What makes litigation so important to our history as a nation is how it reflects the lives and values of ordinary people.

Introduction

Litigation and Honor

MECHELLE VINSON WAS AN ATTRACTIVE bank teller pleased when her boss found her work excellent and promised to promote her. What he did instead, she alleged in a lawsuit, was attempt to seduce her. The case of *Meritor Bank v. Vinson* (1986) left a mark on the corporate business community that spread to higher education, the military, and the media—for it was the first case to include hostile workplace environment in the definition of impermissible sexual harassment.

There had been forms of sexual harassment—offering or trading sexual favors for promises of advantage—in the workplace from time immemorial. Then the Civil Rights Act of 1964's Title VII made such conduct suspect, the Equal Opportunity Employment Act of 1972 threw a spotlight on women in the workplace, and the rise of second-stage feminism raised the consciousness of working women. Sexual harassment became legally actionable. That is, instead of job retention at will, the firing or demotion based on a woman's refusal to accept sexual favors, or based on her objection to sexual advances, or even a sexual innuendo that made a workspace a hostile environment was grounds for relief in federal courts. That is what happened when Mechelle Vinson filed her lawsuit in 1978.

Fired from her job, even after the District of Columbia (federal) district court dismissed the suit, she persisted. Finally, in 1986, the U.S. Supreme Court found in her favor. A hostile work environment was grounds for a harassment lawsuit thereafter. What had happened was that a new cause of action (i.e., grounds for a suit) arose when one woman adhered to the new rules of women's place, and when her employer clung to the older customs of sexual conduct.

In a larger sense, litigation like Vinson's expresses a plaintiff's sense that the defendant's conduct imperils the community itself. The plaintiff comes to believe that he or she speaks for the community when he or she brings a lawsuit in its courts. For their part, defendants force the issue because they believe that their rights are the rights of everyone around them; they hold fast for the sake of the community as well as for their own. Individualized in this way, rises in litigation rates not only reflect societal influences upon groups of potential litigants but also express individual litigants' attempts to restate and reinforce the social values of their society when it appears that these values are under attack.

Litigation enables an individual or an entire community to explore and test the boundaries of permissible personal conduct. When large segments of the population experience these feelings, litigiousness swells. These occur in periods of cultural and social change and evidence a temporary disparity between new and old social norms. When the boundaries become indistinct or too many people seem to be crossing the boundaries, litigation will increase. When the values of a community are under attack or are changing too rapidly for potential litigants—plaintiffs or defendants—to control, men and women will troop to the courts to reassert traditional, unwritten rules.

Removed from procedural technicalities into its social and cultural context, litigation appears as one of the many paradoxes that dot the landscape of American history. Embodying this simultaneous adherence to opposites—like freedom and slavery, individualism and the need to belong to organizations, optimism and insecurity—litigation is a phenomenon that brings us together in the very act of pitting us against one another. A people of laws and lawyers, we are addicted to lawsuits—watching them, starting them, and defending them. Litigation is more than a ritualized form of civil combat; it is also a measure of our commitment to a rule of law. While no one can ignore examples of domestic insurrection and vigilantism like the Civil War and lynching, at our best we look to the law to formulate and carry forward our quarrels with one another and with those who govern us. Litigation is not just part of the American way of life. It is an emblem of the American way of life.

—␣℩␣—

Mechelle Vinson was not alone in bringing her plaint to court. We are a litigious society. One scholarly study, while admitting that it was difficult to quantify rates of lawsuits, still found that the United States led the way in the western world in civil litigation, with 5,806 suits filed per 100,000 adults in a sample year, compared to 3,681 in the United Kingdom, the nearest competitor. In 2017, according to the U.S. courts website, federal noncriminal (civil) filings in the district (trial) courts numbered over 292,000 cases. Federal criminal prosecutions initiated in the same year numbered almost 76,000. These numbers vary from year to year, but the ratio of civil to criminal is more or less stable.

To handle this tide of lawsuits, lawyers were multiplying in numbers and importance in our professional world. In 1870, Wisconsin had only 784 lawyers (men who identified themselves as lawyers on the census at least) for a state population of a little over a million people. The numbers for Michigan, Illinois, and Minnesota were similar. In 2014, there were 91,000 registered lawyers in Illinois alone. More than 30,000 of them practice in greater Chicago. "The amount of litigation, the number of lawyers, the density of legislation and regulation, the expenditures on law, and its presence in public consciousness," according to one expert observer, were all climbing throughout the past quarter century.

The number of lawsuits filed each year does not increase in straight-line fashion, however. Instead, it waxes and wanes. For example, looking just at civil cases in the federal trial courts, the war years 1942–1945 saw an average of twenty thousand cases filed each year. In the postwar period through 1958, that number averaged over thirty-five thousand cases, peaking in the years 1957 and 1958 at over forty-five thousand. Then, for the period 1959 through 1962, the number fell to thirty-eight thousand, after which it began a steady march upward into the two hundred thousand range. On its face, a linear increase in cases filed makes sense, for the population of the nation was rising too. Given this, the rate of cases—the number of cases filed divided by the number of people who could file cases—remained stable, then declined noticeably in the 2000–2017 period. If within these figures there were surges and ebbs, the sheer numbers were still staggering. Add the federal criminal cases, from 1996 to 2017, and over 4.5 million were cases filed. Then, turn to the state cases, with data from the National Center for State Courts, there were 18 million civil cases in 2007, "leveling off" to 15.3 million in 2016. Some fluctuations might be dismissed as random variation, but others hint at historical shifts in the way Americans see one another's conduct, and misconduct, which we explore in the chapters that follow.

—⁕—

The cast of characters in the story of American litigation includes clients, lawyers, and judges. Cases usually begin, as did Vinson's, with an aggrieved person. Alas for our understanding of the roots of litigiousness, in law-school teaching and law books, the client as a living, breathing, unique person tends to disappear. Only the law is important. The slave Dred Scott vanishes after the first round of suits for his freedom in Missouri, even though the case *Dred Scott v. Sandford* (1857) was a leading cause of the secession crisis three years later. In *Plessy v. Ferguson* (1896), Louisiana mulatto Homer Plessy brought a suit to end Jim Crow segregation in railroad cars, but when his suit to end segregated seating was appealed to the U.S. Supreme Court, he dropped out of the picture. What remained was the pernicious doctrine that separate but equal satisfied the Equal Protection Clause of the Fourteenth Amendment.

In theory, lawyers are the agents or representatives of clients. Clients are individuals or groups who instruct lawyers to do what the client wants. In this sense, the lawyer is an intermediary. Instead, as legal expert Robert Dinnerstein reported in 1990, most lawyers act as the protagonist, speaking for both plaintiff and defendant. "The Lawyer is concerned with the Client's reaction to his advice but tends not to value client input, for he believes that the client has little of value to contribute to the resolution of his legal problem."

Legal historians have tried to recover the client's story as she or he told it to the lawyer. Fictional accounts of lawyering, and documentaries on famous law cases, get us close to the client, although the imagination of the media makers has to fill in gaps where the historical record is lost. In books and movies like Harper Lee's *To Kill a Mockingbird* and Scott Turow's *Presumed Innocent*, the reader/viewer does get to meet the client. In the cases discussed below, the historical record does not afford a similar intimacy.

Sometimes the surviving record allows the historian to watch over the shoulder of the lawyers, however. This perspective can help reconstruct the relationships between the lawyers and their clients as well between lawyers and judges. We can see that lawyers approach relationships with clients in different ways. Law professor Deborah Rhode suggests that there are four major types of such lawyers, or rather, lawyering styles. The first is the lawyer who is an intimidator. S/he bullies the other side, makes threats, and may even do this with his or her own client (in their best interest, one supposes). Famous "tort" (civil harms like slip-and-fall cases) lawyers like Melvin Belli and Louis Nizer were examples of this style. The second style is the "authoritative stance," in which the lawyer leads by linking the particular case to higher principles. Civil rights lawyering often exhibited this style, as lawyers for the Legal Defense Fund of the National Association for the Advancement of Colored People (NAACP) like Thurgood Marshall departed from the details of a case to limn out the larger goals of equality and fair treatment. A third style is one in which the lawyer is the client's friend. These lawyers not only engage in representation of clients, but they also sponsor social and cultural events around the cases and often engage in public service. Finally, there is the lawyer as coach. One sees this most often not in courtrooms, but in fields of law teaching and mentoring. They help other, usually younger lawyers set out in their careers. Before the advent of law schools, young lawyers learned their trade by working in an established counselor's chambers. As bar associations began to demand law degrees, this function shifted to the shoulders of law professors. Many of these professors would go on to sit on the bench, where they engaged in another form of coaching—working with newly graduated law student "clerks."

Whatever their personal inclination and choice of role, more and more often lawyers have become the managers of litigation. In particular, lawyers for large entities, like corporations, banks, insurance companies, manufacturers, and the government, have replaced the client as the center of the suit, making key decisions with minimal or nonexistent client input or approval.

The last of the formal players in the legal system is the judge or justice. We think of the judge as the robed, impartial umpire behind the raised bench at the front of the courtroom. We expect judges to be fair, learned, and respected. Most judges are just that. Some are not, and their failings are cause for public outcry. Judges have two additional jobs that are not so familiar to the layperson. The first is managing the litigation, working with clients and lawyers to reduce the time and cost of the trial or the appeal. The second is writing opinions on issues raised during the litigation.

There are important differences between state and federal judges. State trial and appeals court judges are elected, sometimes after an initial appointment. Federal judges are nominated by the president, confirmed by a majority vote of the Senate, and appointed by the president (he signs their commissions). Most federal judges are either assigned to district courts, whose purpose is to try cases, determine facts, and render verdicts (if a jury trial) or bench decisions (if no jury), or to various special kinds of courts, for example bankruptcy courts. Today, most cases that go to district courts are settled before the trial stage. State court systems have more or less the same hierarchical structure—many trial courts, a few courts of appeals, and one supreme court—as the federal court system.

Appeals court judges sitting in the twelve federal circuits hear a much smaller number of cases based on some disputed point of law. The appeals can come from lower federal courts or from state courts. They can be based on disputes over the application of the law to the case at hand or over the meaning of the law itself. The U.S. Supreme Court is the highest appellate court in the land, and since the latter portion of the twentieth century it can hear or not hear an appeal as it wishes. In earlier days, however, it could not avoid appeals and so had a much heavier load (actually about ten times as heavy) as it does today. Then as now its most important product is the written opinions of the justices that accompany their votes on cases.

As federal appeals court judge and law professor Richard Posner has written about judging, in rendering a decision, the judge can take into account a wide variety of information. The "rules of the game" require the judge to look at precedent (earlier cases' opinions on the same subject), black letter law (codes and statutes), and the various briefs of the counselors in the case, as well as briefs of "friends of the court" (amicus curiae), and legal scholarship. Even "externalities" like the political and economic impact of any particular decision can figure into the judge's decision. Judges are constrained in the latitude of their decisions by their concern for their reputation among their peers and among expert observers of the court. Some judges were innovative legal thinkers. Some refused to color outside the lines. Some were liberals. Most were conservative. We shall meet both kinds in the pages that follow.

Legal scholar Robert Cover wrote that there is a kind of "violence" in judging, for in the American adversarial system there are winners and losers. Judges are not supposed to be part of the adversarial system. They are above and outside of the process of advocacy. At his confirmation hearing, future chief justice John G. Roberts Jr. called this "calling balls and strikes." But as every fan of baseball knows, the hardest job in umpiring is calling balls and strikes, because the strike zone of every home plate umpire is a little different. Baseball technology has narrowed those differences, but a similar effort at lockstep formulas, for example congressionally imposed sentencing guidelines, has not worked as well in the real world of judging. As Posner and Cover agreed, judges are real people living in a real world, and their decisions will reflect the values of that world. Although the opinions of judges and justices in the cases that follow appear almost Mosaic in their authority, in fact they were products of a time and place, and subject to interpretation and, over time, reversal.

—⚏—

It would be nearly impossible in the format of a book for the general reader to trace the full complexity and detail of American litigation. A differently organized book can make the point as effectively. By focusing on a particular topic in each chapter, and following the evolution of that area of law over time, one can show how litigation represented changing American ideas of self, American business practices, and American notions of right and wrong.

At the core of each of the topics in the following chapters are case studies. The cases exhibit the contest of values that are typical of the litigation of the period, humanizing and deepening our understanding of those times and places. Each chapter concludes with a coda bringing the story of that kind of litigation up to date.

In part I, the first chapter tracks an explosion of defamation suits in the seventeenth-century colonies, wherein servants, mistresses, and masters who had in England known and more or less accepted their place in the social order, in the New World accused one another of all manner of mischief. East Hampton Township on Long Island was one focal point of this miniature status uprising. The ruckus would lead to the first colonial witchcraft scare. The coda shows how defamation of public figures today demonstrated changing notions of right and wrong.

The second chapter follows a major shift (what I have called a "phase change") in the way the American colonists did business, focusing in particular on land disputes in eighteenth-century New Jersey. Real estate transactions whose principals did not know one another partially supplanted older customs of face-to-face exchanges of plots. The former involved documents that ordinary people did not understand. Plaintiff and defendant had to hire trained lawyers to carry on the litigation. A coda returns to litigation over mortgages, descendants of lawsuits over title.

The third chapter turns to slave sales and estate disputes in the antebellum South, tracing a striking rise in suits for fraudulent sales and contested wills. This spike in litigation reflected the southern slave society's shift from vigorous self-confidence to defensive anxiety. The courts were a cockpit of these often bitterly contested cases. The coda returns to the issue of reparations for slavery.

Chapter 4 turns to the rise of free labor, focusing on suits for back pay, the appearance of craft unions, and damage awards for accidents. It closes with the most important of the modern version of these lawsuits—guest worker suits.

In part II, we encounter a spurt of railroad shareholder suits, as new kinds of corporate business organizations replaced older partnerships. In the Gilded Age, railroads were the leading edge of these new kinds of corporate entities, and the creation of the Northern Securities trust became the nation's great test of the tactics of the owners. The coda returns to the *Regional Rail Reorganization Act Cases* (1974) and a foreboding omen of corporate malfeasance for which the shareholders paid, the Enron scandal.

Chapter 6 follows a rise in divorce suits in the first years of the twentieth century, as changing views of marriage and gender roles worked themselves out in the courts. Among the most reform minded of all the states' tribunals, the New York courts experienced this shift in attitudes in telling fashion. New York was also the origin of *U.S. v. Windsor* (2013), the case striking down the Defense of Marriage Act (1996).

Chapter 7 turns to the civil rights suits of the second half of the twentieth century, surveying how a gradual change in race relations spurred litigation over school segregation and public accommodations. The key cases are *Briggs v. Elliot* (1953) and *Bell v. Maryland* (1963).

The final chapter examines an explosion in consumer tort cases, showing how the world of consumption habits in everyday life had become at the same time more faceless and more deeply personal. Called mass products liability, these involved some of the most wealthy corporations and thousands of the most ordinary Americans. The Dalkon Shield class action suit of the 1970s and 1980s captured all of these elements.

A conclusion returns us to the themes of honor and phase change in values, featuring *Boy Scouts of America v. Dale* (2000).

Why defamation, land speculation, slavery, labor, railroading, divorce, civil rights, and mass products litigation? Because all of these types of lawsuits brought ordinary people into the legal records, and this in turn made the legal record a record of ordinary people's concerns.

Part I

Litigation Defines a Nation

CLAIMING THAT LITIGATION DEFINED the new American nation seems both vague and overbroad. It is neither. From the inception of the English colonies, the settlers demanded laws that they could understand, retooled the charters the crown gave into miniature constitutions, fashioned local and colony-wide courts, and gave to justices of the peace and judges great discretion. In turn, those justices and judges strove to keep order and, in the main, to adjudicate disputes among their neighbors fairly and expeditiously.

Of course, the relative status of the parties before the court mattered—as it mattered in politics, marriage, commerce, and occupational opportunity. When the fourth and fifth generations of these colonists concluded that they would no longer be a part of the British Empire, they turned to law to define their controversy and claim their independence. The Declaration of Independence was a legal document crafted by lawyers like Thomas Jefferson, John Adams, Edward Livingston, and Roger Sherman. The fifth member of the drafting committee, Benjamin Franklin, was not a lawyer and had little to do with the actual wording of the document. In the meantime, another lawyer, John Dickinson, shaped the Articles of Confederation that held the sovereign states together until delegates to a constitutional convention in 1787 fashioned a more permanent federal government.

The whole of the revolutionary constitutional achievement, the basis for republican self-government, rested on the concept of rule of law. States no sooner accepted the separation from Britain than they wrote their own constitutions. The legislative branches of those new governments got busy recasting the English common law into an American mold. As I have written in another context, "The revolutionary lawyers stepped into the role of constitution drafters and lawgivers. The revolutionary lawyers' participation in the new confederated and state governments set a pattern, a precedent if you will, of a public role for lawyers outside of the courts." It was the trust that ordinary colonists and colonial leaders, revolutionaries, and nation builders placed in law and tested in litigation that underwrote this grand experiment in republican self-government. Going to court, wagering one's law, accepting the outcome or at least the authority of the law—these were the struts and beams on which the new nation rose.

The proof of revolutionary legalism lay in the hands of a new generation of Americans. Led by lawyers like John Quincy Adams of Massachusetts, John C. Calhoun of South Carolina, Henry Clay of Virginia and Kentucky, Andrew Jackson of South Carolina and Tennessee, Martin Van Buren of New York, and Daniel Webster of New Hampshire and Massachusetts, Americans continued to take their woes to court. A third generation, including Edward Bates of Missouri, Salmon Chase of Ohio, Stephen Douglas and Abraham Lincoln of Illinois, William Seward of New York, and Alexander Stephens of Georgia went from the bar to public service. All of them were litigators before they were political leaders, and in litigation they learned that law and democratic republicanism were inseparable.

In 1860, the U.S. census showed over one hundred thousand lawyers servicing the litigation needs of a free white adult population of seven million. The counselors were busy, for in addition to filing and arguing in court, they advised clients in the increasing variety of potential lawsuits. The rise of insurance companies, rail and canal corporations, and new kinds of financial products opened up challenging avenues of litigation. A great sectional conflict between slavery and free labor loomed on the horizon, and this too found its way into the courts. Secession by eleven southern states would test the commitment to conflict resolution by litigation—though few at the opening of 1860 anticipated the catastrophe to come.

1

Defamation

DEFAMATION IS THE TERM THE LAW USES for slander by word of mouth and libel in print. Today it is a part of "tort" litigation, suits for damages or injunctive relief against a person, persons, or a corporate body for saying or printing untrue statements that harm the plaintiff's reputation. The offense was a civil one in old English law, but it had a criminal cousin. If one published a criticism of the government, it was the felony of seditious libel.

Both of these offenses came with the law the first English colonists brought to America. Here they took new forms. Defamation was the most common civil complaint in the seventeenth-century colonial courts and demonstrated that English social caste could not survive intact in the New World. In the eighteenth century, the defamation of public figures became much more prominent on the courts' dockets and provided a test of a new idea of freedom of speech. Modern defamation suits are still with us, and once again they show how sharp and sudden changes in attitudes can spur litigation.

—⁂—

In many ways, the English migrants to the first North American colonies were representative of the home population. The majority of the newcomers, reflecting the economic demography of England, were bound labor. A few among the immigrants to New England had been substantial homeowners and brought with them or summoned from England household servants. They knew their place in society, and their betters expected the lowly to behave in an appropriately servile manner in the New World. In the southern colonies, contract laborers, called indentured servants, worked the fields alongside landowners' family members. In the Tidewater edge of the Chesapeake Bay, the farms of the better sort, called plantations according to the custom of the Caribbean, were unlike any in England in their adoption of slave labor. The planters, perhaps even more than the family farmers to the north, brought with them a vast array of social and cultural assumptions about the ordering of society.

As in rural England, the new colonial settlements were face-to-face societies. One did business with one's neighbors on a barter basis—labor in exchange for labor or goods. Parties recorded these exchanges in ledgers or other books of obligations. A person's reputation for honesty and fair dealing, or, on the contrary, for sharp practices, would have been well known by neighbors. There was little privacy in these settlements, with the result that everyone pretty much knew everyone else's sexual proclivities. Elizabethan moral codes made premarital and extramarital sex taboo, and accusations of such conduct were another fertile source of defamation suits. In such a face-to-face society, with reputation meaning so much to people, defamation, accusations of moral misconduct, or other slurs were not only hurtful to the victim; they were a peril to the very basis of social order.

Initial expectations to one side, the newcomers' ideal of an ordered society of rank and status soon began to fray in the colonies. Servants who did not know their place challenged their masters in court. Masters and mistresses libeled one another's families. Although deference was the rule in public conduct, in private there was little resembling class solidarity and less enforcing rank. Words were the weapons of those who felt aggrieved, and the local courts were soon nearly swamped with defamation suits. In a face-to-face world, gossip and rumor had a force that today manifests itself in blog trolling and other forms of online insult.

The town and county courts were among the first and the most visible institutions of local government in the early colonies. In them, rumor, gossip, and insult climbing up and down the social ladder led to lawsuits, with masters suing their servants and servants suing their masters. Families broke apart over these lawsuits, as the lawsuits brought into public infamy what previous generations had concealed or negotiated privately. The county court records show that most of the plaintiffs won their suits, but most of the damages awarded by the juries of their peers were small. As far as the justices of the peace sitting on the bench were concerned, the point of the exercise was to keep order. For the plaintiff and defendant, however, the defamation suit had a different and far more intimate purpose.

In some way the most potent of these suits was an accusation of sexual misconduct. Not that the English in America were prudes. Premarital and extramarital sex was fairly common, and about half of all births came before betrothal. But from the first, accusations of sexual misconduct seemed to provoke the most virulent responses. No sooner was the court assembled at Accomack County on the eastern shore of Virginia, in 1634, than Edward Drew swore that Joane Butler had called Drew's wife Marie a "common carted hoare." Not only was the accusation slander per se (in itself), but it suggested that Drew and his wife were members of the lower class. Butler admitted to using those words and in court begged pardon for them. In the meantime, her husband, Thomas, filed a slander suit against Marie Drew. Apparently she had started a rumor that he had slept with Bridgett Wilkins. At the time, the county had a little more than a few hundred English settlers, but that was enough to sustain a vigorous rumor mill about sexual incontinence. In England these sexual slurs would have been handled in church courts under canon law, but in early Virginia there were no such courts (and no clerics to sit in them). Instead, the cases went to the common-law courts of the colony.

There were also slander cases that began not in the bedroom but in the shop. The Derbys of Salem, Massachusetts, were a merchant family. Rival shopkeeper Thomas Maule allegedly persuaded customers not to trade with the Derbys. Such words might have proved the Derbys' ruin and had to be scotched. Folks who should have been doing business with one another according to the fair-trade principles of the day instead flew at rivals in *Derby v. Maule* as "base, cheating, Rogue and one eyed doggs." When the Essex, Massachusetts, county court met in Ipswich in 1663, a commercial dispute merged into a social one and instead of being settled in the town court went to a jury at the county sessions. It seemed that one John Hathorne, a merchant of means (and later a judge in a more infamous trial for witchcraft), had taken offense at his treatment by the town's marshal, a social inferior, and warned, "I hope to make a fool of you before I have done with you."

Surges of defamation suits came at particular moments in what one might call the life cycle of a settlement. After the initial labor of clearing land, when life was a little less precarious and the settlers had a little more time on their hands, the old social rules brought from England began to fray. That happened at different times in different colonies. For example, travel back in time to 1638 and down the coast from Ipswich to the newly founded town of New Haven at the mouth of the Quinnipiac River. New Haven was supposed to be a godly commune. Its minister expected piety, and its magistrates expected obedience from all the men and women gathered there—particularly the better sort of settler. The court records from 1639 to 1672 are complete and demonstrate that the wealthier members of the colony were the most frequent plaintiffs, far outnumbering their lower-status neighbors. The wealthiest were also disproportionately defendants in lawsuits, the result of what historian Mary Beth Norton called a "temporary condition of unusually intense conflict" within the upper tier of the population.

Soon after the founding, cases of slander among the members of the extended Pinion family showed how town members breached the traditional boundaries of private quarrels and animosity. When in court Patrick Moran dodged any fines for allegedly slandering Goodwife Hannah Pinion and her sisters, he brought a lawsuit of his own against all three of them for slandering him as "a base rogue and rascall." Caught in the middle, Hannah's husband Nicholas Pinion told the court he wanted nothing to do with the lawsuit. In the meantime, all the venom among what should have been godly neighbors spilled out into the public arena.

The Pinions were only one of the many families whose members suddenly found themselves in court accused of or accusing others of defamation. Even married women, who were supposed to be represented in court by their spouses, brought such lawsuits in their own name, although more than two-thirds of the parties in these slander suits were men. The gravamen (accusation) was sexual misconduct, financial malfeasance, and lying in court (usually in an earlier slander suit).

Take the case of Richard Beckley, whose feud with neighbor Francis Hitchcock exploded into a cascade of insults and landed Beckley in the New Haven court in 1659. It all started with gossip among the womenfolk, the widow Hitchcock whispering a rumor to Beckley's wife who promised to keep silent but then told Beckley all. Hitchcock learned of it and was furious. She accused Beckley's wife of prattling. Not willing to let this pass, Beckley sued Hitchcock for slander, and arbitrators told Hitchcock to apologize. Hitchcock refused and upped the ante by adding to her charges against Beckley's wife that she was a liar and trouble-maker. Beckley confronted Hitchcock, and the two went at it, according to Beckley's later testimony. The widow allegedly uttered provocative words and wished that he and his wife would be hanged. What for? Well, Hitchcock told neighbors that the Beckleys were thieves and Sabbath breakers. Hadn't she seen their children picking blackberries on the day of worship? But evidence presented in court, for now the magistrates could not let the quarrel continue, convinced the court that Hitchcock was poisoning the public peace with her venomous contumely.

The backstory: when Hitchcock's husband was alive, he and Beckley argued on a regular basis. Beckley was no stranger to the court either, suing and being sued for slander. Beckley, as it happened, was a figure of some importance in the colony; the Hitchcocks were of lower social and economic status. The quarrel demonstrated that people were sensitive about their relative ranks, even in the frontier colonies, and tried to use the courts to protect that status from attacks, but the protection went both ways—lower-status individuals like the Hitchcocks were having none of the airs of their supposed betters.

As the Hitchcocks of the early colonies discovered, defamatory speech could blow up in one's face. Defense of one's reputation and status could lead to a spiral of retaliation, including public revelations of one's or one's family's own slanderous conduct. Call someone a bastard or the mother of a bastard and be prepared for mudslinging from the accused, their friends, and their family. The very act of setting neighbor against neighbor, as Hitchcock and others found, was grounds for fines or a more serious punishment in court. A slander suit could silence rumors, or ignite them. Common ill fame may not have rested on evidence, but that was no bar to its rearing its head in court. There were really no rules of evidence as there are today—the slander case was simply an argument in front of the magistrates.

Clues to when and how defamation contagions erupted come from a close reading of early legal records. They are tantalizingly incomplete, but one can tease out what happened when men and women could not temper their words. Timothy Breen's research into the history of one Long Island Puritan community reveals what happened when the authorities could not quash an epidemic of defamation. On the south prong of Long Island (N.Y.) Sound, in East Hampton, in the 1650s sat a young community of

English men and women, almost all of them farmers. Some were well-to-do; others were servants or day laborers. All were Protestants. A godly community in theory, in practice they seem to have enjoyed nasty gossip and malicious accusations. Given the size of the population, a remarkable number of these landed in court. Fragmentary trial records redound with accusations of theft, verbal assault, and, sometimes, witchcraft. In the village, female servants who did not get along with one another, or with their mistresses, and goodwives sometimes had little good to say about one another. Whether the fluidity of status, the newness of the settlement, or the nearness of danger loosened tongues, the defamation cases began to pile up in the early 1650s.

The epidemic of lawsuits began when two farmers, Benjamin Price and William Edwards, went to court to settle a dispute over a business deal. Edwards's wife was not a party to the transaction, but she soon had a part in the court case. She told everyone that Price and the township had no authority to bring a legal action against her husband. He was soon back in court with an accusation of his own, against Price's wife for slandering Goodwife Edwards. Neighbors summoned to court testified that both women were breaking the peace with their words. Edwards's wife was the older woman and expected deference from Price's wife. The young should respect their elders. Price's wife's reply was that Edwards's wife was a base liar, and he brought witnesses to court to prove it. As the charge and countercharge of defamation spiraled out of control, a new and more potent accusation arose: witchcraft.

The contagion of whispered slander and angry accusation soon infected leading men like William Mulford. He accused the servants and the householders of the Garlick farmstead of slandering Mulford's wife. This would not do—the Garlicks were a family of far lower status than Mulford, and servants should mind their tongues. In the meantime, the founder of the village and its only aristocrat, Lion Gardner, denounced two of his neighbors, Goodwife Simons and, once again, Goodman Garlick. It was true that both had shown contempt for the well-born Gardner, a disease that the Gardners' servant John Wooley caught as well. According to one witness, he was prone to make barking noises when Gardner's wife's back was turned.

All of which fueled the ill feeling that spread through the community in the waning days of the harsh winter of 1658. Elizabeth Howell, Gardner's daughter, fell ill that cold and damp season. Just having delivered a child, she feared for herself and her newborn. Her illness, perhaps postpartum infection, developed into mortal fever. Delirious, Howell announced that she was the victim of witchcraft, the culprit as yet unknown. To protect her, Goodwife Simons agreed to stay at her bedside, and Goodman Simons kept his wife company. Although they saw and heard nothing as Howell passed into eternity, Goodwife Simons had a good idea of who the witch was—none other than the generally disliked Goodwife Garlick.

The accusation required the attention of the leading men who doubled as the village's judges. They soon discovered, if they did not already know, that Garlick had been the target of a spate of rumors and suspicions long before Howell fell ill. The investigation empowered the women of the village to voice their own concerns, for witchcraft was a very domestic, private offense, occurring in homes, at night, when the villagers were most vulnerable. It was all hearsay, however, particularly the parts about devilish familiars and death-dealing potions. The town, overwhelmed by the case, turned it over to the authorities in Connecticut, across Long Island Sound. There it was settled, distance quieting the tongues of Garlick's accusers.

Witchcraft accusations in New England always began with slander raging out of control. Consider the case of Eunice Cole of Hampton, New Hampshire, recounted in the research of historian David D. Hall. Cole was in and out of courts in Massachusetts because her neighbors shared stories of her witchlike powers. According to John Mason, she cursed him and he fell ill. Elizabeth Pearson refused to help, and she came down with aches and pains. Jonathan Thing saw Cole appear and disappear ahead of him on the street as if by magic. Elizabeth Shaw swore that she heard puppies whining near Cole, but saw nothing. On the basis of these accounts, the court tried Cole by a jury but found her "not guilty but suspicious." Cole was lucky. In Salem, Massachusetts, nineteen years later, eighteen other women and men were convicted in court on the basis of similar defamatory testimony and hanged as witches.

Cases like Goody Garlick's and Eunice Cole's connect many of the dots of an American way of litigation. Plaintiffs brought suits when they thought that a malefactor had wronged them and in the process endangered social order. Defendants refused to settle when they thought that plaintiffs were violating community standards and needed to be taught a lesson. In the process, whole communities became involved. Civil litigation was never just about mine and yours—individual winners and losers. Though ultimately resolved in a legal setting, it always contested larger social and cultural norms in the legal arena. In the first years of East Hampton, good behavior of servants, sexual continence among young people, and obedience to one's betters was the code of the upper class, and when the lower classes rebelled against that code, litigation for slander and ultimately for suspected witchcraft showed the gulf between the old and the new sets of social mores.

Hundreds of defamation cases littered the county courts of Massachusetts before 1680, and there were 145 lawsuits for defamation in Maryland between 1630 and 1680. No one, even a magistrate, was safe from these suits. Then, almost as suddenly as it had erupted, the rage of words quieted, and defamation suits took their place as a small part of a much larger local court docket. Something had changed back as the colonies matured—a growing understanding of the new world order of things, in which a rough equality of status and place among free white persons was important, and all parties seemed to get the point. A new class had appeared among them: African slaves. In law, slaves could not be defamed, as they had no legal identity. They could not defame others, as they could not be brought to court to answer the charge. Free persons recognized the danger in defaming one another when slaves could overhear and spread the stories. Slaves who served food or pulled the ropes on ceiling punkahs (fans) in the dining room were often sources of this kind of gossip in the slave quarters. Racial unity required a self-imposed auditory orderliness among whites. In slave country, defamation still reared its head, but only briefly. Gossip that reached the wrong ears, from master to slave, to slave, to another master, might all too easily result in the alternative to the defamation suit—the duel.

—⁂—

Lawsuits for alleged personal slurs continued to roil settler communities in the eighteenth century, but another kind of defamation suit became more common as the number of private defamation cases ebbed. When officials brought lawsuits for defamation, the stakes were higher than in purely private litigation. One of Pennsylvania's first laws near the end of the century forbade "spreaders of false news" and "clamorous, scolding, and railing" against officials. While "contempt of authority" was a criminal offense, and offenders might be fined or corporally punished, an official could also bring a civil suit for defamation against a private person.

Nathaniel Byfield's litigiousness demonstrates what such a suit could bring. Byfield came to Boston a young man and quickly established himself as a leading merchant in the emerging Anglo-Massachusetts trade network. He would enjoy a long career in law and politics as a representative to the General Court and then as a member of the colonial council. At various times he was also a judge of the court of common pleas and probate for Bristol County and a judge of the vice admiralty court for the colony. He was a lay judge—he never practiced law, save when he went to court to plead his own cases. One of these ran on for almost two decades and shows the close tie between public office and legal influence in this era of litigiousness. (Note that there was no bar to multiple office holding in the colonies. That came with the checks-and-balances system of the first state constitutions.)

Byfield was one of the founders of the town of Bristol, gaining from the General Court (in which he then sat) permission to lay out a town and distribute land within its borders. Byfield was not a humble or conciliatory man, and soon he and the other founders of the town were quarreling. The townspeople took sides, local government was in an uproar, and Byfield found himself backed to the wall. A rugged antagonist emerged in Nathaniel Blagrove, owner of the town mill and other property in Bristol. Blagrove was the administrator of the estate of the Hayman family, and in that capacity he brought a private action against Byfield for failing to make payments on a mortgage. In fact, Byfield had tried to make good the missed payments, but Blagrove wanted the property, not the payments. The superior court gave judgment to Blagrove. Byfield struck back through the General Court, of which he was currently the Speaker, inducing that assembly to pass an act allowing those owing money on mortgages (including Byfield) to prevent foreclosure by paying what they owed. The act also specified that foreclosure proceedings begun during the previous two years (a period covering the time that Blagrove had filed his suit) could to be retroactively brought under the new rule.

Byfield sought an equitable remedy for his missing mortgage payments called "equity of redemption," which allowed late payments. Procedure in equity was far simpler and more accessible than procedure in the law courts. In law, a case started with the filing of a "writ" with the clerk of the court. Every case had to fit one of the preexisting categories of writs. In equity, the petitioner made out a complaint in ordinary language and named a remedy and filed it with the clerk. In a law case, evidence was presented at the trial. In equity suits, the parties took depositions and presented them in court. The law courts had jurisdiction over things, for example goods or property in dispute. In equity, the judge had jurisdiction over persons. Judges sitting in equity might order a wide array of remedies not available to parties in law, including injunctions. These were commands to the parties to do or not do some act. The injunctive relief of the court of equity is the grandparent of the civil rights injunction, for today all federal courts are courts of both equity and law.

The act did remedy a genuine problem—Massachusetts temporarily had no courts of equity to offer the equity of redemption (preventing foreclosure on mortgages)—but Byfield was not a disinterested do-gooder. Barbara Black, who has traced his twists and turns, ties Byfield's thinking to the issue of dignity and good faith: "From Byfield's perspective, Blagrove's behavior was villainous, an unconscionable attempt to take improper advantage of accidental circumstances [that is, the temporary absence of a court of equity] to impose the full rigor of the common law [which did not allow equity of redemption]."

Byfield was not finished with Blagrove. Byfield not only had "pull" in the General Court; he was also a valuable ally of Governor Joseph Dudley. From the governor he obtained the post of judge of probate (wills and estates) in Bristol County, and then Byfield turned the tables on Blagrove. While sitting as judge in the probate court, Byfield convinced one of the heirs to the Hayman estate to sue Blagrove for mismanagement in the probate court. Brought before Judge Byfield, Blagrove knew he was in trouble. Byfield demanded that Blagrove give a full account of his administration of the entire estate. When Blagrove delayed, Byfield arranged for the governor's son, Paul Dudley, to act as counsel for the heir. At the same time, Byfield himself brought an action against Blagrove for £6,000 in the court of common pleas for not fulfilling his duty to the heir in Byfield's court. Blagrove was being squeezed between his personal enemy Byfield and Byfield the judge. Blagrove tried to appeal to the governor and council, but Governor Dudley, after hearing his son, lawyer Dudley, speak against the appeal, ruled that the common law must take its course without interference from the executive.

Blagrove had one hope left: just as equity jurisprudence could allow a defaulting mortgagee to redeem a piece of mortgaged property, in equity one could reduce ("chancer") a penalty bond down to the actual debt owed. Blagrove pleaded that the administration bond of £6,000 was just like a penalty bond, and he should only owe to the heirs what the will promised them, a sum considerably smaller than £6,000. Alas, after hearing this argument, the justices of the Superior Court of Judicature, all friends of Byfield, declared that they could not chancer the administration bond because they did not know what the underlying debt was.

The story might have ended there, with Blagrove a crushed victim of highly partisan justice, had Blagrove not been so tenacious. Instead, he resisted paying the £6,000 to the court of probate while he petitioned the General Court to instruct the justices of the superior court to chancer the bond. At last they agreed and so informed the justices. In effect, the General Court, a legislature, had acted as an appellate court. Now the tables had turned on Byfield. Ordered in his capacity as probate judge to obey the higher court, he refused, and for his refusal (expressed in very intemperate language) he was removed from his post as probate judge. *Byfield v. Blagrove* demonstrates the way in which personal dignity wove its way into litigation. It also shows that public officials were not above using their offices for private purposes. In a time when the distinction between public office holding and private interests was not so well drawn in public law, litigation provided an opportunity to draw that line in individual cases.

Where was the phase change? It was the blossoming of a new conception of officeholding, in which colonial elites were beginning to regard public office as a public trust rather than a patronage plum, and colonial voters were beginning to insist that electees represent the interests of the voters. The assembly insisted on this. Byfield resisted it. After all, he was well connected with the governor and through him with the imperial authorities. That did not matter to the colonial assembly. They wanted offices in the colony to be responsive to the people. One can see the colonial crisis of the 1760s looming in the distance. In it, the crown's officials clung to the orders of their distant masters, while colonial assemblies demanded that offices in the colonies belonged to the colonists.

One could say that the crisis of the 1760s in the colonies rode a wave of defamation. Defamation of character and reputation had become a standard tactic of political rivals by the middle of the eighteenth century. Anonymous pamphlets and newspaper editorials routinely called opposing politicians villains, rascals, and cads. During one Connecticut race, young Benedict Arnold was dismissed as a "designing man" who only sought money and popularity. No longer was the basis of calumny exclusively sexual (although the language might suggest it). Now it was alleged political corruption that was the target.

When England's prime minister, George Grenville, decided to reform the colonial system by forcing colonists to pay taxes in 1765, angry colonists replied with a campaign of public vilification. Across the neck of land that connected Boston with the rest of Massachusetts there appeared "liberty poles" and effigies festooned with intemperate language. Accusing government officials of corruption, even if true (especially if true), was the crime of seditious libel, but fortunately for the Sons of Liberty, Grenville and his minions were three thousand miles away. The calculated insult, shouted by the mob or published anonymously, became a potent political weapon against the British authorities: those "fawning scriblerius . . . that infamous miscreated leering Jacobite . . . that stamp man" were insults that worked the mob into a fury and directed its energies against Parliament and the crown. There was no counter to it in law if the governor or the sheriff could not bring the defamers to court.

—⁓—

In the 1790s, defamation would become a mainstay of early national politics, ultimately leading to the first national experiment with anti-defamation law and litigation. The decade was a time of domestic furor and international war familiar to Americans today. The Treaty of 1778 that brought French funding, supplies, troops, and a navy to the aid of the American revolutionaries included a mutual defense pact between the United States and France. Its terms were limited to the duration of the War for Independence, but in honoring those terms the French government nearly bankrupted itself. That fiscal strain in part led to the calling of a National Assembly, and then to the creation of a constitutional monarchy. By 1792, the French political crisis had turned revolutionary, and with radicals leading the way, a republic replaced the monarchy. Radicals executed the king and the queen the next year, and a reign of terror descended upon the nation. Asked by the French for support in its war against Britain, President George Washington demurred. He judged that neutrality was the safest course for the new nation.

In Congress, James Madison, joined by Secretary of State Thomas Jefferson and their supporters, feared the British and saw the French Revolution, despite its excesses, as an experiment in liberty similar to America's in 1776. Secretary of the Treasury Alexander Hamilton and his allies, calling themselves the Federalists, favored Britain. They feared the antireligious sentiments of the French radicals and benefited from trade with Britain. In 1794, domestic divisions and foreign policy controversies led to the formation of electoral parties. Both parties sponsored newspapers that defamed the other party's leaders and policies. Alexander Hamilton, writing in the Federalist *Gazette of the United States* on June 13, 1798, warned that "the French Faction in America would go all lengths with their imperious & unprincipled Masters . . . ready in the gratification of ambition vanity or revenge, or in compliance with the wages of corruption, to immolate the independence and welfare of their country at the shrine of France." Republican Benjamin Bache's *Philadelphia Aurora* thundered back that President John Adams and the Federalists were "hatchers of conspiracy" to destroy American liberties.

On the floor of Congress, defamation led to physical confrontations. Matthew Lyon, a Republican who had fought in the War for Independence, incensed at what he thought was the condescending manner of fellow representative Roger Griswold, insulted Griswold. Griswold replied that Lyon was a coward. Lyon then spat in Griswold's face. On February 15, 1798, the battle resumed, as Griswold entered the Independence Hall chamber where the lower house met and beat a seated Lyon on the head and shoulders with a cane. Lyon roared back defiance and leapt to the fireplace, where he armed himself with a poker. The two men then engaged in a duel with hickory and wrought-iron weaponry. The choice of weapons was telling: Griswold, a Federalist from one of the elite families of the Nutmeg State, and Lyon the upstart Vermont brawler, were appropriately armed. No one was hurt, and the House amused itself by debating whether Lyon, the instigator (he spat in Griswold's face), should be censured or expelled.

President John Adams, elected in 1796 after a hotly contested election, was stung by the insults, but it was the leaders of the Federalist Party in Congress rather than Adams who proposed a solution to the problem of inflammatory public language. The First Amendment to the Constitution that Madison introduced and Congress passed in 1789, and the states ratified in 1791, barred Congress from abridging freedom of speech or of the press. One way around the amendment was the resurrection of an older but never quite forgotten English concept of free speech: no prior censorship. On June 23, James Lloyd of Maryland introduced legislation that made any publication of "false, scandalous, and malicious" statements that defamed the government, or brought it into contempt or disrepute, or caused anyone to "hate" the government, subject to fines and imprisonment. Truth was a defense, but the truth of political opinions was hard to prove. Was John Adams really a "rascal"? Were the Federalists really trying to undermine American liberties? Hamilton, whose pen was as busily scurrilous as any of the Federalists, nevertheless was appalled at the new law. On June 29, 1798, he wrote to Oliver Wolcott, his successor as secretary of the treasury, "I hope sincerely, the thing may not be hurried through. Let us not establish a tyranny." Republicans in and out of Congress protested, to no avail.

The bill passed. Adams (somewhat reluctantly) signed it. Federalist federal marshals were soon rounding up Republican editors and writers for trial before handpicked Federalist juries presided over by Federalist judiciary. Vice President Jefferson left Philadelphia and returned to his home outside of Charlottesville, stopping briefly on the way to consult with James Madison at his Montpelier estate in the summer of 1798. Madison was already preparing a set of resolves against the act for the consideration of the Virginia House of Delegates. Jefferson prepared his own response and, after some delay to test the temperature of opposition to the acts, gave it to Kentucky's attorney general John Breckinridge, a friend and fellow former Virginia planter and politician. Breckinridge was also a member of the Kentucky assembly. Jefferson asked Breckinridge to present it to his state's assembly, but to keep Jefferson's authorship secret. It was not revealed until after his death. Breckinridge did as

Jefferson asked, only making one notable change in the draft—he took out the word "nullification."

In the meantime, Madison was working away on a draft of his own resolves. He was the author of the First Amendment and presumably knew what it meant. He presented a set of resolutions to the Virginia House of Delegates that winter of 1799 condemning the act. It clearly violated the First Amendment. The freedom to offer opinion on politics was the only sure foundation of liberty in a republic. That was why freedom of speech, the press, assembly, and petition were all vital to the survival of a republican government. He expanded on these views in 1799: "This security of the freedom of the press requires that it should be exempt not only from previous restraint by the Executive, as in Great Britain, but from legislative restraint also; and this exemption, to be effectual, must be an exemption not only from the previous inspection of licensers, but from the subsequent penalty of laws." He was consistent when he reminded the Virginia legislators that "in the United States the executive magistrates are not held to be infallible, nor the Legislatures to be omnipotent; and both being elective, are both responsible."

By contrast with Madison's temperate writing, Jefferson's resolves packed a wallop, for they not only concerned the Federalist legislation; they concerned the very nature of the federal government. In them one can see how far the controversy over defamation had spun out of control. Jefferson wrote that "the several States composing the United States of America, are not united on the principle of unlimited submission to their General Government; but that, by a compact under the style and title of a Constitution for the United States, and of amendments thereto, they constituted a General Government for special purposes." Later thinkers with different purposes would expand this notion into "states' rights," the theory that the Constitution bound together sovereign states by their own consent, and the federal government could exercise only those powers "delegated" to it explicitly in the Constitution. All other powers were reserved to the states. "Whensoever the General Government assumes undelegated powers, its acts are unauthoritative, void, and of no force."

Jefferson added that "the government created by this compact was not made the exclusive or final judge of the extent of the powers delegated to itself." He went on to argue that "all their other acts which assume to create, define, or punish crimes, other than those so enumerated in the Constitution, are altogether void, and of no force." This doctrine, later and in another context, became the basis for the doctrine of "nullification," although Breckinridge had removed that word from Jefferson's draft. (It mysteriously reappeared in a revised set of resolves the assembly debated the next year, in 1800.) Under this interpretation of federalism, a state government could announce that a federal law was null and void within that state. It was a potent intellectual weapon in the hands of those who feared federal legislation, but where might it lead if pushed to an extreme? Kentucky passed the resolutions, the last of which asked other states to chime in. A number of them did, but none went as far as Jefferson and Kentucky.

Despite Madison's and Jefferson's efforts, aided by Republicans all over the country, the sedition act led to fourteen prosecutions, and as many more indictments, in which not every one convinced the grand jury to indict, but every one that did go to trial resulted in a verdict of guilty. In these cases, the new world of the First Amendment met the older standard of seditious libel. The honor of both parties vindicated, in their own minds at least, the contest of values. The Republicans looked forward to the idea of a free press and the Federalists back to an era of deference to those in authority. In this sense, the trials for defamation of political figures at the end of the eighteenth century were much the same as the litigation over reputation in the seventeenth century.

With the war scare ending in 1800, the act itself going out of existence the next year, and Jefferson winning the presidency (and pardoning the Republicans still in jail), the immediate crisis ended. But its emanations did not. What had happened? Another major shift in political practices had intervened. With the election of Jefferson, the very idea of democratic political campaigning had gained traction. In subsequent elections, both sides would engage in derogatory speeches and newspaper editorials, but no one would face prosecutions. Political speech of the most defamatory sort would go unpunished, except during wartime. After all, in 1801 Jefferson entered the White House for the first of his two terms. Jefferson's first inaugural address promised that erroneous political opinions would not be suppressed; "let them stand undisturbed as monuments of the safety with which error of opinion may be tolerated, where reason is left free to combat it."

For some involved in the defamation crisis, the outcome was not so hopeful. Defamation was the occasion, if not the root cause, of the Alexander Hamilton–Aaron Burr duel. Hamilton had allegedly defamed Burr in public; Burr demanded an explanation. Hamilton refused it. Letters were exchanged by seconds, and the two men settled the matter with pistols on the New Jersey shore instead of going to court, although they were both lawyers. Hamilton died the next day. Burr's reputation never recovered.

Political defamation had even more frightening consequences in the years to come. Some historians argue that the Civil War was the result of perceived slander—Republican politicians slandering the honor of the South. In 1856, with politics set aflame by the "bleeding Kansas" issue, Massachusetts senator Charles Sumner treated the upper house to another of his daylong orations, this one entitled "The Crime against Kansas." He not only accused slaveholders and their Democratic Party supporters of immorality; he called out former South Carolina senator Andrew Butler by name. Butler had suffered a stroke and drooled when he spoke. Congressman Preston Brooks of South Carolina, Butler's cousin, decided to punish Sumner for defamation, not by bringing a lawsuit, but by approaching the seated senator from behind and beating him senseless. (Brooks's fellow South Carolina representative James Keitt stood nearby with a loaded pistol in case anyone came to Sumner's aid.) The caning nearly killed Sumner. A war of words followed in northern and southern newspapers. With the election of Abraham Lincoln, defamation descended into secession. Lincoln, caricatured as an ape, and Jefferson Davis, satirized as an old woman, never brought their cause to court. How much better it would have been to find a legal solution to the problem of defamation.

—⚓—

Although not nearly so important as they once were, defamation cases continue to make news. Under modern law, a plaintiff must not only prove defamation, but real damages to himself. Hurt feelings, diminished reputation, or lingering resentment will not do. Some categories of defamation, including the assertion of sexual misconduct, mental illness, or professional malfeasance, carry the suit over the threshold, but that just shifts the burden to the defendant to show that he was acting in good faith, or speaking the truth, or was offering a legitimate opinion. Under the First Amendment's provisions for freedom of speech and the press (imposed on the states by the Fourteenth Amendment), such speech is generally privileged. Academic freedom, a component of free speech in educational settings, includes the same protections.

The rise of celebrity journalism, moreover, has led to another twist in the legal nature of the defamation lawsuit. The difference was enunciated in *New York Times v. Sullivan* (1964) and explained in Justice William Brennan's opinion for the Court. Absent actual malice, that is, reckless disregard for the truth, the defendant was safe when he or she made statements of opinion or purported fact about a public figure.

The facts were these: in a *New York Times* advertisement, a group of four Alabama clergymen, joined by another sixty-four leading civil rights figures, made allegations against the police commissioner of Montgomery, Alabama, one L. B. Sullivan. In the course of public protests against segregation there, he used excessive force to disperse civil rights demonstrators. The advertisement included certain claims that were not precisely accurate. For example, the protesting students did not sing "My Country 'Tis of Thee"; they sang the National Anthem. The inaccuracies were not particularly substantial, but Alabama libel law, under which the commissioner brought a lawsuit for libel, required that all such claims be exactly true. This was a return to much older English law and was generally discarded in other states. The Alabama trial judge instructed the jury that it did not have to find that the commissioner had suffered real damages, and the jury found for the plaintiff to the tune of $500,000. The Alabama Supreme Court affirmed the verdict.

The U.S. Supreme Court reversed and remanded (sent back) the case to the Alabama courts, in effect saying that the Alabama law had violated the First and Fourteenth Amendments. Brennan began, "We are required in this case to determine for the first time the extent to which the constitutional protections for speech and press limit a State's power to award damages in a libel action brought by a public official against critics of his official conduct. . . . Respondent [Sullivan] made no effort to prove that he suffered actual pecuniary loss as a result of the alleged libel." The newspaper retracted the advert when Governor James Patterson, a veteran defender of segregation when he was the state's attorney general, made an official request, but the four ministers and the signers did not retract what they had said. Brennan continued, "We reverse the judgment. We hold that the rule of law applied by the Alabama courts is constitutionally deficient for failure to provide the safeguards for freedom of speech and of the press that are required by the *First* and *Fourteenth Amendments* in a libel action brought by a public official against critics of his official conduct."

Alabama's attorneys had argued that even if the authors and signers of the advertisement were protected, the newspaper wasn't, because the advertisement was commercial speech. Brennan and the Court disagreed. "The publication here . . . communicated information, expressed opinion, recited grievances, protested claimed abuses, and sought financial support on behalf of a movement whose existence and objectives are matters of the highest public interest and concern. . . . To avoid placing such a handicap upon the freedoms of expression, we hold that if the allegedly libelous statements would otherwise be constitutionally protected from the present judgment, they do not forfeit that protection because they were published in the form of a paid advertisement."

The standard that the First Amendment imposed was that only reckless disregard of the truth was grounds for a lawsuit. "The general proposition that freedom of expression upon public questions is secured by the *First Amendment* has long been settled by our decisions. . . . Thus we consider this case against the background of a profound national commitment to the principle that debate on public issues should be uninhibited, robust, and wide-open, and that it may well include vehement, caustic, and sometimes unpleasantly sharp attacks on government and public officials." The Court recognized that civil rights was one of, perhaps the most important of, the political issues "of our time, [and] would seem clearly to qualify for the constitutional protection. The question is whether it forfeits that protection by the falsity of some of its factual statements and by its alleged defamation of respondent." The truth of a political opinion was always problematic, "but the people of this nation have ordained in the light of history, that, in spite of the probability of excesses and abuses, these liberties are, in the long view, essential to enlightened opinion and right conduct on the part of the citizens of a democracy." The public interest in hearing differences of opinion outweighed the private interest of public figures in protecting their reputations. "Errors of fact" in these exchanges were "inevitable." The constitutional standard the Court imposed was one of "actual malice"—the speaker or author knowingly and wantonly disregarding facts. Only then would the publication or speech be actionable. Others members of the Court, agreeing with the decision, in concurring opinions went further than Brennan to offer that every political opinion was protected.

For Sullivan and his fellow commissioners, honor and public office were intimately connected. The *Times* advertisement, whether true or false, called that honor into question. The *Times* was a national paper, and the commissioners knew that it, along with television coverage of the protests, in particular the role of the police, brought dishonor on them and their fellow southerners. They turned to the courts, whose judges and juries were like themselves believers in white supremacy and segregation of the races, to defend that contested honor. The ministers and civil rights workers were also defending honor, an honor that the fall of Jim Crow restored. In this case, as in the desegregation cases accompanying it in the 1960s, an entire social order built on Jim Crow vanished, and the beginnings of a new one, based on equality and dignity, took shape.

No one on the Court anticipated the rise of social media, however, and the potential for abuse of the First Amendment in anonymous postings to blog sites. But that is the world of defamation in which we now live, and the opinions are less political than they are matters of sexual abuse and otherwise private misconduct. The victims remain anonymous, and the accused are not political figures at all.

Sometimes, however, a blogger reveals himself. The social media site requires real names, or the individual who posts is trying to sell himself as a product. Dignity and honor may not seem at the root of the defamation suit against a conspiracy theorist, but it is. In 2018, three parents whose children were killed at Sandy Hook Elementary School in 2012 filed a defamation lawsuit against Alex Jones, a conspiracy theorist who had previously claimed the shooting was "completely fake" and a "giant hoax" perpetrated by opponents of the Second Amendment. Jones used his radio show and his website, InfoWars, to promote the claims and sought evidence in various news and video sources. While these sometimes got facts wrong or clipped images, they did not sustain his attacks on the veracity of the parents or the genuineness of their grief. They were not actors, and the deaths were real, removing the defense of truth from his remarks, while the tenor of his remarks not only undermined the parents' campaign for the regulation of guns; it assaulted their moral character by calling them "vampires."

In *Pozner v. Jones*, the plaintiff family claimed that "the gist of these statements was that the Sandy Hook parents . . . are participating in a sinister manipulation plan to fool the public. . . . The statements were a continuation and elaboration of a years long campaign to falsely attack the honesty of the Sandy Hook parents, casting them as participants in a ghastly conspiracy and cover-up." All the elements of defamation were present, including the fact that the plaintiffs were private individuals, not public officials or public figures.

> Defendants' defamatory publications were designed to harm Plaintiff's reputation and subject the Plaintiff to public contempt, disgrace, ridicule, or attack. . . . Defendant acted with actual malice. Defendant's defamatory statements were knowingly false or made with reckless disregard for the truth or falsity of the statements at the time the statements were made. . . . Defendant's defamatory statements constitute defamation per se. The harmful nature of the defamatory statements is self-evident. The defamatory statements implicate the Plaintiff in heinous criminal conduct. False implications of criminal conduct are the classic example of defamation per se. . . . Defendant publicly disseminated the defamatory publications to an enormous audience causing significant damages to the Plaintiff. Defendants' defamatory publications have injured Plaintiff's reputation and image, and they have exposed Plaintiff to public and private hatred, contempt, and ridicule.

What could be more plain an assault on the dignity of the parents than the boldface accusation that they had lied about the assassination of their children? But such is the nature of blog and attack radio conspiracy theory today. Jones thereupon conceded his error.

Not every social-media-spawned defamation suit is so clear-cut, not when new world of online reviews of services meets older standards of medical care. Michelle Levine went to gynecologist Joon Song to have what she thought was her annual pelvic exam. Instead, she reported on Yelp and Zocdoc, she was given an ultrasound test. She assumed that the visit was free, according to her medical insurance plan. Instead, the doctor charged her over $400. She gave him one star on Yelp. Had she made her complaint to New York's state medical board or even the district attorney's office, she would have been protected from retaliation. Or she could have sued him for malpractice. Instead, she simply shared her opinion on the websites. Websites like Yelp are full of negative as well as positive reviews of restaurants and other public establishments. Dr. Song could have lumped the comments, but instead he filed a suit against her for libel. He sought $1 million in damages to his reputation. According to further online journalism, she was out of pocket $20,000 defending herself. Dr. Song's bad publicity got a lot worse when Levine revealed the details of the episode online and mainline news sites picked it up.

—ɯ—

If one could predict the future, one could easily see a spate of similar defamation cases, as those who feel wronged by bloggers and other social media authors bring suits to restore their reputations and punish the defamer. Defamers could avert the suit by apologizing and retracting, but if they feel ideologically or financially bound to what they have said, as most conspiracy theorists seem to do, they will defend their suits. The phase change is the rise of electronic media, with instantaneous publication and ever-increasing levels of vituperation. But most of us do not want to be victimized by whoever posts these comments, and we will begin to seek redress in the courts under pre–electronic age ideals of dignity and privacy.

2

Land-Grabbing and Money-Grubbing

IN WOODY ALLEN'S NAPOLEONIC-ERA Russia spoof *Love and Death* (1975), the chief character's father walks about with a clump of sod under his coat. His son explains that his father always wanted a piece of land, even though it was small. Thomas Jefferson, who inherited a somewhat larger Virginia estate from his father, Peter, nevertheless praised the small farmer as the bulwark of a free nation. "Those who labor in the earth," he wrote in his *Notes on the State of Virginia* (1782), "are the chosen people of God." By the end of the colonial period, the mainland colonies were a patchwork of family farms, great plantations, stands of wood and vales of swamp, and Indian lands. Everyone from the lowest to the grandest in the colonies gloried in landownership.

Occupiers of land did not always have title, however. In English law, all the colonies belonged to the crown. Kings James I and II and Charles I and II gave much of North America in "proprietorships" to their noble friends. Proprietorships at one time included Nova Scotia, Maine, New York, New Jersey, Pennsylvania, Maryland, and the Carolinas—millions of acres. The proprietors had a problem, however. They were land rich and labor poor. Settlers they sent to work the land for the benefit of the proprietor soon battled with the proprietor's agents over title to the land. Some proprietors like William Penn and his sons clung to the title but sold pieces of the grant to prospective settlers. Others, like the proprietors of New Jersey and the Carolinas, gave the land back to the crown. New York, taken from the Dutch by James Stuart, was for a time a proprietorship, then became a royal colony.

The one uniformity was that every colony found ways to dispossess the native users of land from their possession of it. Individual colonists and colonial governments alike viewed Indian occupation as unworthy of ownership. Indians cleared land, gardened on it, and then moved on when the fertility of the land decreased. Periodic burns cleared brush in new sites, and the natives established residence there. Indian hunting grounds were seasonally occupied, but not "improved" (farmed) in the sense that English farmers understood land use. Although the first colonists survived in part because Indians traded corn and other products of the land for European consumer durables, soon the demands of staple crop production of tobacco and rice in the South and family farming in the North convinced the colonists that the Indians had to go. Although colonial governments sometimes interceded to regulate (as opposed to actually protecting) Indian land claims, such regulations actually restricted Indian claims as well as colonial land avarice. If Indians tried to reclaim ancestral lands or assert rights to land through force, the game changed entirely, and the result was the dispossession of the native peoples and the occupation of their land by settlers. In times of peace, unfair treaties and subterfuge did what war had not.

The result of these multiple occupiers of land over time was a crazy quilt of titles, some written and recorded, some oral; some from Indians, others from earlier settlers. Title to land in the colonies came in a process far simpler than in England. By the eighteenth century, the deed of sale for land had to be in writing and then registered in the county court. In the seventeenth century, men completed these purchases face-to-face. In the new century, the entire market system was undergoing a sea change. Mortgages for land loans served as bank checks that passed through many hands. More and more of these sales became enmeshed in the interpersonal dynamics of distance trading, and a larger and larger number of disputes over land turned into formal lawsuits. When residents of different towns, counties, parishes, or colonies began to contest one another's claims, and their quarrels more and more often concerned speculation over lands to the west, litigation ceased to be the last chapter in a communal story and became a detached, abstract legal episode.

All of which meant that parties to the litigation needed trained legal counsel. In the seventeenth century, New England statutes had barred legal practice for money. Attorneys could represent others, but not for pay. Virginia strictly regulated law practice, for example in 1645 finding that "whereas, many troublesome suits are multiplied by the unskilfulness and covetousness of attorneys, who have more intended their own profit, and their inordinate lucre, than the good of their clients; Be it, therefore, enacted, that all mercenary attorneys be wholly expelled from such office." This admonition notwithstanding, by the end of the century there were about thirty of those mercenary lawyers practicing in the county courts and the supreme court in Williamsburg. So, too, lawyers arrived in Charles Town, South Carolina, shortly after the colony was established in the 1670s, although the profession was first regulated in 1712. Lawyers were practicing in New York by the 1670s, the city soon becoming the capital of the West Indies trade and requiring knowledgeable counselors. The same lure for lawyers brought them to Philadelphia soon after it was founded in 1682.

In the eighteenth century, lawyering became legal and lucrative because there were new kinds of business to sustain legal practice. Defamation accusations and defenses did not require the presence of lawyers, and even if a lawyer or two were involved (usually because he was defamed as a pettifogger or liar), there was no money to be made representing parties in defamation suits. Land title suits were a different matter, and one could say that the colonial bar grew to maturity (and wealth) representing parties in title disputes. In land law, the gradual intrusion of a money economy, of trade with strangers, undercut face-to-face alternatives to formal litigation in the courts. The rise of busy and relatively impersonal commercial centers increased the number and complexity of land transactions among strangers. Lawyers managed the transition from rural to urban practice, collecting fees along the way.

In court, counsel tried to answer the question to whom the land on the deed or the mortgage document belonged. In other words, whose title was better? Did it belong to the Indians, and thus those who bought it from the Indians? Did it instead belong to settlers who had gained title from the governors of the colonies or their agents? Did it belong to farmers who improved it, or to speculators who sought to flip it?

Even if original title was assured, retaining real estate in the colonies rested on market forces, geographical limitations, and demographic pressure out of the possessor's control. Evidence that historian Allan Kulikoff has assembled shows that the cost of land steadily increased through the eighteenth century as the availability of land along the Atlantic coast decreased. Fewer and fewer families occupied more and more large bundles of land. Those families who could stay on small plots subdivided their land into smaller and smaller parcels for their children. The children then had to grind out a living on farm plots that barely supported mother, father, and children—or move west to cultivate lands occupied by native peoples. Where once Goody Garlick could tend her garden and, if she kept her tongue, fear no one, by the middle of the eighteenth century, family farmers faced almost insuperable population pressure and soil depletion.

In the meantime, land speculators in the eighteenth-century colonies and in the home islands formed companies to gobble up land, either to resell to farmers or to exploit resources like timber and bog iron. Speculation appealed to the wealthy, for even the wealthiest landholders were in debt and dreamed of new streams of income from undeveloped lands. Land speculators like Benjamin Franklin, George Washington, and Alexander Hamilton eyed opportunities for profit in developing Ohio and Canadian lands. Future revolutionaries like George Mason of Virginia joined with royal governors like Robert Dinwiddie and leading English politicians to fund the Ohio Company as soon as the French and Indians were removed.

Under whose law were the land companies to operate? Colonial land law varied, as each of the colonies had evolved different forms of land use. In New England, colonial assemblies abandoned the old rules that passed land on to the oldest son (primogeniture). The oldest son simply got a double share. Debts that burdened owners were discharged when the former owner died. The record of the transfer of title (the deed) in the county court was sufficient evidence of ownership, another New England innovation. The southern colonies retained the old law of primogeniture, ensuring that the plantation lands accumulated by one planter would be kept intact in the next generation. Southern landowners saw land as more than proof of a gentleman's standing in society. It was private property. In Maryland, for example, one could simply write the details of the sale on the back of the original grant document. This facilitated the easy transfer of land, making it a commodity on the market instead of proof of one's social status.

—⁓—

The grand changes in the way the colonists did land buying and selling, and with whom, and the variations in colonial land law framed the outer contours of the litigation explosion, but they do not explain why individuals decided that no recourse was open to them in a dispute but a lawsuit. The surge in litigation can be seen as a shifting of the border between such disputes and actual lawsuits. Why did proportionately more people insist that disputes be taken to court in the 1710s through the 1740s than in prior years? There are many answers, but one that seems to stand out is that people who gained land from government grants resented the intrusion of those whose title came from alleged Indian purchases. The grantees thought that the Indians were never the owners of the land and so could not transfer title. Farmers who had occupied the land and improved it resisted the claims of those who had paper titles but never set foot on the land. They were just speculators. Farming was good. Speculating was bad. Thus was framed an American meme—the yeoman farmer was the basis of republican government according to Jefferson. Speculation was a contagion of corruption.

The suits over landownership thus fed into a larger process, which surely influenced potential litigants. When a changing economy threatened communal values, potential plaintiffs grew anxious that potential defendants were trying to get away with something. Potential defendants themselves, bewildered by the speed and scope of economic and social changes, resisted confession of their supposed delicts and debts or referral of the disputes to arbitration. They resented what seemed to them to be plaintiffs' suddenly unreasonable demands. The defendants forced a day in court to prevent the plaintiff from breaking the old rules.

In the period from 1710 to 1740 when litigation rates first surged, the long-term expansion of commerce and its instrumentalities—combined with the growing breakdown of traditional institutions of social control—created a crisis of social values similar to the crisis that led to the surge in defamation. In the decades when new ways of doing business first gained the approval of the courts, neighbors still believed that strangers were using law to violate older norms of conduct. Courts' dockets began to fill. For example, New York's overcrowded supreme court dockets in this period mirrored the struggle between a new commercial elite, tied to the crown, and a corps of artisans and small landholders. The courts became one battleground for these forces as artisan and yeoman debtors struck back at wealthy merchants and landlords. When a new alliance of artisans, yeomen, and anti-crown elite families, principally the Livingstons, formed in the 1740s, the litigation rates leveled off.

As the boundaries of acceptable behavior (acceptable, that is, to individuals defending an extended dignity) were gradually redrawn, the gross number of disputes increased, but the rate at which they were taken "to law" diminished. Individuals again knew what to expect and where they stood. The number of unconceded and unresolved claims between strangers always remained higher than between neighbors because, as Christine Heyrman has written, the boundary of acceptable behavior is harder to see when it goes beyond the "town borders."

—៣៣—

Now let us return to the New Jersey shore. As in most of the colonies in the eighteenth century, a gentleman's status in New Jersey depended on landownership. But landownership could be highly contentious, and nothing illustrated this more, or drove litigation rates higher, than multiple parties disputing the same parcels of land. One would naturally expect quarrels over land and its uses to find their way into colonial and early national courts, and they did. Titles, boundaries, use of natural resources (timber and water), and trespass of persons and animals were the chief causes of disputes. Tracked in Brendan McConville's definitive detective work, the long-running dispute over the Elizabethtown land grants (the so-called Clinker Lots) adjacent to Perth Amboy on the New Jersey shore illustrated the lengths to which the settlers would go to validate their titles in, and out of, court.

The East Jersey settlements, first platted by the Dutch, and later occupied by English settlers under grants and purchases made by the Quaker Proprietors of East Jersey, were the seat of the troubles. After the proprietary colony became a royal colony in 1702, some of the families retained their titles from the Quaker Proprietors in the last two decades of the 1600s. Some had their claims from the Delaware or Leni Lenape Indians, whose idea of selling land included multiple sales to various buyers. There were over 150 of these transfers in the surviving records, all prior to 1715, the Indians signing by their mark and not understanding that they had given away the land, rather than allowing the buyer to hunt, fish, and traverse it. Some of the settlers had deeds from the later proprietary government of William Penn, after 1681, or from the royal colony of New Jersey's governors after 1702. Four sets of overlapping and competing titles, themselves being sold and bought after 1702, led to a confusion that exemplified the worst in colonial land law and polished the skills of three generations of colonial lawyers. Many of the most famous names in the colonial bar, including James Alexander and William Livingston, cut their teeth on the Elizabethtown litigation.

Alexander's involvement is worth pursuing as it demonstrates how patronage, ambition, and lawyering overlapped. He came from a good family in Scotland (minor officials and landowners) to Perth Amboy, one step ahead of English prosecution for his support of the ousted Stuart family, and then to New York City in 1715. He "read law" in a practitioner's office and was admitted to practice in the colony's courts in 1720. Thereafter he became a member of the council of the colony and was soon a part of the New York governing junta led by Lewis Morris. Along with Morris, Alexander acquired a good deal of land and dozens of slaves in both New York and New Jersey. He married well into the colony's mercantile elite. A poor public speaker but learned in law and other subjects including surveying (a most useful skill for a man on the make, as young George Washington discovered thirty years later), when Lewis Morris became governor of New Jersey, Alexander became the point man of the East Jersey Proprietary Board's legal campaign to acquire and sell lands.

Alexander's choice of debarkation port of Perth Amboy made sense, for the Scottish community dominated Perth Amboy's local politics. Insofar as it (along with Burlington City) was one of the dual capitals of the royal colony, it remained a center of political and economic activity throughout the colonial era. Its population also remained different in ethnic composition and political affiliation from the West Jersey colonists. Closer to New York and New England in settlement patterns, more likely to be Presbyterian or Dutch Reformed rather than Quaker, the East Jerseyites of Perth Amboy quarreled over everything with the West Jersey officials, including where to draw the survey line between the two halves of the colony. The line ran right through the Elizabethtown grants around what is now Elizabeth, New Jersey, many of whose holders had questionable titles.

Making matters more complicated, many of the East Jersey faction held their land titles from only one faction of the original proprietors, the so-called English faction. The royal appointment of Alexander as surveyor general in 1715 (he was as adept at currying favor in the home country as in the two colonies) was supposed to quiet the dispute over titles and rents (a form of taxation), but did little to reduce tensions, as Alexander was himself a landowner and as a lawyer would represent others who had title from the original proprietors. It was a clear conflict of interest in today's terms, but common in a world in which multiple office holding was the norm.

In the meantime, some of the deed books had disappeared. Everyone went to court to vindicate their rights, but just as often disputants took matters into their own hands. The latter had become a custom of the residents, and sometimes appearing in disguise, armed with clubs, they dispossessed families who had gained possession through the agency of the other faction. Various governors colluded with various parties, using patronage to gain political support. The fact that the governor also presided over the court of chancery, whose task it was to determine who had title, undermined the credibility of the court.

On top of all this, there were squatters on the land who wanted to buy title, tenants who had not paid their rent, title holders who were eager to sell or subdivide, and a sharp division between absentee and resident holders. Historians tracing the conflict have also suggested that a kind of aristocracy of property and political status had arisen by the mid-century, and the large estates of these men were eyed covetously by smaller stakeholders—just as the large landowners tried to gobble up smaller parcels of land. Other historians dispute this characterization, suggesting that class was not as important as personal allegiances.

The most active and perhaps the most aggressive of these factions was the Elizabethtown Association, who claimed land based on grants that even antedated the East Jersey Proprietary government. If this failed to win favor in court, individual members offered proof of purchase from the Indians. Given that English law did not regard individual Indians as having title to anything, these claims were highly unlikely to win in court. Nevertheless, the Association continued to survey, divide, and sell off parcels of its alleged grant, even though men living on the land under proprietary titles had to be ousted from their homesteads. Without legal justification or authority, the Elizabethtown men harassed and threatened the proprietary settlers. Although the men on both sides of these quarrels came from the same middling (lower middle class) strata of society, class did not matter so much as individual prospects. On both sides were family heads who had improved their lands and depended on its produce to support their families.

When men lost in court, they turned to self-help. Essex County courts indicted more than sixty alleged rioters. They confessed and submitted to the mercy of the court. The justices of the peace fined the rioters and ordered that they produce surety bonds for their future good behavior. They complied and paid the costs of prosecution. Elsewhere, plaintiffs won their cases and were settled on disputed lands. Rioters accepted the verdict of the juries and agreed "to contend no farther against so clear a title."

If the proprietary point of view prevailed in Middlesex and Hunterdon Counties, the majority of the people of Essex County had not yet, according to the proprietors, become "sensible of their errors." The unrest continued into the 1740s, as squatters and renters refused to pay quitrents to the proprietors. Into this fray once again came the ubiquitous James Alexander. Representing the proprietary faction, organized as the Eastern Board of Proprietors, and himself a large landowner, he wanted to protect the sales of his own lands (a far more lucrative operation than trying to collect rents from tenants).

One might wonder why such conflict existed between the Association and the Board, but the answer is not hard to find. New Jersey was attractive to families who wanted to farm the land, merchants who saw in the region's resources a way to make profits, and former servants who wanted to start families. Population grew rapidly, from 15,000 souls in 1700 to 61,383 in 1740, the latter figure based on the first actual census. The fastest-growing communities, or townships as the law provided, were those along the northeastern coast and inland from the coast. Population in these increased over 4 percent a year. Some of this growth was due to in-migration, but more of it came from natural increase. New Jersey was part of an Atlantic World system in which the wheat-growing colonies of North America, principally New York, Pennsylvania, New Jersey, and Delaware, supplied England's (and in violation of the Navigation Acts, France's) West Indian plantations with bread. Wheat culture in the middle colonies was not nearly as profitable as sugar cultivation on the Caribbean islands, but the slaves who turned the cane into sugar and molasses had to eat. What was more, some of the most desirable parcels in East

Jersey still had stands of hardwood. Timber for ships masts, houses, fur-niture, and other purposes was another valuable staple for Atlantic World marketplaces. Finally, under some of the land were mineral resources like copper and iron ore. Mines, furnaces, and forges dotted the landscape. All of this attracted the attention of speculators and entrepreneurs and added another layer of conflict.

In addition to its litigation with the Board, the Association was still caught up in older suits going back to the earliest years of the century. For example, in *Vaughn v. Woodruff* (1718), a superior court in the col-ony held that proprietary title trumped Association title. Such decisions became commonplace in the 1730s and could have gone the other way, but the judges were the appointees of the crown, and they came from the great proprietary landed class. Indeed, the majority of all judicial and peacekeeping officials in the colony were members of the large landhold-ing class and held proprietary lands. This included the supreme court justices. Whether bias or a strict application of land law enabled the pro-prietary faction to win ejectment suits in the regular courts is a question that the winners and losers answered in opposite ways. It also helped that the proprietary faction employed skilled lawyers like Alexander, where the squatters and Association title holders could not afford such counsel.

The litigation was remarkable in another way: a series of lengthy let-ters containing the chancery pleadings, as well as depositions taken in aid of the petitioners' litigation, were published by the Board of the pro-prietary faction at the behest of Alexander, while other documents were published by the Association. These publications turned on and reflected how private litigation could become a public quarrel. They also reflected the special nature of proceedings in chancery courts.

Colonial lawmakers adopted in various ways the functions of the English courts of chancery. Here, as in courts of law, procedure was simplified and relief made more accessible than in the English court of chancery. Equity, a parallel but distinct jurisprudential system to "law," was dispensed by chancellors. They determined the facts in a suit through direct interrogation of parties and witnesses or written accounts (depositions) read into evidence in court, rather than a trial based on the much narrower "writ" (a formal document fixed in content in which parties filled in the blank spaces) in a common-law court. The chan-cellor could intervene in a lawsuit at any time in its process, enabling the parties to obtain relief not available at that time from courts of law. Parties could apply to the chancellor to compel their legal adversaries to produce documents, give testimony, and remain in the jurisdiction. Chancellors could enjoin or mandate that parties do or not do something—for example, not waste the assets of an estate until the legal issue of its ownership was settled or perform the terms of a contract. Parties to the suit disobeyed the chancellor at their peril. He had jurisdiction over their persons and could fine or imprison those who disobeyed his decrees. The chancellor of England was a learned judge, and process in his court was often long and costly as well as thoughtful and realistic.

In Maryland, New York, the Carolinas, Virginia, and New Jersey, the governor or the governor and his council sat as chancellors. Their equity was swifter but less predictable than the work of the English chancellor and could be abused (as it was notoriously for a time in New York) by a partisan governor. For a brief time, Pennsylvania experimented with a separate central court of equity. So did Rhode Island and New Hampshire, but these courts failed for political reasons. In Pennsylvania, Delaware, Massachusetts (until 1691), and Virginia, county justices performed the functions of chancellors. The colonial assemblies of Massachusetts (until 1691), Connecticut, and Pennsylvania doubled as courts of equity, another example of the general jurisdiction common in American courts. Local equity was plainly spoken, similar in outline to English equity but much less technical.

For himself and his faction, Alexander authored an over-one-hundred-page bill for the chancery court to consider, a miniature history of landownership in the state concluding that the contested lands were always the proprietors' to grant. The legal process was not neutral—it never is. For Alexander knew that the best chance for his clients lay not in the local courts, whose jury boxes were filled with the other side's men, but with the governor himself. On April 13, 1745, Alexander brought the document to the clerk in chancery, Thomas Bartow. The title of the bill ran as follows: "A Bill in the Chancery of New Jersey, at the suit of John Earl of Stair and others, Proprietors of the Eastern Division of New Jersey; against Benjamin Bond and some other Persons of Elizabethtown, distinguished by the Name of the Qinker [Clinker] Lot Right Men. With three large Maps, done from Copper-Plates, to which is added; The Publication of the Council of Proprietors of East New

Jersey, and Mr. Nevill's speeches to the General Assembly, concerning the Riots committed in New Jersey, and the pretenses of the Rioters, and their Seducers."

The reader was likewise advised that "these Papers will give a better Light into the History and Constitution of New Jersey, than anything hitherto published, the matters whereof have been chiefly collected from Records." The document was published by subscription (that is, like newspapers at the time, Alexander got people to pay in advance for copies) and printed by James Parker. Parker and Benjamin Franklin were to sell a few copies, the "Price bound and Maps coloured, Three Pounds; plain and stitch only, Fifty Shillings, Proclamation Money." The bill was an exhaustive defense of the proprietary claims, signed by James Alexander and Joseph Murray, "of Council for the Complainants."

After the case of the plaintiffs had been fully set forth, the bill concluded, praying that the defendants be commanded to appear on a certain day in "His Majesty's Court of Chancery of this Province, then and there to answer the Premises." The governor—like Alexander an omnipresent Lewis Morris—was asked to grant writs of injunction, commanding the defendants and confederates to commit no further "Waste or spoil upon the lands in question, by cutting of timber or otherwise howsoever, until your Excellency shall have given farther directions therein." The Association engaged William Livingston and William Smith Jr. as their counsel, to prepare an answer to the proprietary document. Both men were Yale educated and part of the so-called triumvirate (the third was William Morin Scott) who practiced in New York. Livingston was the son of one of New York's largest landholders and would, in 1770, move to Elizabethtown; become a benefactor of the new College of New Jersey (later Princeton); and, during the Revolution, become governor of New Jersey. He was also something of a wit, his *Independent Reflector* essays taking on controversial topics with sharply pointed satire.

Livingston's "An Answer to a Bill in the Chancery of New Jersey" was not completed until August 1751, and printed the following year by subscription. Affixed to the "Answer" were the signatures of 449 freeholders and inhabitants of Elizabethtown. Like the original, its title more than hinted at its purpose: "An Answer to a Bill in the Chancery of New Jersey, at the suit of John Earl of Stair, and others, commonly called Proprietors, of the Eastern Division of New Jersey, against Benjamin Bond, and others, claiming under the original Proprietors and Associates of Elizabethtown, to which is added; Nothing either of the publications of the Council of Proprietors of East New Jersey, or, of the Pretences of the Rioters, and their Seducers; except so far as the persons, meant by Rioters, Pretend Title against the Parties to the above Answer; but a Great Deal of the Controversy, though much less of the History and Constitution of New Jersey, than the said Bill."

When the litigation commenced, Governor Morris was the chancellor. Himself a lawyer and, like Alexander, Livingston, and Smith, a veteran politician, Morris knew that whatever he decided was going to be controversial. In theory, equity in courts of chancery was supposed to do justice when a common-law decision might not. It would find a way to bring everyone together. But with riots and threats of riots in the air, and the land's value as timber and garden produce rapidly diminishing, King Solomon himself would have had a hard time finding a solution that satisfied everyone. In any case, Morris died in 1746, and the problem passed to the hands of his successor, Governor Jonathan Belcher. Belcher was a New Englander, a New Light evangelical, and he leaned to the side of the defendants. Time aided him as well, as the death of many of the leading men of the Association, and some of the rioters, allowed him to delay his decision. Then a new peril threatened the colony. Although it was no longer a frontier, its neighbors, New York and Pennsylvania, lay exposed to depredations from the French and their Indian allies on the frontier during the French and Indian War. The war carried on until 1763, followed by an Indian uprising in 1763 that raged for two years. During the War for Independence from 1775 to 1783, there was a suspension of legal business, and after the colonies had gained their freedom and New Jersey had become a state, the lawsuit was not reopened.

It may hardly seem that these chancery suits were about honor. The term and its usual accompaniments were entirely absent from the bills in chancery as they were from the contest of clubs and insults in the streets of Elizabethtown. But honor was at the center of the dispute. The dueling chancery complaints, first filed in 1745, replied to in 1751, and then refiled by the original defendants in 1754, were alternatives to duels. When one thinks of these suits in terms of honor and values changes, they explain themselves. In publishing, the Board and the Association crossed over the line from private litigation to public law adjudication. In other words, they made a private quarrel into a public issue. Of course, because of the riots, the issue was already highly publicized. What is more, given Alexander's, Livingston's, and Morris's public standing, the dispute could hardly have been kept private. Historians of law have argued that the line between private litigation and public policy litigation was rarely crossed until the twentieth century, but the Elizabethtown chancery suits show that this line was drawn in very shifting sands as early as the middle of the eighteenth century.

By publishing, both sides were making an appeal to public opinion outside of the courtroom. Here was the phase change. The rise of public opinion as a political force dates from this time. While the rise of public opinion has been tied to the increasing influence of newspapers like Benjamin Franklin's *Pennsylvania Gazette*, which, as it happened, carried full coverage of the Clinker Lot riots, the separate publication of the bills and answers served a similar purpose. In fact, Franklin was the Philadelphia printer and publisher (along with a New York City press) of the court documents. Although, compared to modern politics, the public sphere of the eighteenth century was limited, in New Jersey and the other northern colonies the right to vote was shared by all white male property holders. In a series of issues involving paper currency (colonial paper currency emissions made it easy for colonists to pay debts, including debts to English creditors), proto-political parties had emerged in New York, New Jersey, and Massachusetts. By publishing the bills and answers in chancery, the two factions in the Elizabethtown land dispute acted like proto-political parties. The impact of this division in East Jersey was already apparent in voting for the lower house of the colonial legislature. The assembly of the colony was divided between the two factions. In a way the dueling publications acted as a kind of platform for the two factions in their campaign for votes.

For the Association, ownership of land, and even more important, the entire autonomy to buy, sell, and place its tenants on the land, established their honorable place in society. Status depended on absolute control of land. They were honorable not because they were wealthy, but because of the way in which they could—or tried to—exercise this control. This was not a throwback to the older feudal ideal that the lord of the manor had honor. That concept was based on the notion that the manor lord was also a commander of men in the king's service—a martial ideal of honor. In the New Jersey land wars of the mid-eighteenth century, the landed aristocracy had honor because they could give land to (and take land away from) their clients. It was clientage and patronage through the medium of real estate that conferred honor.

The Elizabethtown Association were not the victims of greedy and all-powerful proprietary functionaries. The Association were themselves land speculators eager to improve their own holdings, and willing to use violence to underwrite their claims. Indeed, after 1735, it was the Association's initiative to expand its claims that drew Alexander and the proprietary faction back into the fray. The Association protected the claims of those within the township, but those who had entered lands the Association eyed, without accepting the Association as their landlords, were dispossessed. Even within the Association, there were factions, for these men were not communally motivated—they were proto-capitalist agrarian businessmen. Small committees of men within the contested tracts associated themselves into larger collectives, using legalesque formularities—"pacts" that members of the committees signed and sealed in public ceremonies. These legal steps were joined by illegal gatherings when members of the committee were arrested and held in jail for armed trespass on proprietary grantees' land. Indeed, it was from these committees, rather than the Association, that the plans for resistance to the officials arose. Thus even the public demonstrations of lawlessness had a patina of legality, at least in the minds of those who saw the labor of their hands as the basis for private property, rather than grants and deeds in the arcane language of the lawyers.

For the Board, the committeemen signers of the pacts, and even the squatters on the Clinker Lots, honor had a different connotation. A man had honor because he worked the land. The notion of yeomen liberty associated with agrarianists from Jefferson through the Vanderbilt University poets, the "Fugitives" of the early twentieth century, ran through the rhetoric of the anti-proprietary party. Again, this was not some form of communitarian, anti-modern strain of thinking. These farmers did not yearn for a precapitalist time of self-sufficiency and mutual aid. Quite the contrary, they understood that they were growing wheat and cutting timber for faraway markets and reinvesting profits in their enterprise. Their honor arose from their autonomy, from control of their own parcels, and with that, of their own futures. They were no one's clients, and though they understood patronage, they embraced a different ideology of individual worth and achievement.

—⟋⟋⟋—

Disputes over vacant lands, title to improved lands, and real estate development went west with the nation. The first stop in the 1780s was the Wyoming Valley lands in Pennsylvania, to which alleged purchasers with Connecticut Company titles went to legal war against squatters who claimed possession because they had been promised the land by Pennsylvania's revolutionary government. Prior to the Revolution, both colonies had supposedly purchased land in the Valley of the Susquehanna from the Indians, but the title depended on the prerevolutionary charters of the two colonies, and the Revolution had thrown all titles up for grabs, as it had for the Elizabethtown litigants. After the war, during the so-called Confederation Period of American history, the Articles of Confederation held the states together loosely. The Articles' Congress had no courts to settle interstate quarrels (one of the reasons why real estate lawyers like Alexander Hamilton wanted the new nation to have federal courts). A commission tried to bring the two sides together. Following its recommendations, the Connecticut claimants agreed to become citizens of Pennsylvania and accept title from it. Nevertheless, the Pennsylvania residents of the Wyoming Valley refused to give up their titles. Gangs of men from both sides carried on a miniature civil war for years, and the quarrel went on until 1810, when the state's courts settled claims individually and leading Yankees agreed to work with leading Pennsylvania men.

The land disputes traveled all the way across the country by the 1850s, when throngs of American settlers in California asked newly established federal courts there to settle claim disputes with Mexican inhabitants. Some of the Mexican titles went back to Spanish colonial days, while others rested on the Mexican Republic ousted from California during the Mexican-American War. The disputes echoed similar quarrels arising earlier from the Louisiana Purchase, the acquisition of Florida, and the annexation of Texas. In all these, there was no clear set of rules to settle quarrels over foreign titles to land acquired by the United States. Congress stepped in with the Land Act of 1851, essentially transferring all the questions to the federal district courts in Northern and Southern California, flooding those courts with tangled controversies. Some of the Mexican ranchos had ill-defined boundaries and stretched for hundreds of square miles of unsurveyed territory. Other, supposed grants were outright frauds. The problem was compounded by Mexican land law, which was different from the quit-deed and file requirements of American land law. Before the act, Congress had handled the clashes poorly. Now the courts had the task, and jurists like district court judges Ogden Hoffman and Matthew MacAllister treated the near endless suits of disputed claims with care. The result was that some but hardly all of the older titles were sustained, opening the way for what might reasonably be called a California land rush.

—⁓—

Such issues of foreign real estate titles as confounded the courts in Pennsylvania and California in the antebellum years are no longer central to the development of American law, but there are occasions when one aspect of land disputes does have a galvanic impact on the entire nation. Land title is now not as important as the means by which the purchase of real estate is financed. At the heart of the Elizabethtown parcels and the Wyoming Valley land war were financial arrangements called mortgages. A mortgage is a loan wherein the loaner (the mortgagee) retains legal title to the property but the recipient of the loan (the mortgagor) can occupy and use the land so long as he or she pays a portion of the loan each stated period of payment. When the mortgagor pays the full amount of the loan, title transfers to the mortgagor. If the mortgagor fails to pay for any length of time, he or she still has what is called the equity of redemption—an extension to make good the delayed payment.

Mortgage was everywhere in American life—slaves were mortgaged; railroad rights of way were mortgaged; homes and farms were mortgaged. Without mortgages there was insufficient capital for most free Americans to take part in the real estate market. One of the pervasive and genuine grievances of newly freed slaves was their inability to get banks to give them mortgages to start or expand businesses or buy homes. That racial profiling goes on to this day, despite federal regulations against discrimination in lending.

Mortgages fall under the category of secured transactions in the mercantile codes of the twentieth century. A secured transaction with regard to land is one in which the property may be sold if the underlying loan is in default. The foreclosure of mortgaged homesteads (where the bank, the holder of the mortgage, threw farm families off the land for nonpayment) was a hotly contested feature in rural areas during the Great Depression of 1929–1939. States passed "mortgage moratorium" laws barring holders of mortgages from foreclosing. Banks brought lawsuits by the dozens to fight against these statutes.

In *Home Building Association v. Blaisdell* (1934), the U.S. Supreme Court upheld one state law from Minnesota as a necessary temporary measure to relieve homeowners behind on their mortgage payments. Chief Justice Charles Evans Hughes, New York's former Progressive governor, delivered the opinion of the Court. He agreed with the state's own highest court that

> upheld the statute as an emergency measure. Although conceding that the obligations of the mortgage contract were impaired, the [state] court decided that what it thus described as an impairment was, notwithstanding the contract clause of the Federal Constitution, within the police power of the State as that power was called into exercise by the public economic emergency which the legislature had found to exist. . . . The [state's relief] Act provides that, during the emergency declared to exist, relief may be had through authorized judicial proceedings with respect to foreclosures of mortgages, and execution sales, of real estate; that sales may be postponed and periods of redemption may be extended.

In short, homeowner litigation against the mortgage holder, the mortgage and loan associations and the banks, was a way to keep the wolf from the door. The "Contract Clause" of Article I, section 10, of the federal Constitution, which guaranteed that states would not impair the obligations in contracts (of which mortgages were a type), had to be read as part of a living Constitution, a document and system of law that took into account the needs of the people it was framed to serve. When the Depression had ended, homeowners were once again expected to pay their mortgages on time.

Then it all happened again, as the real estate boom of the early 2000s collapsed and balloon mortgages too easily given out in the years before 2008 exploded. Hundreds of thousands of homeowning families' mortgages, nearly 1 percent of all homeowners in the nation, were foreclosed for nonpayment. In the present region where the Elizabethtown suits took place (Elizabeth city in Union County), 186 mortgages obtained from 2001 to 2008 were foreclosed in 2009. State figures corresponded to Union County's—indeed, New Jersey led the nation in 2016 and 2017 foreclosures, averaging over seventy thousand per year. This was one in every fifty-nine homes. More than half were mortgages written between 2004 and 2008, at the height of the real estate boom. The collapse in the housing market was profound. The author's auto trip to Salem town in Salem County in 2009 showed rows of private homes unfinished or unoccupied because the financing for them had disappeared. The bubble had burst, and with it the hopes of many for a piece of the American dream.

The balloon mortgage had payments tied to the prime rate offered by the federal bank, called a balloon because the biggest payment comes at the end of the mortgage. Savings and loan firms were giving these out without adequate security for their payment. Then brokerage firms and major banks began to trade in "bundles" of securities including these nearly worthless mortgages. Worse, some of these same firms, including the largest in the country, began to buy the securities. This time the federal government stepped in, with TARP (Troubled Asset Relief Program) to buy the defective securities, in effect loaning federal funds to banks and brokerage houses to cover their losses with relatively easy terms for repayment, and the MRSA (Mortgage Relief Stabilization Act) and Hope for Homeowners program aimed at enabling homeowners facing foreclosure to refinance. This national program of refinancing mortgages never solved the problem, but it demonstrated how general legislative solutions had replaced individual litigation.

The larger difficulty for the would-be homeowner lay not in the perils of high-level finance, but in the elusive social status of post–World War II America. What ownership of a farmstead had been for the nineteenth-century American, owning a home was for the twentieth-century suburban dweller. Honor lay in owning one's own home. It gave the homeowner a membership in a community of homeowners. The bigger the home, the more visible the status of the family. The "McMansion" of the 1990s was proof that a family had arrived in the middle class. The IRS tax code's exemption for mortgage interest payments, not allowed for rental payments, underwrote the cultural and social status of the homeowner.

Losing one's home, consequently, was a mark of shame. The very act of leaving it behind was a public affirmation of failure. That it fell upon those least able to pay for the balloon mortgage and whose home investment was "underwater" (the value of the home on the market falling below the substance of the mortgage) was a further demonstration of the growing wealth inequality in twenty-first-century America. Insofar as honor was reflected in property holding, those Americans cast out of their homes had no way to restore it. The popular protests of the Elizabethtown settlers were no longer available as a means of redress, and the homeowner threatened with dispossession had only one recourse—the courts.

The legal battles over financing property ownership continue. Today, boundaries of the contest are set by regulations of the financing industry, the successors to the Proprietors' Association of the 1740s. In *Beard v. Ocwen Loan Servicing* (2015), one sees echoes of the Elizabethtown cases. Ocwen is a loan servicing company, a middleman picking up mortgages, arranging for refinancing, and charging fees to discharge the mortgage. It advertises itself as "helping homeowners" to refinance mortgages through its lending affiliate, Homeward Residential. It is the defendant in many suits, including one from the Third Circuit (which includes New Jersey).

Ocwen was sued by Jaynie Beard, alleging that the company had violated the Fair Debt Collection Practices Act (FDCPA). That federal act protects borrowers against unfair, abusive, and underhanded collection tactics. Ocwen wanted the federal court to dismiss her suit out of hand. The facts were familiar to anyone who had watched the real estate bubble collapse. She owned property in Harrisburg, the capital of Pennsylvania, purchased with a loan from Columbia National Bank, a savings and loan institution. The mortgage was an "adhesion" or "boilerplate" contract (small print, lots of clauses, full of technical language) designed to hide and confuse the borrower. Paragraph 14 stated that "Lender may charge Borrower fees for services . . . performed in connection with Borrower's default . . . including, but not limited to, attorneys' fees." Paragraph 14 goes on to limit this authority, however, by stating, "Lender may not charge fees that are expressly prohibited by this Security Instrument or by Applicable Law." In 2010, by which time the mortgage had passed to American Home Mortgage, Beard defaulted. She agreed to a modification of the loan and tried to keep up payments, but in 2012 again she defaulted. By this time the mortgage was held by Homeward, Ocwen's subsidiary.

This shell game, in which mortgages pass like bank checks from one refinancer to another, is so common as to be the rule in the mortgage business. Ocwen then stepped in and offered yet another refinancing scheme, so "unpalatable" to Beard that she asked for a statement of the outstanding amount necessary to fulfill the prior agreement and was prepared to pay it. Ocwen sent her a statement through its lawyer that included over $8,000 for fees, including its legal fees (though it had only held the loan for a short time, and in that time its lawyers had little to do with the transaction) in addition to the principal of the loan. The statement ended with a demand for payment in its New Jersey office within two days or Ocwen would foreclose. By comparison, James Alexander's timetable for compliance with the Association's claims for the Clinker Lots was very generous.

The federal judge in Beard's case, William Caldwell, found that Ocwen's statement was a communication to the borrower, and so fell under the federal statute, rather than a legal document, which would have been exempt under the federal law, even though Ocwen's lawyers had sent it. The scheme to bilk her for lawyers' fees had failed.

In protecting the borrower, a regime of regulation by statute replaced both the common law and the equity of the chancellors courts. But one had to litigate. Beard had to hire a lawyer and sue Ocwen in federal court to protect her honor against what she saw as an unscrupulous corporation. By contrast, Ocwen looked at the record and saw a borrower who could or would not pay what she owed. The contest of the Association and the Committee over the Clinker Lots lay in the distant past, or did it? Ocwen tried to finagle the new regulatory regime, a phase change that Beard and her counsel, by contrast, appreciated.

3

Slavery and Honor

MUCH HAD CHANGED IN AMERICAN LAW between the 1740s and the 1840s. A new nation was born in revolution, and it survived because of state constitutions and a confederation based on Articles of Confederation that a lawyer, John Dickinson, had crafted. The Constitution of 1787 created a regime of federalism, in which both a central government and an array of state governments were simultaneously sovereign. Once again, lawyers like Gouverneur Morris played key roles in framing the new law. The nation prospered despite vicious political partisanship and another war with Great Britain. Through all of this, one body of substantive law had not changed. Despite Dickinson's anti-slavery posture in 1776 and Morris's opposition at the Philadelphia constitutional convention, the federal Constitution conceded that some people could hold other people in perpetual bondage, exploiting their forced labor and withholding their civil rights.

In the antebellum period (1800–1861), state law determined the legal status of persons. States gave or withheld privileges and immunities from women, servants, immigrants, and children. Even Native Americans, whose status was in theory defined by treaties between native peoples and the federal government, found themselves subjects of state regulation. The most striking of these "domestic" or "municipal" regulations were those imposed on people of African origin.

—⁂—

State law empowered white men and women to keep black men, women, and children in bondage. This was called "chattel slavery" because the slaves had the legal status of personal property or chattel. (In Virginia, slaves were real estate—a way of protecting the slaveholding widow from her late husband's creditors.) Slaves could be bought, sold, leased out, given to relatives by testamentary gift, mortgaged, insured, and otherwise transferred or held as property. No one else faced these legal impositions. Slaves could be "corrected" without punishment by any free person, although some slave states' laws prohibited the killing of slaves without justification (to protect the master's economic interest in the slave). Slaves could not own or bear arms, practice medicine, congregate in groups without supervision, or go about freely without passes from their owners. They could not sue or be sued, having no civil rights or liberties. Free blacks also labored under great disadvantages in the South, always prey to reenslavement, and in the free states persons of color were denied many of the basic rights of citizens. For the states also determined who could and who could not be citizens, indeed, who the law regarded as fully human and who not.

Slaves constituted the most important portion of personal property in the antebellum South. On the market they were worth more than the land and its products. What was just as important, the expansion of the nation to the west and the profitability of almost all commercial ventures, that is, the success of the nation's experiment in capitalism itself, was linked to the further deployment of slavery into new lands. The internal slave trade was one of the most lucrative of all businesses in the antebellum period. This in turn rested on another economic fact: intensive labor on an extensive scale was necessary if landowners were to benefit from the vast expanse of new territory brought under cultivation in the South.

Historian of slavery Edward Baptist has summed up the relationship of slavery and freedom: "Planters assumed they needed slave labor just as they needed soil and rain." From the rice lands of the Low Country of South Carolina and Georgia through the cotton lands of the Black Belt of Alabama and Mississippi, down to the sugar plantations on the Gulf of Mexico, slave labor drove the staple crop export market. Cotton was the largest U.S. export crop, and the profits of cotton enabled planters to expand slavery into newly settled areas. No sooner was land acquired, for example Florida from the Spanish, than slavery established its firm foothold. For what drove capital investment was the prospect of wealth, and staple-crop-based wealth required labor—and slaves, it turned out, were exceptionally able laborers.

What made slaves into slaves was not race—there were free blacks in the South just as there were in the North. True, dark skin created a presumption that an individual was a slave, but it was law that made slavery stick. Law enabled slavery to exist in the stream of commerce. Law monitored the internal slave trade when federal law barred the importation of slaves from abroad. Curtail the buying and selling of slaves, and much of their value disappeared, but the legal regime facilitated the movement of slaves from place to place and from owner to owner by policing slave sales and other transactions. Whether by simple sale, auction, or inheritance, law instructed the buyer and seller, testator and inheritor. All this would end with the Thirteenth and Fourteenth Amendments during and after the Civil War, but for the period from the founding of the nation through 1865, millions of dark-skinned Americans were slaves under the legal regime of the slave states.

On its face coherent and potent, slave law had at its core a fundamental contradiction. In law, slaves were objects, but in fact—as every master and mistress knew—they were people. Masters and their agents had to recognize agency in individual slaves. Unlike other forms of chattel, slaves could negotiate for personal space and time, withholding or offering their services in return. As a result, some masters treated slaves well (according to law) within the system of bondage, while other masters added brutality to the everyday iniquities of the system. A few masters bought slaves intending to sexually abuse them. Some masters tried to mitigate the rigors of statute law regarding slavery by providing in their wills freedom and monetary rewards for individual slaves. These benevolent instincts led to litigation when heirs and creditors swarmed over the estate and sought to convert its property in slaves into their own property, as in the Alabama case of *Atwood's Heirs v. Beck* (1852).

In 1843 Henry S. Atwood appointed executors to fulfill his dying wish that after the sale of his property and most of his 250 slaves to pay his debts and leave a bequest to his heirs, "certain slaves" be freed and legacies set aside for them. He wished that they be taken out of the state and freed. Alabama law did not allow him to free slaves in the state. He died in 1851, and his lawyer set up a trust to protect the slaves from the claims of the heirs. A challenge to the will went to the court of chancery. Chancery courts used equity rules in cases of trusts, to ensure that the assets of the trust were not wasted and the purpose of the trust was affected. Some of the slaves were Henry's own children, according to Bryan Prince's scholarly account in *My Brother's Keeper*, for Henry was one of the wealthiest cotton planters in the state, and he had many children by his slave mistresses. In and around planters' mansion houses were extended interracial communities. Some of the planters regarded themselves as patriarchs, much like the biblical Abraham, and they lived openly with their mulatto children and mixed-race mistresses. In vain white wives and daughters protested against this very visible exhibition of upper-class white privilege. Atwood's two sisters objected to the will's provisions, as they no doubt had objected to his sexual practices during his lifetime.

The court of equity heard intentions in detail. Courts of equity had charge of the testator's motives and the context of their wills, in order to effect the old English doctrine of *cy pres*—the intent of the donor or the testator. In other words, Atwood created a trust whose beneficiaries were the slaves. Note also how the slaves were changed from chattel to human third parties by the will. Some were already free. Others were undoubtedly his children, living with their mothers on his plantations. Still others were their relations, or favored house servants. The will gives the historian a chance to get to know a little more about them:

> a mulatto boy named Alexander, aged about fifteen years, also to his sister, a mulatto girl aged about twelve years, named Ann, who are now residing in the State of Ohio, in charge of Lemuel Brown, near Aberdeen, in Adams county; also to their sister, named Cebille, aged about nine years, also to her brother, named Julius, aged about eight years, also to his brother, John, aged about five years, the three latter children being on my plantation, near Prairie Bluff, and all of the aforesaid children, namely, Alexander, Ann, Cebille, Julius and John, being children of a negro woman belonging to me, and known by the name of Candis.

Atwood was notorious for philandering, and he had no hesitancy in revealing his sexual relations with his slaves. "I also give and bequeath to a mulatto boy, named William, aged about six years, and to his brother Daniel, aged less than one year, both being children of a slave of mine named Mary, who resides at my plantation at Chilachi, six miles from Prairie Bluff." The tipoff is that these were mulatto, that is, mixed-race, children, and he wanted to remove them from the reach of creditors, his heirs, and Alabama authorities. To do this, he not only had to arrange for them to be freed out of the state, but he also had to provide for them, lest they be treated as paupers and reduced to virtual slavery. "To each and all of the before mentioned children, I give and bequeath the sum of eight thousand dollars each, to be appropriated and invested in such manner as hereafter described . . . for the purpose of my said executors removing said children as aforesaid . . . to a free State." He enjoined the executors of the will, acting as the trustees, to "give to each and all of the children before named their freedom, as also the sum of eight thousand dollars each, to be invested as hereinafter named." The will's beneficence was not limited to his children by slave mothers. Favored members of his extended household were included in the will. "I also will and bequeath to nine of my servants their freedom, and hereby invest in my said executors, as hereinafter named, the control and ownership of said negroes, so far as it may be necessary to remove the said slaves to a free State."

Although he left to his sisters more than enough to sustain them, they appealed the chancellor's decision in favor of the will to the Supreme Court of Alabama, and its opinion clarified the relationship between statute law regarding slavery as an institution and the wishes of an individual slave owner regarding the disposition of individual slaves. Masters had an absolute power over their chattel.

Chief Justice William Parish Chilton wrote the opinion. He served on the court for one term, from 1852 to 1856, after which he returned to private practice with William Lowndes Yancey. Yancey was already well known as one of the Deep South's "fire-eaters"—an early and vocal supporter of secession. When Alabama seceded, Chilton accepted election to the Confederate Congress. After the war, he returned to private practice. A strong supporter of the state's need for slavery, he nevertheless did not accede to the heirs' argument that the trust violated the law. The state law was clear that the master could do what he wished with the slaves, including freeing them and providing for them, so long as he or his agents did it outside of the state. Chilton's opinion was not the last word on the subject, but the case was widely cited in the slave states.

According to Chilton, Atwood did not have to obtain the consent of the state legislature for the manumission of his slaves. "It is most unquestionably true, that slaves are now regarded by our law as chattels, and the owners thereof have an absolute unqualified property in them. . . . The master, having an unqualified property in his slaves, may dispose of them in any way he pleases, unless restrained by some rule of law, or fixed and settled policy of the State. The *jus disponendi*, or right of disposing of his property, is an inseparable incident to its absolute and unqualified ownership." The legislature and the constitution of the state guaranteed this power to the slave owner, subject to certain checks. This was another of the ironies in slave law. The slave was the chattel of the master. But the state had the power to regulate what the master did. Public policy in Alabama dictated that the master not free his slaves in the state. Too many free blacks raised dangers to public safety, according to this reasoning, "prompted alike by humanity for the slave and security for the State."

Chilton, who practiced in the state and was familiar with the paradox of slave law, conceded, "In considering the rules which apply to, and regulate this peculiar species of property, we must look upon them in the double capacity of chattels and intelligent beings. Considered in this latter capacity, our law, pervaded as it is by the spirit of christianity, and founded on principles of humanity and benevolence, throws around them its protection." Clearly, Chilton was not just writing about this case, but about the entire institution of slavery in the South. His audience was not just the parties to the cause, but jurists as far away as England (whose laws he cited) and the North. He ranged, thus, over the common law, Justinian's code, and other sources of slave law in a miniature version of a treatise on slavery to reinforce the authority of his opinion and to gain for Alabama slave law a place in the law of nations.

He also canvased the precedents in Alabama and its neighbors. For example, he added, unnecessarily for the resolution of the suit, but in defense of slavery itself, "The master is bound both morally and legally to supply the slave's necessary wants, and he may not avoid this liability by voluntarily putting the slave away from him, without providing some one to occupy the relation of master to him." The master class was merciful and the law benevolent:

> and but for the inhibition created by the statute laws, he might at pleasure renounce his property in them by manumission. . . . We are, therefore, of opinion, that as between the master and his slave, aside from all statutory prohibition, the right of manumission does exist, and is deducible not only from the absolute ownership of the master in the slave as a chattel, but from analogous rules applicable to slavery as it has obtained in every civilized country, as far as our researches extend, and as sustained by numerous adjudications of our own country.

The only bar to the absolute power of the individual slave owner lay in the general statute law of the state of Alabama. A short history lesson explained how the statute law evolved. At first, the law was resistant to manumission, but over time its face softened. Chilton: "Diverse applications were made under it to the legislature, by the owners of slaves, for their emancipation." The legislature granted such requests, and finally, "these frequent applications becoming inconvenient, it was deemed proper to vest the power in the judge of the County Court, which was done by statute in 1834." Prospective freedmen and women had to be removed from the state. Free blacks were a potential danger, perhaps stirring the restive spirit of slaves and fomenting disobedience or rebellion. Still, the will of the master, embodied in the master's will, was absolute if provision was made to remove the slaves to free territory.

The court was not about to set itself up as a legislative body. If Alabama lawgivers wanted to bar all emancipations, they would be thwarting the absolute power of the slave owner. "We can only ascertain the policy of the State from the laws which have been enacted by the legislature, or set forth in the Constitution." Chilton's own views were clear, however. "For, were we to go outside of these for a rule of decision, and look to the conflicting views of politicians, as to what line of policy is most prudent to be pursued by the State; or disregarding these, should ourselves determine that it is wise and politic, as tending to guard the institution of slavery, that no slaves should be permitted to be taken from the State for the purpose of emancipation, we should manifestly assume the functions of legislators, and not judges."

The court knew what everyone in Alabama knew. In 1852, the congressional debates over the admission of California as a free state, and the creation of the Fugitive Slave Act of 1850, had set teeth on edge in both free soil North and pro-slavery South. The number of contested slave cases in the state courts zoomed up in the year after the fiercely debated compromise. Many in the South, including Chilton's friend Yancey, pressed for secession to protect slavery. The movement for disunion was thwarted not by a spirit of compromise, but by the intervention of unionists like John C. Calhoun of South Carolina and Jefferson Davis of Mississippi. Nevertheless, both men warned that an assault on slavery by northern free soilers or abolitionists would result in secession. Thus every slave case was now resolved in the shadow of a national debate over the South's "peculiar institution."

Justice Chilton used the case to rehearse the nationwide debate over the expansion of slavery to the new western territories. Alabama had once been a part of that movement, its rich bottom lands luring masters and slaves from Virginia, the Carolinas, and Georgia. Now Alabama was a cotton state, and its slaves were immensely valuable; freeing them rather than allowing heirs and creditors to redeploy them was an act of immense generosity, not least to the slaves, but also to those who watched Alabama with critical eyes. In the national debate over the morality of slavery, the resolution of the Atwood bequest was a more important event than a simple lawsuit.

Chilton addressed these facts obliquely, indeed grudgingly. "The legislative authority has said, that slaves in this State shall continue such while they remain here, unless for good cause shown to the Probate judge, upon the petition of the master, after due publication made, they are set at liberty by the decree of such judge, and then, on condition of their removal without the State in twelve months; but the right of the owner to take or send them off as slaves so long as they remain in this State, but for the purpose of emancipation in a State where, by the law, this may be effected, has not been prohibited." The court knew the value of the slaves in question; indeed, of all the slaves in the state. "However much we might desire the law to be different, however much we might suppose sound policy requires that a restraint should be imposed upon this natural right of causing one's property to be removed to another State where it may be dealt with injuriously to our institutions, still, it is not for us to change or make the law."

Chilton could not forbear a last swipe at the policy that allowed benevolence in a time when abolitionist and free soil writers questioned the morality of the slaveholder, concealing his personal views in a riff on checks and balances in Alabama's self-government. "It is not for the court, but for the legislature, to determine whether there is too great a disproportion between the white and slave population of Alabama, or what number of slaves would best contribute to the security of the institution, and to the development of the wealth and agricultural resources of the State." Alabama needed its slaves. Alabama needed to show that its slavery was not inhumane. Alabama masters needed to know that the state would not so intrude into their property rights as to deny the right to do with their slaves as they wished. One can almost see Chilton gritting his teeth as he found for the trust to free and remunerate the freedmen and women: "because it would to this extent lessen the number of slaves, and, consequently, the wealth of Alabama, and would be adding to the free negro population of some sister State persons who may contribute to incite our slaves to insubordination or insurrection."

The Atwood slaves, freed in Ohio, would go on there and in Canada to careers of ability and repute. Perhaps Atwood knew this. After all, they were his progeny. Slaves had value on the market for their individual abilities. They were not interchangeable. For those who knew or could manipulate these facts, the internal slave trade was lucrative. As a whole it facilitated market exchanges, providing a labor supply for developing areas of the country. Robert Gudmestad's magisterial study of the internal slave trade used census and other data sets to estimate that over 350,000 men, women, and children moved from the Upper South to the Lower South, cutting ties of kinship and friendship. While it is difficult from the records to determine how many of these slaves were sold or sent on consignment and how many traveled to or with family members, there is no question that the buying and selling of slaves was a vital and profitable part of the "peculiar institution." Slaves took part in this enterprise, seeking to keep families together, to stay with or leave particular masters, or to negotiate in certain ways for themselves—even though, again ironically, the names of slaves at the center of the disputed sale most often did not appear in the case citations.

—⁂—

The statute law of slavery promoted the larger goal of complete control of slaves by their owners. In individual cases—that is, in the matters that ended up in the courts—one saw the ragged edges and the contradictions in the law of slavery by those who contrived to bend the law to their advantage. In one well-documented case, a buyer had just left the auction house with a young slave purchase when a passerby told the buyer that he had purchased a dead man; "the boy was sick, too sick to be cured." Lawyers for the buyers well knew the tricks of such sellers, using cod liver oil, for example, to give a semblance of life to a slave already dying from consumption.

As the anecdote above, widely shared at the time, indicates, in custom and self-definition, slave owners associated honor with fair dealing in slave sales and treatment. Indeed, so prevalent were these transactions, and so sensitive were white southerners about honor, that the two could hardly have been separated. But lawsuits between sellers and buyers of slaves illustrated all of the practices of the time—good faith and bad faith, risk taking and profit taking, and the movement of capital and labor over the land. Insofar as slavery as a system was profitable, and it was, slave selling and buying was an essential practice, but a number of these suits exhibited misrepresentations of various kinds.

Antebellum slave sales law adopted the doctrine that the law would protect a buyer from the seller's misconduct. Modern law deals with this under the classification of implied warranties. Buyers rely on the seller's information and probity that the purchase is suitable for the particular purpose the buyer has in mind. It is thus an irony that modern law matched slave law. There were protections for the buyer. If a seller represented that a field hand had certain characteristics of strength, endurance, and know-how, while a blacksmith or a cook had other skills, the purchaser might rely on the seller's presentation. The representation of the slave as being suited for a particular purpose would, were it taking place today, create an implied warranty of fitness for that purpose. If the seller knew and the buyer did not that the slave was unfit for that purpose, the sale was fraudulent.

The reason for these protections in the law of slave sales was that the buyer was also a slave owner or a slave trader, and the law was pro-slavery. A law that left the buyer without recourse in a fraudulent slave sale was not a pro-slavery law. Of course, a seller could aver that the defect in the product—the slave—was unknown to him, or, conversely, that the buyer knew and went ahead anyway. Even the claim that the price the parties agreed on included some sense of the slave's incapacity was subject to litigation. A parallel issue, whether the seller had good title to the slave, was similarly subject to litigation. Parole (oral) evidence of who said what to whom, as well as written evidence in contracts and bills of sale, were admissible in court. In any case, these questions were left to juries to decide, and jurors were most often slave owners themselves.

Elaborate rules for such transactions evolved in leading slave markets like Natchez, Mississippi; New Orleans, Louisiana; and Charleston, South Carolina. Sellers were not supposed to conceal infirmities when they presented their slave property for auction or private sale, but they did so. To bring a suit for "redhibition" under Louisiana law, voiding the sale and returning the purchase price, the new owner had to demonstrate that he had taken all reasonable measures to find out the condition and state of the slave. This included physical and emotional defects and behavioral problems (running away, for example). The same was true if the seller said that he either had title to the slave or represented someone who owned the slave. If the slave was stolen from its legal owner, or the title to the slave was unclear (for example, in a contested estate proceeding), then the sale was fraudulent. Thus honor, a cultural construction, became a legal precept—good-faith dealing on both sides aided the slave system in functioning smoothly.

The litigation surrounding these cases reveals how a society supposedly based on honorable dealings actually rested on fraud, peculation, and speculation. The estate cases confuted the much-touted values of family and family sentiment. As Alabama slaveholder Gabriel Thomas wrote to his sister regarding one potential suit, "View the whole ground—ponder well your footsteps—commune with your own heart" before you go to court. What made these cases significant, however, was not mere duplicity, but the surge in numbers in the 1850s. As in *Atwood*, it was the debate over the Fugitive Slave Law of 1850, the limitation of the expansion of slavery into the territories, the sudden rise in the price of slaves, and the increasingly potent campaigning of the abolitionists that made every dispute over the conduct of slave sales so fraught. With so much at stake in purely financial terms, it was no wonder that the courts heard case after case of fraudulent sales—a phenomenon not unknown to courts today.

In Alabama, civil disputes over slave sales and other such matters came to the attention of the lower state courts. More and more of the time, losing parties carried the case to the state's supreme court. From 1820 to 1860, there were sixteen hundred of these cases, including disputes over hiring slaves, sales, inheritance, and the negligence of slaves. A review of the case numbers in Lexis shows a distinct bump at the start of the 1850s, followed by a leveling off.

Many of the cases in this bump concern the hiring out of slaves, particularly in the urban areas of the state, and disputes over the condition of slaves sold. The former arose out of the abuse of hirelings, hence the damage to the property of the master. There might be violations of the terms of the agreement for hire, for example using the slave for a job not contemplated by the owner or failure to provide for the health and welfare of the hired slave, or failure to pay for treatment, returning the slave to the owner worse for wear, or not returning a deceased slave at all. Leasors and hirers seemed less concerned about the welfare of the slaves, even though a law in 1852 enjoined them to be more vigilant and gave expanded grounds for suing to the owners. In general, when such laws appear, the underlying social fact is that there are more cases of that type happening.

An additional eighty cases, almost all in the decade, concerned fraud in sales of slaves, many of these cases coming in the last years before the war, as prices for slaves, hence the motive for fraud, soared. For example, between 1850 and 1860, twenty-five cases of diseased slaves sold supposedly in good health came before the Supreme Court of Alabama. In all of them, seller and buyer disputed both ordinary observations and expert medical testimony about when and how the slaves became ill. Sellers were passing off slaves with persistent ailments as sound, including a number of cases in which, shortly after the sale was consummated, the slave died of the ailment. While some of these cases might be attributed to the notorious fast dealing of auctioneers, most involved sellers who had some reputation in the community.

But slaves were commodities, sales were commercial transactions, and despite the ideal of gentility and the mores of trustworthiness, money was always useful. As James Oakes has concluded in his *Ruling Race*, even slave-owning professionals, the lawyers, doctors, and merchants who rose to the top of society alongside the great planters, were willing to go into debt to buy their way into the landed gentry. In need of money, and willing to sell slaves to repay what they owed for their other purchases, they had little scruple about a little fraud. Indeed, slaves were the best security against bankruptcy, for they retained their value even in hard times—except when they were sick. After all, the nutrition of slaves did not promote health, nor did working conditions, nor did medical care for pregnant women, the very young, and the very old. And even when average diets were fairly nutritious, not every slave had an adequate diet. Thus the doctors who found slaves sound at the time of sale had an interest in the sale as well as in the health of the slave patient. As the numbers of slaveholders grew, with some 170,000 people entering the slaveholding class between 1830 and 1860, the numbers of such suspect sales naturally grew apace (this is called trended data), but as the number of fraudulent sales became larger, the specter of fraud became more common. With that, the underpinnings of a society supposedly built on trust and honor fell away. The slaveholding culture of master and servant had become a culture of buyer and seller.

What all of these cases demonstrate is, as legal historian Ariela Gross has written, that "the road from the slave market in southern towns inexorably led to the courthouse." Following the romantic mischaracterization of slave society by contemporary apologists, some historians have argued that honor for the slaveholder meant avoiding litigation. Honorable men did not sue one another. The slave cases paint a very different picture. They show that honor and litigation were intertwined. An honorable seller did not hide defects or lie under oath when these defects were revealed. An honorable buyer made every effort to inquire into the real condition of slaves. Honorable men treated slaves in the stream of commerce properly, not breaking up families or sending away slaves who did not consent to go. Of course, students of the slave trade have seen the ugly truth behind these claims. Sale and purchase was a necessary evil of the commerce in slavery, and fraud was common. Honor became a defense in litigation, a pose, in the words of Gross, that "spilled in and out of the courtroom." Indeed, the very terminology fashioned to "dishonor" a transaction became a term of art in these cases.

Viewing the numbers of cases and looking inside individual cases suggests that something was going wrong in the slave society that the cases themselves cannot explain. There was something that aggravated suspicion of fraud and made buyers more eager to go to law rather than to settle out of court and made sellers a little more unscrupulous. As Chief Justice Chilton hinted, the closing of the southern frontier after the Compromise of 1850 had something to do with heightened social tension, for now the slave population increase that had fueled expansion looked more ominous. Without new lands to cultivate with slaves, the density of slaves on existing southern lands would grow, and that raised the specter of slave rebellion.

Making that specter the more real in southern minds was the growing anti-slavery sentiment of the North. What once had been a small and largely despised abolitionism had become a major force in northern society. In 1854, the newly formed Republican Party, a party with no grass-roots support in the South, made free soil a centerpiece of its platform.

The free soil movement called for an end to the expansion of slavery. Free soil was not the same as abolitionism, but abolitionists like John C. Fremont found a home in the Republican Party, and in 1856 he gained a near majority of votes for president in the North. Fremont, whose adventures had taken him to the Deep South and the Far West, would be one of the first Union army generals to free all the slaves that came into his camps. Southern anxiety had a political side to it—growing secessionist sentiment—but because it was southern slavery that was under siege, another by-product of the siege mentality was litigiousness over slavery. No one was safe from it, certainly not the most distrusted whites in the South, the slave traders and their agents, nor even the topmost figures in society.

In all these ways, slavery litigation was both private—involving buyers and sellers, testators, creditors, and heirs—and public. Slavery could not exist without the power of the state behind the power of the slave owner and slave trader. When slavery was ended by the Thirteenth Amendment, it was the federal government and the Constitution as amended that stood behind universal emancipation. The Thirteenth Amendment was at the time and for many years thereafter the most extensive "taking" of private property in our history. It exceeded in total financial value the taking of native peoples' land by the first European settlers, the acquisition of land from Mexico as a result of the Mexican-American War in 1848, and the imposition of income taxes in the first income tax statutes after the Sixteenth Amendment. The Thirteenth applied not just to former rebels, as a form of confiscation of contraband in time of civil war, but to everyone who owned slaves and to every slave. Those slaveholders who remained loyal to the Union in the South and in the North were similarly affected. It was for its time the largest imposition on private property rights, dwarfing other Civil War confiscation and sequestration (including the seizure of ships and cargos in the blockade of southern ports), taxation, the issuance of federal "greenback" paper currency as legal tender, customs duties, and fines.

—⁂—

Suits for remission of the rigors of slavery continue today in the form of suits for reparations. The concept of reparations is a legal one, derived from the same jurisprudence of "equity" as practiced in the New Jersey colonial courts of chancery. Federal courts gained equitable jurisprudence in the federal Constitution and in the 1789 Judiciary Act. State courts also exercised the old powers of the king's chancellors. These federal and state courts, like the colonial courts and the court held by the king's secretary, or chancellor, derived their basic precepts from older ideas of doing justice in individual cases where going to law offered no relief.

Restitution, a form of equitable relief, was designed to give to aggrieved parties what had unjustly been taken from them. Thus, if a contract worker had largely but not wholly completed a task and was denied any payment because she failed to fulfill the terms of the contract, an equitable suit for restitution would gain the worker payment for the services she had performed. The essence of restitution is to prevent the defendant from being unjustly enriched by the plaintiff's labor. What if the defendant stripped the innocent of their possessions down to the gold in their teeth, or grew rich on the forced labor of others? Would the petitioner in equity seeking restitution not be entitled to it? History offers many cases of this very injustice, and the collaboration of equity and history affords the descendants and survivors of those so deprived of a remedy. This kind of remedy would and could not be the making whole of the victims in every case of historical injustice, for in most of the cases the victims have gone to their final reward. But their families and descendants can bring suits in equity for reparations.

Reparation suits of this kind can reach back into the distant past. The trigger for reparations for this kind of harm is proof of past injustice with continuing consequences in the present. Reparations may be financial. In 1971, congressional acts provided $1 billion in reparations, along with forty-four million acres of land, to Alaskan native peoples. Courts returned tribal lands to other native peoples throughout the 1970s and 1980s. After a lawsuit seeking an equitable remedy, Japanese Americans interned during World War II were given reparations by Congress in 1988 to the tune of $1.6 billion (or $20,000 for every survivor of the so-called relocation camps). In determining the amount and the recipients of these reparations, historical records and historical research was crucial, and historians played a pivotal role.

Reparations for American slavery and the slave trade are an even larger challenge to the collaboration of equity and history, for slavery in America was impossible without the active assistance of the law. Let's review:

Slavery was a divisive question at the federal constitutional convention of 1787. There the framers, with the exceptions of anti-slave spokesmen Elbridge Gerry, Rufus King, and Gouverneur Morris, sought a compromise between freedom and free labor, on the one hand, and slavery and slave labor on the other. The federal Constitution never mentioned slavery, but it provided for a three-fifths portion of total slaves to count in states' apportionment; it allowed the despised international slave trade to continue until 1808; and, most controversially, it provided for the rendition of those "owing labor" in one state who fled to be forcibly returned to the state from which they came. Slavery was to be legal where state law established it and illegal where state law barred it.

In antebellum federal slavery cases like *Prigg v. Pennsylvania* (1842), the federal courts not only acceded to the "peculiar institution," they protected it. Justice Joseph Story, who wrote the decision of the high court in *Prigg*, was a professional from head to toe, a law professor at Harvard as well as a respected member of the Supreme Court, and the author of commentaries on the Constitution and other legal subjects. He abhorred the institution of slavery and said so in his private correspondence. He nevertheless recognized slavery's constitutional posture—the Rendition Clause dictated, "No person held to service or labour in one state under the laws thereof, escaping into another, shall in consequence of any law or regulation therein, be discharged from such service or labour; but shall be delivered up, on claim of the party to whom such service or labour may be due." Story felt obliged by his professional duty as a judge to opine that the state of Pennsylvania could not try a slave catcher for kidnaping an alleged runaway. As he wrote to a friend, shortly after the Court announced the decision and Massachusetts abolitionists' voices rose to condemn him, "You know full well that I have ever been opposed to slavery. But I take my standard of duty as a judge from the Constitution."

Although slavery ended with the Thirteenth Amendment to the federal Constitution, its lasting impact continued in the Jim Crow era from the end of Reconstruction through the 1950s. It was an instance of unjust enrichment (see *Britton v. Turner* in chapter 4 below), when the descendants of slaves were forced by racialist state laws into tenancy, sharecropping, and cheap manual labor. In 2002, nine suits were filed around the country by groups of litigants collectively termed African American

Descendants of Slave Families against existing tobacco, bank, finance, and railway corporations whose origins and economic viability allegedly rested on the slave trade or the products of slave labor.

The theory behind the suit was that every slave family was victimized by predatory antebellum capitalism, and thus any of the descendants had a legitimate claim against the companies that profited from slavery. It was a class action suit, but it lacked proximate cause—that is, the proof that any particular defendant had harmed any particular ancestor of the class plaintiffs. In effect, plaintiffs contended that slavery itself was the harm that the companies had perpetuated. One defense would have been that slavery was legal at the time, and companies benefiting from legal activities could not be forced to pay reparations for what was a moral delict rather than a legal one, but that was for the courts to decide in litigation.

These suits were consolidated and heard in the Northern District of Illinois federal court, Judge Charles R. Norgle presiding. Norgle had long experience on the bench in DuPage County, Illinois, and was elevated to the federal bench by President Ronald Reagan in 1984. Sometimes controversial, always conservative, he worried that the plaintiffs could not produce evidence to show that they, in their own persons, had been harmed by the misconduct of the corporations. When plaintiffs asked for a ruling requiring defendants to preserve their relevant records so that counsel could search for the required personal connection, Judge Norgle recognized that the plaintiffs "identify themselves as formerly enslaved African-Americans or descendants of formerly enslaved African-Americans and seek monetary and injunctive relief against various corporate institutions, Defendants, for present and past wrongs in connection with the institution of slavery," but did not offer evidence that they had themselves been harmed by the defendant corporations. That gap in the plaintiffs' suit would become crucial.

Norgle continued, "No party disputes the evils of slavery. One specific remedy Plaintiffs seek is that Defendants be 'compelled to produce documents that reveal crucial information surrounding the institution of slavery and the economic benefits that flowed therefrom.'" In short, the plaintiffs wanted the court to aid them in pointing the finger of blame at the defendant corporations. In similar suits, courts ordered "discovery" of documentary evidence in the hands of one party sought by another.

This was a power that courts of equity had for nearly a thousand years, and it was incorporated in the Federal Rules of Civil Procedure in 1938.

Under modern rules of pleading, defendants must produce documents they would have asked for had they been plaintiffs, but the case did not get that far, because Judge Norgle ruled that "Plaintiffs' fail to specifically identify what documents they are seeking to preserve or what time frame the document preservation order should encompass." One might wonder how the plaintiffs could be specific without access to the documentary evidence in the hands of the defendants, but Judge Norgle did not weigh that possibility. Instead, he implied that the plaintiffs' attorneys were going on a fishing expedition, hoping to find evidence of defendants' complicity. "Plaintiffs merely present an overly broad and vague statement as to the documents that they are seeking and assert that document preservation is needed." The defendants' counsel had already told the judge that they had searched for the relevant evidence in good faith when the plaintiffs had first asked for it, and could not find it. The records of their pre-1865 business had been lost or destroyed.

The judge was not persuaded that the defendants were acting in bad faith, that is, that they were lying about the existence of the pre-1865 records. The historical record, as opposed to the legal records, was clear. Everyone knew that the defendants had a hand in profiting from slavery in a general way, for example lending money to slaveholders or handling slave sales or the sales of the products of slave labor, but for the suit to proceed, plaintiffs had to prove that the defendants had a direct connection with the forebears of the plaintiffs. Even were the records intact and produced at trial, most slaves were only distantly connected with the companies that sold tobacco products, or with the banks that financed those sales, or with the railroad lines that carried the products to distant markets. It would take a far more inventive and sweeping reading of the role of courts, the use of evidence, and, at the end, the arrangement of remedies to connect these dots.

Judge Norgle subsequently ruled that the case had no merit on its face and dismissed it. The Court of Appeals for the Seventh Circuit upheld his ruling. Judge Richard Posner wrote the opinion for the Court of appeals. Posner is one of the leading exponents of the law and economics school of tort jurisprudence. That school, associated with the University of Chicago School of Law, argues that the economic consequences of legal decisions should be factored into them. Here, the hidden issue was the economic impact of reparations on the present-day commerce of the nation. Judge Posner did not begin with that issue, however, instead reserving it for the very end of his opinion. He began with the history of the lawsuits. "Nine suits were filed in federal district courts around the country seeking monetary relief under both federal and state law for harms stemming from the enslavement of black people in America. A tenth suit, by the Hurdle group of plaintiffs, makes similar claims but was filed in a state court and then removed by the defendants to a federal district court. The Multidistrict Litigation Panel consolidated all the suits in the district court in Chicago for pretrial proceedings."

Posner then summarized the gist of the suits with an almost studied dispassion. The law for him was not about the immorality of slavery or the complicity of early national business firms. "The suits are a series of mostly identical class actions on behalf of all Americans descended from slaves with whom one or more of the defendants or their corporate predecessors may have been directly or indirectly involved. . . . The defendants are companies or the successors to companies that provided services, such as transportation, finance, and insurance, to slaveowners. At least two of the defendants *were* slaveowners; the predecessor of one of the bank defendants once accepted 13,000 slaves as collateral on loans and ended up owning 1,250 of them when the borrowers defaulted, and the predecessor of another defendant ended up owning 346 slaves, also as a consequence of a borrower's default." But slavery was legal, wasn't it, and its profits therefore legal? "Even before the Thirteenth Amendment, slavery was illegal in the northern states, and the complaint charges that the defendants were violating the laws of those states in transacting with slaveowners. It also claims that there were occasional enslavements long after the passage of the Thirteenth Amendment and that some of the defendants were complicit in those too. By way of relief, the complaint seeks disgorgement to the class members of the profits that the defendants obtained from their dealings with slaveowners."

Posner's elucidation of the historical question was crystal clear, a product of years of writing books for general readers on how judges think. The legal question, however, was not so easily parsed. "The legal basis for the plaintiffs' federal claim is [the federal statute] which provides that 'all citizens of the United States shall have the same right, in every State and Territory, as is enjoyed by white citizens thereof to inherit, purchase, lease, sell, hold, and convey real and personal property.'" Here was the problem: "A claim based on a federal statute invokes the federal-question jurisdiction of the federal courts. But since most of the conduct of which the plaintiffs complain occurred prior to the passage of the Thirteenth Amendment, and indeed prior to the Civil War, does not provide a sturdy basis for the retention of federal jurisdiction over the plaintiffs' nonfederal claims." What seemed to be an "aha" was in fact a crucial matter of federalism—the division of suits between the two judicial systems. That division was even stronger before the Civil War than it is now.

Posner opined that the case did not belong in federal court because the grievance of slavery was not a federal one. According to the antebellum U.S. Supreme Court, slavery was a matter of state law. That is, federal law passed to the states the choice of being a free state or a slave state. There was a loophole for the plaintiffs. If the plaintiffs were citizens of one state and the defendant corporation was chartered in another, plaintiffs could bring the suit to the federal courts under the rule of "diversity" of residence of the parties. But even this loophole could be closed if the corporation did business in the state where a plaintiff lived. Judge Norgle had ruled that the suits did not belong in the federal courts because there was no diversity and because the matter was political rather than judicial. In effect, he left the plaintiffs to seek a legislative remedy, much as the victims of Japanese relocation camps during World War II gained reparations from Congress. Posner agreed.

Now came Posner's treatment of the economic question:

> A case that sought reparations for the wrong of slavery would encounter financial obstacles, but the plaintiffs have been careful to cast the litigation as a quest for conventional legal relief. All they are asking the federal judiciary to do is to apply state law (plus the one federal statute), to the defendants' conduct. They face, of course, formidable obstacles, quite apart from the severely limited applicability [of the federal laws]. To name just one of those obstacles, it is highly unlikely that antebellum laws in northern states were intended to confer financial or other benefits on the twenty-first century descendants of slaves.

Still, those damage awards would have been limited to the actual slaves harmed.

But the slaves did not have standing to bring the suit in the first place, as they were not citizens of the United States or foreign nationals. They were property. Property cannot sue persons. Posner relied here on *Dred Scott v. Sandford* (1857), although he did not cite this infamous case in his opinion. In it, Chief Justice Roger Taney, for himself and one other justice, Peter Daniel of Virginia, said that African Americans could never be citizens. This obiter dictum (a statement not necessary to settle the case) was answered by the first clause of the Fourteenth Amendment (anyone born in the United States was a citizen of the United States and the state in which that person resided). That amendment came after the end of slavery, but Judge Posner did not note that birthright citizenship applied retroactively—that is, men and women freed by the Thirteenth Amendment who were born in the United States were made citizens by the Fourteenth Amendment.

Posner conceded that the legal iniquities that slavery imposed on the slaves continued to injure the descendants of slaves. Take the case of Aetna Insurance, one of the defendants. "Aetna is alleged to have written several insurance policies on slaves in the 1850s in violation of state law applicable to the company, and to have obtained premiums from the insureds—the slaveowners—that (we'll assume) exceeded the cost of the insurance to Aetna (its expenses plus the payment of proceeds if the insured event came to pass). The plaintiffs argue that Aetna's net income from this insurance was a wrongful profit that the company should be ordered to restore to the plaintiff classes." The judge's law and economic analysis was stated as though it were legal doctrine rather than economic theory: "If the insurance business was competitive back then (and the plaintiffs do not argue that it was not), Aetna did not profit in an economic sense from the transactions of which the plaintiffs complain (its "profit" would just be its cost of equity capital), and in any event it would have distributed any profits from the transactions to its share-holders long ago."

An even more sophisticated set of circumstances, all of which were hypothetical, followed: "The plaintiffs introduce another claim of injury by asserting that had the defendants refused to violate their own states' laws by doing business with slaveowners, there would have been less slavery because the refusal would have been tantamount to subjecting the slaveowners to a partial boycott." In other words, denied the services of companies, slave owners would have found the "peculiar institution" more expensive to operate, "and, by making slavery less profitable, might have reduced the amount of it." Or, Posner posed, such deprivation might simply have depressed the purchase price of slaves. In any case, "this causal chain is too long and has too many weak links for a court to be able to find that the defendants' conduct harmed the plaintiffs at all, let alone in an amount that could be estimated without the wildest speculation." In passing, one might add that Posner, a sophisticated and insightful exponent of law and economics, did not address the question of the inherited wealth that generations of persons of color could have passed to their children and grandchildren—had all of these generations of men and women not been bound in slavery.

—⁊⁊⁊—

A nationwide campaign of litigation to right a hundred-year-old wrong had failed, or had it? For if litigation in the twenty-first century still rests on a sense of wronged honor, the reparations suits did do something that the plaintiffs wanted. Many of the companies, including major banks and financial institutions, accepted the blame and apologized. Although not part of the *In Re African American Descendants* litigation, Brown University, whose eponymous founder, the Brown family, was a major player in the American slave trade, recognized the core values of the lawsuit. Reparations to the victims of the slave trade would involve an astronomical amount of money, but another kind of restitution remedy was available. Payouts were not an option, but part of this apology was an attempt to retrieve the history and apply it to the remedy.

Brown University's coverage of the reparations debate at Brown was exhaustive and, though in some ways self-serving (after all, it exonerated one of the biggest slave traders in early American history and the college that slave-trading profits made possible), gave evidence of the seriousness with which the university took its legal and historical obligations in the shadow of the courthouse. In 2003, Brown University president Ruth J. Simmons appointed a Steering Committee on Slavery and Justice to investigate the university's historical relationship to slavery and the transatlantic slave trade. On October 18, 2006, the committee reported its findings. These were released to the public. In short, using history itself as a kind of restitution brought together the skills of the historian, preparing and displaying the materials, and the conceptual virtuosity of the law. For "the committee was also asked to reflect on the meaning of this history in the present, on the complex historical, political, legal, and moral questions posed by any present-day confrontation with past injustice."

The last three pages of the eighty-eight-page report lined out the recommendations of the Committee on Slavery and Justice. Every one of the recommendations rested upon the assumption that public awareness and expert judgment were both essential components of the legal idea of restitution. Litigation was not necessary to "acknowledge formally and publicly the participation of many of Brown's founders and benefactors in the institution of slavery and the transatlantic slave trade, as well as the benefits that the University derived from them." Nor to "tell the truth in all its complexity." Nor to engage in making Brown University into a "living site of memory." Such steps, "without provoking paralysis or shame," restored honor to those from whom it had been taken.

The proposals were an alternative to litigation for monetary damages, based on the idea that information was itself a remedy to the damages that slavery had imposed on an entire people. These were the very qualities that had caused the buyers and sellers of slaves to bring suits in the first place, now extended to the slaves they bought and sold. Whether such remedies replaced the lost value of slave labor, much less the thousands of everyday indignities of slavery, remains an open question. While this list of reparations did not arrange to repay unpaid wages or restore lost goods, it did seek to do equity in a broader way. If equity reunites what past injustice has torn asunder, the institutional support of historical studies of slavery and the slave trade restores something of great value to the descendants of slavery's victims. It gives them back a history; indeed, it reminds everyone, white and black, of the contributions of the slaves to the American economy, of the ways in which slaves created their own culture and family life in the midst of their travails, and it reminds us of the courage of those who risked life and limb, and left parents and children behind, to flee slavery or to rebel against it. Restitution reunites what had been unjustly severed—the story of one part of our people from the rest.

4

Free Labor?

IN THE 1830S, THE DEFENSE of slavery spilled over into the free states as anti-abolitionist mobs attacked anti-slavery speakers and destroyed abolitionist presses. The mobs' purpose was not so much to defend slavery as to protect jobs against competition from slaves. In response, "free soil" politicians denounced slavery not because of its injustice to the slave, but because of its affront to the ideal of free labor. It was this pride that infused Abraham Lincoln's speech at the Wisconsin State Fair in 1859: "Men, with their families—wives, sons and daughters—work for themselves, on their farms, in their houses and in their shops, taking the whole product to themselves, and asking no favors of capital on the one hand, nor of hirelings or slaves on the other." Lawyer William Henry Seward, campaigning for candidates of the new Republican Party in Rochester, New York, in 1858, put the contrast between the two systems of labor starkly: "It is an irrepressible conflict between opposing and enduring forces, and it means that the United States must and will, sooner or later, become either entirely a slave-holding nation or entirely a free-labor nation."

Over the same course of time from 1800 to 1860 as slavery entrenched itself in southern state law, wage earners in the North became self-conscious defenders of the virtue of free labor. Just as the southern courts recognized the vital importance of slave labor to the economic life of the South, so courts in the free states began to credit the importance of free labor. This was something new, for although in northern states slavery was outlawed, most laborers were not exactly free, at least not at first. At the outset of the nineteenth century, many workers in the North were servants, or apprentices, or contract laborers. The law of labor, as legal historian Robert Steinfeld has reminded us, favored the employers. They could bring suit against workers who did not finish jobs or who left the vicinity. Indentured laborers, brought to the new nation to carve out its canals and built its first railways, responded by claiming that they were not slaves, and should not be treated as such. Female domestics agreed, announcing that they were maids rather than servants.

In the first decades of the nineteenth century, wage labor, with a fixed compensation for daily performance, was replacing the indenture, under which a contract for labor extended for a fixed term of months or years. Native-born and imported laborers were paid their agreed-upon wages at the completion of a specified job. Nevertheless, there was no way in which most employers could enforce the terms of the wage contract save refusal to pay what was owed for partial completion of the contracted labor. Laborers could simply walk off the job. Even closely watched workers like those in the first textile mills could simply find other employment, sometimes with rival mills, because the demand for labor exceeded the supply of willing hands. Workers, particularly farmhands, bargained with their feet. This kind of freedom—freedom to leave— did not translate into bargaining power for wages or work already done, however.

Even as farm labor was freeing itself from the constraints of indentured servitude, mill and factory workers were finding that their bargaining power was diminishing. As immigrants poured into the nation's ports and young men and women left the farms to seek employment in the cities, the supply of industrial laborers began to match the demand. By the end of the 1830s, the machinery of the mills and the wheels of the railroads were spinning faster and faster, increasing productivity, lowering costs, and causing accidents. Employers relied on the courts to protect industry by attributing the fault of accidents to workers' fellows, rather than their employers. This was a subsidy to industry paid by the workers. The lawsuits workers brought to recover for these accidents reflected the workers' determination to assert their value as individuals even as that individuality was constrained by mass production.

The struggle of labor to control the conditions of the workplace, to gain equal footing with their employers, in short, to be free, remains a constant. From the Irish guest workers who dug the Erie Canal in the 1810s and cut the Pennsylvania Railroad's right-of-way through the Alleghany Mountains in the 1840s, to the guest workers from the Caribbean and Mexico who plant and harvest sugar and lettuce in Florida and California today, the litigation begun in the first decades of the nineteenth century continues.

Unlike the public figures in the defamation cases, the leaders of land revolts who landed in the criminal courts, and the wealthy slave owners whose names fill court dockets, the ordinary laboring men who filed lawsuits for themselves and their fellow workers have left little trace in the historical record. Akin to the cynical English philosopher Thomas Hobbes's men in a state of nature, the laboring masses were born to nasty, brutish, and short lives, and died almost anonymously. I say almost because they lent their names to the lawsuits in this chapter. Thus, Hobbes was wrong about these men in one respect. They were never just solitary objects of the law; through their litigation they were also makers of the law.

In the New England and Pennsylvania textile industry of the 1810s and 1820s, workers were hired under "entire contracts." These mill hands, most often young women from rural areas who had come to labor in factories to supplement family income, could not recover back pay if they left before the end of each year. By the 1850s, this had changed. In a myriad of suits in Massachusetts and Pennsylvania, lawyers obtained partial wages for their clients. Often the lawyers had ambitions that extended beyond the courtroom. These lawyer-politicians saw workers as voters and lawsuits for back pay as vehicles to publicize their attachment to workers' rights. The judges in these cases were also politicians, for state judicial office was elective. But the two political tracks were separate, with lawyers like William Seward of New York and Alexander Stephens of Georgia going on to seats in the state and federal assemblies and governorships, and, in the case of Abraham Lincoln, the presidency. Most of the judges, by inclination, remained in the judicial branch or returned to private practice.

In *Britton v. Turner* (1834), the New Hampshire Supreme Court signaled this shift to favor the rights of workers. Associate Justice Joel Parker wrote the opinion. Hardly a pro-labor radical, he served briefly in the state assembly and then for the rest of his life on the bench. He

also taught law at Dartmouth College and Harvard Law School. Parker
began with an assumption of fact, "that the labor performed by the plaintiff, and for which he seeks to recover a compensation in this action, was
commenced under a special contract to labor for the defendant the term
of one year, for the sum of one hundred and twenty dollars, and that the
plaintiff has labored but a portion of that time, and has voluntarily failed
to complete the entire contract." This was the "entire contract" theory.
"It is clear, then, that he is not entitled to recover upon the contract itself,
because the service, which was to entitle him to the sum agreed upon, has
never been performed." Britton had voluntarily broken or "breached" his
contract with Turner and, under contract law, was entitled to nothing
for his labor. Now came Parker's bombshell. "But the question arises,
can the plaintiff, under these circumstances, recover a reasonable sum for
the service he has actually performed, under the count (the legal argument) in *quantum meruit* (for the work he did). Upon this, and questions
of a similar nature, the decisions to be found in the books are not easily
reconciled."

Parker saw this as a new and important question. Such hard cases do
not always produce good law, but he was undeterred. Time has proven
his innovative reasoning a lasting contribution to labor law. First, he had
to deal with the contract question. "It has been held, upon contracts of
this kind for labor to be performed at a specified price, that the party who
voluntarily fails to fulfil the contract by performing the whole labor contracted for, is not entitled to recover any thing for the labor actually performed, however much he may have done towards the performance, and
this has been considered the settled rule of law upon this subject." Parker
replaced the unjust rule with a just one in one sentence. "That such rule
in its operation may be very unequal, not to say unjust, is apparent."
Instead, the worker who partially performed a task was only liable for
"the damages which the other party has sustained by reason of such non
performance," that is, more or less, finding someone else to finish the job,
"whereas a party who in good faith has entered upon the performance
of his contract, and nearly completed it, and then abandoned the further
performance" loses all the pay to which he was entitled for his labor. He
bears the entire loss of the value he added to the job. It made no sense
to Parker. It was a mere "technical rule" from a time gone by in a place
across the ocean, a time when workers were regarded as servants and a

servant who ran away from a job could be jailed for not finishing it. A further irony was that "by the operation of this rule, then, the party who attempts performance may be placed in a much worse situation than he who wholly disregards his contract" or does nothing to fulfill it.

Parker treated the case before the court as an illustration of his reasoning. The defendant gained unjustly from the worker's labor if the defendant did not have to pay anything. "If the defendant can succeed in this defence, he in fact receives nearly five sixths of the value of a whole year's labor" for nothing. He gains unjustly. In fact, if employers could drive off contract workers before they had fulfilled their contracts, and then win when the employee sued, they would be enriched by the labor and not have to pay a cent for it. That is exactly what some unscrupulous shipowners were doing with their crews—contracting for the entire voyage, then applying such savage discipline to members of the crew that some jumped ship before the end of the return voyage. They did not get a cent for their labor. In the same year that Parker announced his decision, Richard Henry Dana, a young Boston lawyer, signed on board a merchant ship to document this abuse of sailors. His *Two Years Before the Mast* (1834) was a pioneer whistle-blower book and led to legal reforms, for "sailors need most the protection of the law. On such voyages as these, there are many cases of outrageous cruelty on record, enough to make one heartsick, and almost disgusted with the sight of man; and many, many more, which have never come to light, and never will be known, until the sea shall give up its dead."

Parker told the employer "who contracts for labor merely, for a certain period, does so with full knowledge that he must, from the nature of the case, be accepting part performance from day to day, if the other party commences the performance, and with knowledge also that the other may eventually fail of completing the entire term." Free labor flowed through the country like a current. Farmers' sons from Parker's New Hampshire, like Daniel Webster, went to Boston, or, like future Supreme Court justices like Stephen J. Field, to far-off California gold fields. Entire families packed up their household goods in farm wagons, rechristened prairie schooners, and headed to the Midwest, or took the overland trail to Oregon. Everywhere, free Americans were in motion. The law of labor must account for this constant ebb and flow of men and women. "This rule, by binding the employer to pay the value of the service he actually receives, and the laborer to answer in damages where he does not complete the entire contract, will leave no temptation to the former to drive the laborer from his service, near the close of his term, by ill treatment, in order to escape from payment; nor to the latter to desert his service before the stipulated time, without a sufficient reason; and it will in most instances settle the whole controversy in one action, and prevent a multiplicity of suits and cross actions."

Britton was a craftsman, an artisan from a world in which individuals worked alone or with a handful of others building, forging, or fabricating objects of use one at a time. Perhaps this made his case, and that of his fellow craftsmen, atypical of the experience of the factory workers. But the precedent applied to them as well. It could not give the workingman of 1840 what earlier generations of artisans had enjoyed—a sense of workmanship and pride in the goods they crafted.

—⚭—

When capital investment (in part the return on staple exports like cotton that slavery made possible) and technological advances promoted the growth of industry in the 1840s and after, many workers found themselves little more than extensions of the machines they ran and repaired. This sense that free labor was being dishonored spread throughout the North. Some of the anger at lost status workers displaced into politics, resulting in the creation of popular workingman's parties like the Loco Focos (named after a type of matchstick used in evening demonstrations). Other workers organized to improve pay, working conditions, and hours.

The most visible expression of labor organization in the North was the labor "union." As historian Sean Wilentz explains, "the union formed their own political community," creating a sense of unity, purpose, and equality. The union allowed the rank and file "to have their say in public events." Women in the shoe factories and the textile mills created their own organizations to build unity and protest ill treatment, but the unions were male.

Unions elected officers and published newspapers. Union men paraded and held festivals. Such gatherings fostered a self-consciousness that went beyond the free labor idea. The unions were largely composed of craftsmen, and they saw themselves as above the ordinary day laborer.

This class divisiveness would continue into the craft and industrial union divide in the twentieth century, but for the present, it served to give the union men a sense of dignity that industrialization denied them. When they saw injustice to their numbers, they employed a tactic that brought them into the purview of the law: the strike. Strikes, with picket lines, were a kind of demonstration that the law regarded as proof of restraint of trade, an illegal combination or "conspiracy." Here private disputes overlapped criminal prosecutions. Forming a union was a crime.

In *Commonwealth v. Hunt* (1842), all of these rules about unions were tested. Only rarely do cases result in new law. This occurs when a court of appeals decides that old rules no longer fit new conditions.

Robert Rantoul Jr., counsel for the defendants, was a Jacksonian Democrat, a former member of the state house of representatives, future federal attorney for the district of Massachusetts, and, briefly, U.S. senator. He understood the political as well as the free labor and union consequences of the case. It was the most important of his career. The indictment against the seven union men was harsh, though its language was a formula going back to old English law. The offense was simply their agreement among themselves not to work for employers who paid too little, their creation of the Boston Journeymen Bootmakers Society, and their pressure on shoemakers not to employ anyone who did not belong to their society. They were found guilty and fined at trial. They appealed to the Massachusetts Supreme Judicial Court.

Rantoul's task was easy in one sense and hard in another. It was easy to argue that nothing should be a crime that was not made a crime by statute—that is, by the act of the legislature. Anything else was undemocratic. "As we have no statute concerning conspiracy, the facts alleged in the indictment constitute an offence, if any, at common law. But the English common law of conspiracy is not in force in this State. We have not adopted the whole mass of the common law of England, indiscriminately, nor of the English statute law which passed either before or after the settlement of our country."

That was the easy part. The hard part was that courts throughout the country for the past forty years had adopted the English common-law view of unionization as a criminal conspiracy. So he had to banish the precedent. "The English law, as to acts in restraint of trade, is generally local in its nature, and not suited to our condition. It has never been adopted here." Well, not adopted by statute law, but followed by courts. "All the law we ever had on these subjects was domestic, and is now obsolete." Free labor was a new concept. The old case law on restraint of trade came from a time before free labor, and if it made sense, it made sense when most labor was a form of servitude under the old English statute of artificers of 1563.

Look at the language of that obsolete law (on which the present prosecutions were based), Rantoul told the court, and find admonitions like "that no person retained according to this statute shall depart from his master, mistress, or dame before the end of his or her term." This was precisely what Justice Parker had rejected in *Britton*. "The statutes of laborers were blind struggles of the feudal nobles to avert from themselves the effects of great national calamities. Every one of these statutes had a local and temporary cause." They should not apply in an era of free labor.

Chief Justice Lemuel Shaw was persuaded, but not immediately. He was cautious by nature and conservative in his views, but highly moralistic. He was opposed to the expansion of slavery, finding in *Commonwealth v. Aves* (1836) that no one domiciled in Massachusetts (i.e., living there) could be a slave, and bringing a slave into Massachusetts, even for a short time, freed the slave. In the present case, "we were desirous of examining, with some attention, the great number of cases cited at the argument, and others which have presented themselves in course, and partly because we considered it a question of great importance to the Commonwealth."

He assumed that "the general rules of common law" were in force in Massachusetts, even when they were not embodied in specific legislative acts. But "it will not necessarily follow that every indictment at common law for this offence is a precedent for a similar indictment in this State." Conspiracy, "for two or more to confederate and combine together, by concerted means, to do that which is unlawful or criminal, to the injury of the public, or portions or classes of the community, or even to the rights of an individual," was still an offense, but when applied to "the common law, or early English statutes, which were made for the purpose of regulating the wages of laborers, the settlement of paupers, and making it penal for any one to use a trade or handicraft to which he had not served a full apprenticeship—not being adapted to the circumstances of our colonial condition—were not adopted, used or approved, and therefore do not come within the description of the laws adopted and confirmed by the provision of the constitution already cited." In short, in Massachusetts, the conditions of free labor overturned the old rules of servitude. A conviction in England, where unionization was illegal, under the old rubric of workers as servants, simply made no sense in a world of free labor.

As a matter of law, Shaw found that the alleged offense was too vaguely defined and too broadly drawn—prudential (judge-made) distinctions that would figure in many later labor cases. "The great difficulty is, in framing any definition or description, to be drawn from the decided cases, which shall specifically identify this offence—a description broad enough to include all cases punishable under this description, without including acts which are not punishable." Was free labor itself punishable? Certainly not. Was the gathering of free laborers then punishable if the object was to promote free labor's wages or working conditions? Hardly. If nothing in the association of journeymen boot makers was illegal, was their effort to promote membership by recruiting new members or by calling out those who refused to join illegal? Not clearly. "From this view of the law respecting conspiracy, we think it an offence which especially demands the application of that wise and humane rule of the common law, that an indictment shall state, with as much certainty as the nature of the case will admit, the facts which constitute the crime intended to be charged."

Shaw reported that Rantoul had asked the trial judge to tell the jury just how the act or acts of the union were themselves wrong. "But the judge refused so to do, and instructed the jury, that the indictment did, in his opinion, describe a confederacy among the defendants to do an unlawful act, and to effect the same by unlawful means." In other words, according to the trial judge, the offense was unionization itself. Shaw demurred. "Stripped then of these introductory recitals and alleged injurious consequences, and of the qualifying epithets attached to the facts, the averment is this; that the defendants and others formed themselves into a society, and agreed not to work for any person, who should employ any journeyman or other person, not a member of such society, after notice given him to discharge such workman." But "such a purpose is not unlawful."

Shaw could have added that the 1840s was a time when Americans were joining all manner of societies and associations for temperance, literacy, self-improvement, political action, and religious worship. It was the age of the Church of Jesus Christ of Latter-day Saints, the Shakers, and socialist "phalanxes." Middle-class women like Elizabeth Cady Stanton and Susan B. Anthony were coming together to demand all manner of reforms, including the right to vote. Who could say that craftsmen were doing anything wrong by associating themselves for their mutual advantage? "Such an association might be used to afford each other assistance in times of poverty, sickness and distress; or to raise their intellectual, moral and social condition; or to make improvement in their art; or for other proper purposes." Of course, any gathering might have sinister ulterior motives. "But in order to charge all those, who become members of an association, with the guilt of a criminal conspiracy, it must be averred and proved that the actual, if not the avowed object of the association, was criminal." A good law "looks at truth and reality."

Shaw assayed one final test of the union. "Supposing the object of the association to be laudable and lawful, or at least not unlawful, are these means criminal?" Here he turned to the same considerations of free labor that Parker employed in *Britton*. "The case supposes that these persons are not bound by contract, but free to work for whom they please, or not to work, if they so prefer. In this state of things, we cannot perceive, that it is criminal for men to agree together to exercise their own acknowledged rights, in such a manner as best to subserve their own interests." For the essence of free labor was the essence of the union—serving the best interest of the individual worker. If that could be obtained by voluntary association, the state should not stand in its way. If, in the present case, the members of the union agreed not to work or to cease to work for a master who did not recognize the union, it was the same as an individual worker who did not finish a task. A servant could be held liable in law for not performing as agreed, but a free worker was free to walk away or stay away. "It is perfectly consistent with every thing stated in [the indictment] that the effect of the [workers' union] agreement was, that when they were free to act, they would not engage with an employer, or continue in his employment."

There was a caveat in what seemed thus far to be a total victory for unionization. "We think, therefore, that . . . the legality of such an association will therefore depend upon the means to be used for its accomplishment." In later years, courts would issue injunctions against unions striking for higher wages, safer working conditions, or simply to unionize more of the working force on the theory that the means were illegal. This left considerable discretion to the courts. Some courts, in later years, would find that picketing itself was illegal if it blocked entrances to factories, or that a strike against a railroad was illegal if it prevented the timely delivery of the U.S. mails. Union officials would then be guilty of criminal contempt of court if they knowingly or unknowingly violated the injunction against the picketing or strike—some of which were issued without notice to the union organizers. So often did employers seek this kind of aid from the courts and so common were these court orders that they constituted their own category in equity jurisprudence: the "labor injunction." Unions did not get relief from the imposition of these until the New Deal's Labor Relations Act. Even now, some states prohibit state employees from unionizing at all. Federal and state law is studded with statutes designed to reduce the influence of unions (for example, by requiring "cooling-off periods" and scrutinizing the political views of union leaders).

—m—

Lawsuits for injuries to workers in the course of their employment were another hotly contested subject of antebellum litigation. Early nineteenth-century industrial accident suits were heard under the old doctrine of respondeat superior (the master as responsible for the health and safety of his servant). Newer doctrines crafted in the first years of industrialization gave a subsidy to the employer. The first was acceptance of risk (a contract worker knows and accepts the dangers of a particular job), and the second was the fellow servant rule (if the immediate cause of the injury to a worker is the negligence of a fellow worker, the injured party cannot sue his employer). They were both "prudential"—that is, they were invented by judges to resolve the apparent conflict between the old rule of respondeat superior and the new and more dangerous conditions of working in a factory.

In *Farwell v. Boston and Worcester R.R.* (1842), Chief Justice Shaw demonstrated how perhaps the most respected common law judge in the land handled these cases. The facts in *Farwell* were horrific but increasingly familiar as more and more men worked in railroad yards and around locomotives and rolling stock. Farwell was a contract employee working as an engineer on a train when a fellow worker, allegedly carelessly supervised, threw a switch that caused Farwell to fall underneath one of the rail cars. His hand was crushed. Counsel for the Boston and Worchester argued that Farwell knew about the dangers of the job when he applied for it and even more so when he worked for the company. He had accepted the risk. He simply needed to be a more watchful worker, anticipating that accidents could occur. In any case, if the employer had to pay workers for every injury that fellow workers caused, the company would go out of business.

Charles Loring, a young and already upcoming Boston lawyer, represented Farwell, the plaintiff. His argument was ingenious. "If the plaintiff had been a stranger, the defendants would have been liable; and he contends that the case is not varied by the fact that both the plaintiff and Whitcomb were the servants of the defendants." What was more, "He could not, by any vigilance or any power that he could exercise, have prevented the accident." Finally, Loring called up the old doctrine of respondeat superior, "that a master, by the nature of his contract with a servant, stipulates for the safety of the servant's employment, so far as the master can regulate the matter."

Chief Justice Shaw was not impressed. He conceded that "this is an action of new impression in our courts, and involves a principle of great importance," and thus the old doctrine of respondeat superior did not apply. Instead, Shaw saw the matter as an example of a new type of contract case. "This does not apply to the case of a servant bringing his action against his own employer to recover damages for an injury arising in the course of that employment, where all such risks and perils as the employer and the servant respectively intend to assume and bear may be regulated by the express or implied contract between them, and which, in contemplation of law, must be presumed to be thus regulated." Ironically, the victory that workers had won in cases like *Britton*, claiming that they were not servants but contractees, worked against them in *Farwell*.

Shaw posited a "general rule, resulting from considerations as well of justice as of policy . . . that he who engages in the employment of another for the performance of specified duties and services, for compensation, takes upon himself the natural and ordinary risks and perils incident to the performance of such services, and in legal presumption, the compensation is adjusted accordingly." In the new doctrine of assumption of risk, justice did not weigh the comparative economic positions of the worker and the employer. Farwell had assumed the risk and (theoretically) was paid accordingly. If he were not adequately compensated, he would not (according to free market labor doctrine current at the time) have accepted the position. He should have been more careful himself.

Of course, Farwell could have sued the other worker for negligence, but the other worker was as poor as he was. Only the railroad could adequately compensate him for the injury he suffered, and presumably for his inability to work as an engineer ever again. Shaw was well aware of the tenuous financial status of the state's new railroads, however. In a shift of perspective that was novel at the time but is much more common today, he turned from settled law to policy considerations. "If we look from considerations of justice to those of policy, they will strongly lead to the same conclusion. In considering the rights and obligations arising out of particular relations, it is competent for courts of justice to regard considerations of policy and general convenience, and to draw from them such rules as will, in their practical application, best promote the safety and security of all parties concerned." Policy—that is, what best promoted the economic stability of business—weighed the scales in favor of the railroad. Everyone benefited from the cheap freight rates of the rail lines. If workers could sue for injuries that their fellow workers caused, the railroad companies would soon be driven into bankruptcy, or at least that is what Shaw surmised.

In other words, although not at issue in the suit itself, Shaw believed that the railroad and all who depended on it for freight and passenger traffic had rights too. Everyone simply had to be more careful. "Where several persons are employed in the conduct of one common enterprise or undertaking, and the safety of each depends much on the care and skill with which each other shall perform his appropriate duty, each is an observer of the conduct of the others. . . . By these means, the safety of each will be much more effectually secured, than could be done by a resort to the common employer for indemnity in case of loss by the negligence of each other." What about Farwell, then? What remedy did he have? "Under these circumstances, the loss must be deemed to be the result of a pure accident, like those to which all men, in all employments, and at all times, are more or less exposed; and like similar losses from accidental causes, it must rest where it first fell, unless the plaintiff has a remedy against the person actually in default; of which we give no opinion."

A decade after Shaw's opinion, free labor was gaining political traction, particularly in the Midwest, where an Ohio decision showed the first crack in what had been a well-mortised wall around Shaw's decision. Judges in Ohio were elected, and free labor was the electorate. In *Cleveland RR v. Keary* (1854), Ohio Supreme Court justices Rufus Ranney and Robert Warden found for the injured worker. Ranney, a Democrat, wrote that the conductor against whom the complaint was made was not a fellow servant, but a supervisor, and Warden, a young Republican new to the court (at thirty years of age) rejected the fellow servant rule on the grounds that the entire doctrine was wrong. One might dismiss their opinions as attempts to pander to voters, but in antebellum America, elections were highly popular events and many more eligible voters cast their ballots than do today. No judge could afford to ignore the views of the majority of voters, as Chief Justice Chilton of Alabama no doubt knew as he crafted his opinion in *Atwood*.

Keary was the brakeman on a train, injured, he alleged, due to the negligence of the conductor. The Cuyahoga County jury was instructed in the rule of respondeat superior, from which the defendant railroad appealed to the state's highest court (note that the railroad here is the appellant, and its name comes first in the case title). Ranney's opinion was for the court. He narrowed his opinion to the facts of the case: "The plaintiff below was in the employ of the defendant, as a brakeman on one of their trains, and was very seriously and permanently injured by a collision between the train and a locomotive, also belonging to the defendants." None of this was his fault. Instead, it was the conductor of the train whose negligence caused the injury. The conductor was careless, but if he were a coworker, his carelessness would have been, as with Farwell's coworker, simply an accident.

At the trial, the railroad company's counsel cited *Farwell* and the many similar decisions on the fellow servant rule that used *Farwell* as precedent. But the trial court judge did not so instruct the jury. Instead, the trial judge told the jury they should use the respondeat superior formula, "that, if they were satisfied, from the evidence, that the injury to the plaintiff was occasioned by the negligence or carelessness of either the conductor or superintendent, under whose control he was placed by the company, and acting at the time, and without his fault, he was entitled to recover such damages as would compensate him for the injury." The jury retired, considered the evidence, and returned a verdict for the plaintiff for $6,050.

The train company's counsel appealed the decision on the basis of the trial judge's supposedly incorrect instructions to the jury. Judge Ranney thought the matter over and declined to overturn the jury verdict or return the case to the lower court with instructions to the trial judge to change his charge to the jury. "Where an employer places one person in his employ under the direction of another, also in his employ, such employer is liable for injury to the person placed in the subordinate situation, by the negligence of his superior."

Ranney was not quite done, and what he had to say suggested that the free labor movement, and free labor advocates, had not yet won the day in politics any more than in law. For set against the rights of laborers to control the conditions of their labor was another movement that was fast spreading over the landscape of American commerce. In his address to the Wisconsin State Fair, Lincoln warned that free labor had two battles to fight. One was against slavery. The other was against a heartless class of capitalists and their legal creation, the business corporation. Corporations had in times past been a very limited presence in the nation's economic life. Legislatures only granted charters to corporations when the purpose of the corporate charter was the public good. By the 1850s, they were fast becoming the dominant species of business organization. So-called general incorporation laws allowed corporations for private gain to proliferate. Railroads, canal companies, and industrial combinations took advantage of these general incorporation laws to pay the license fee to the state and gain the protection of the corporate organization model. This included limited liability to the directors of the corporation when their business activities went bust or when their company operations injured bystanders.

Ranney recognized this change in the business world in what amounted to an obiter dictum in his opinion, that is, something in it not necessary to settle the case. He opined, "I shall take no time to prove, that this corporation and every other, prosecuting a lawful business, is entitled to the same rights, and subject to the same liabilities, when not otherwise provided by law, as a private individual. This has been too often affirmed by this court, and the courts of our sister states, to be now a matter of doubt." Well, perhaps it had, but why did he need to repeat it here? He wanted to indicate that, unlike the other cases, here a corporation (the railroad) would be held responsible for injuries it incurred. "Indeed, a corporation is but an aggregation of individuals, to whom legal unity is given; endowed with certain capacities for their own interest and advantage, it would indeed be singular, if they were for that reason, exempted from the liabilities for injuries, to which, without their beneficial capacities, they would be subject." The incorporation did not immunize the corporation from legal responsibility. "We, therefore, treat this case the same as though the road had been owned, and the trains run, by a private individual. If, under the circumstances, such private individual would be liable, the company is liable."

His admonition to the corporate interests was not based on some version of labor radicalism, but a powerful conservatism. If the corporation was no more than an aggregate of individuals, then it must accept the legal obligations of individuals. "Hence, in prosecuting his own lawful business, and in the use of his own property, he must submit to the great social necessity of so using his own, as not to injure others. While they are his legal right, *this* is his legal duty. They go hand in hand, and the law scrupulously respects the one, and rigorously enforces the other."

One almost senses that Ranney, who ran for Congress repeatedly and was, by report, never quite happy sitting on the bench, wanted to turn his opinion in this case into a political address. He certainly wandered far afield of the facts, to argue that the law "treats man as a rational and intellectual being, capable of understanding his duties to his fellow men, and requires of him, in his intercourse with them, to exercise a constant regard for their rights. In the complicated relations of civilized society, no force can be employed, no business pursued, which is not likely to result in injury to others, unless it is controlled and directed by an intelligent will, conscientiously and carefully employed to prevent it." The uncontrolled development of industry had to be constrained by rationality. Free labor, like the corporation, must recognize these curbs on self-interest.

As if recognizing the extent to which he had strayed from the matter at hand, Ranney returned to precedent, and *Farwell*. In a common-law system, precedent can determine the outcome of cases, but *Farwell* was the work of a Massachusetts court and thus did not dictate what Ohio should do. "We entertain the highest respect for these courts, and their undivided opinions upon any question arising upon the principles of the common law, would cause us to hesitate long before we differed from them. But even upon such a question, we should be compelled to follow the dictates of our own understandings; and the more especially should we feel at perfect liberty to do so, when they did not profess to base their decisions upon any settled principle of law, but undertook to declare a new rule for their action." *Farwell* "did not seem to us consistent with the analogies of the law, and calculated to promote justice."

Justice Warden concurred but had some dicta of his own to contribute. "While I agree that this judgment should be affirmed, the ground on which I would place the right of the plaintiff below, is so much broader than that taken by the majority of the court." Warden also left behind the facts of the case to advocate for the rights of workingmen. "The whole history of *tradesmen* and *artificers*, for instance, forbids us to class them with menial servants, no matter what their place in the scale of employment. . . . Men employed in the workshop of the mechanic, or in like occupations, had never been so stamped with the mark of inferiority," as Shaw seemed to imply, in *Farwell*. "The notion of Chief Justice Shaw, that the contract of service includes an undertaking by the servant of all risks, whether of unavoidable accident or of damages arising from the negligence of other servants, is certainly an ingenious invention . . . [but] no such agreement or understanding is ever had, or ought ever to be countenanced by the law. It would be so against reason and conscience as to be void."

The workingman, the free laborer, thus stood on a par with the master of old and the more recent captain of industry. The hidden argument is that no free laborer entered into a contract to be a slave, to give up rights that every free person enjoyed as a matter of reason as well as law. One can see, lurking in the shadows of these opinions, the specter of the Slave Power. If slavery were allowed to expand into the unorganized territories of the West or to acquire new lands in the Caribbean, the rights of all workers would be compromised. If law abetted slavery, than how could law be trusted to protect free labor? The honor of free labor, restated by victories in the courts, was endangered by slavery, just as the honor of the slave master was endangered by the arguments of free soilers. The confrontation of vying ideals of honor would come to a head with the election of Republican Abraham Lincoln and the secession of eleven southern states.

—꿰—

Labor law in the twentieth century changed not because of evolving precedent, but because of federal and state statutory reforms. Horrific violence in the suppression of mining and manufacturing strikes early in the century did not lead to reforms but focused national attention on the failure of law to provide protection for union workers. While craft unions thrived, industrial unions of blue-collar workers faced the combined forces of state and private oppression. The federal courts refused to uphold the Sherman (1890) and Clayton (1914) Antitrust Acts protection of unions against the labor injunction, and child labor restrictions Congress passed in 1916. Federal courts struck down minimum wage and maximum hour laws. There were some improvements in the lot of all workers, however. State worker compensation laws overtook and replaced the suits for industrial injuries. Labor law began to abandon the hire and fire "at will" rule to prevent many of the abuses individual workers had to litigate in the nineteenth century. New Deal labor laws led to genuine reform, in particular the Wagner Labor Relations Act of 1935, upheld by the Supreme Court in 1937, which once again protected workers against the labor injunction. Later acts created agencies to ensure safe working conditions and ended child labor. But all of this did not touch agricultural workers, and that not by accident. For the representatives of the farming interests in Congress were adamant that reform of seasonal workers' conditions and wages would raise farm product prices and put some farmers out of business.

Some laborers unprotected by many of these changes in law were "guest workers." During World War II, sugar plantation owners in the South and food crop farmers in the West were able to employ agricultural labor from Mexico and the Caribbean to replace American farmworkers serving in the armed forces. These "guest workers" came under treaty arrangements with the government of their countries. They did not have individual contracts with their U.S. employers, the arrangement brokered by the U.S. government. These are not illegal or undocumented aliens who have crossed borders; they are documented. The "guest worker" from the Caribbean or Mexico is much prized by the owners of farms because these workers can be returned to their native lands when they are no longer needed or when they are regarded as troublemakers, although their work in U.S. fields continued for years after the war was over. Agricultural union leaders have routinely protested against the importation of laborers for precisely this reason.

Can the courts fill the gap left by statutory inaction in agricultural labor rights? Can they make law, as they did in *Britton* and *Farwell* protecting the rights of field hands? The lead case is *Cruz v. U.S.* (2002), in which a former guest worker for himself and others similarly situated tried to win back pay against former employers. He sued Mexico, the United States, and the Wells Fargo bank fiduciaries for the farm owners who had employed the braceros. The results were sad if predictable. The court initially held that the United States and Mexico were entitled to foreign sovereign immunity. They could not be sued without their permission. The plaintiff could not hold the banks liable because he did not have a contractual relationship with the banks (the banks had a contractual relationship with the United States). Nor did the banks hold funds in trust for the workers. Nor was there unjust enrichment (forget about *Britton*). Nor did the defendants violate any American rules of unfair business practices. Nor was there a statutory cause of action, because the applicable law, passed by Congress in 1942, had long ago lapsed.

Charles Breyer, the district court judge sitting in the Northern District of California, heard and decided the case. He is the younger brother of Supreme Court justice Stephen Breyer and a 1997 President Clinton appointee to the federal bench after service as San Francisco's city attorney. The facts of the case were these: Individuals from Mexico, known as braceros, who worked in the United States during World War II and some period of time thereafter, brought the suit. While working in the United States, the braceros had a portion of their wages withheld. The withheld wages were deposited in a U.S. bank and then transferred to a Mexican bank. The withholdings were to be refunded when the braceros returned to Mexico. The plaintiffs submitted that the funds were never returned. It sounds simple, but it wasn't, because counsel for the braceros had to scramble to find grounds for a suit that should have been filed over fifty years earlier.

Pleading a case "in the alternative," that is, basing it on a variety of grounds, some of which might be mutually contradictory, is permissible under modern rules of pleading. But the facts of the case made any strategy of pleading dicey. Braceros were still at work in the fields into the 1950s, presumably under the 1942 agreement with Mexico, but by 1951, negotiations with Mexico to continue the program had broken down. Nevertheless, braceros continued to work in U.S. fields until 1964, when the accord was finally repealed.

Judge Breyer offered a clear summary of the facts as he understood them, but the preliminary hearing (to repeat, the case never went to trial) was not over the facts but the various defendants' motion to dismiss the suit before it even went to trial. Thus, the plaintiff had little chance to illuminate all the facts. What stood in the place of a full exploration of the conditions of the work and the missing money was a bare-bones version of the events. The original (1942) agreement between Mexico and the United States provided a standard contract governing the relationship between all the workers and the United States. That agreement made the workers a third party in the subsequent handling of the 10 percent of each worker's wages. These monies were to be retained and deposited into a savings fund. The conditions of that deposit rested on contracts between the United States and the various banks, not on contracts between the workers and the banks. The savings fund deductions were to be returned to the bracero when he returned to Mexico. These funds were in effect held as an inducement for the individuals to return to Mexico when their temporary stay was over. The men could get another "ticket" to return to the United States. Every worker had to cycle in and out of the country. Some came over and over, as the growers handpicked the workers they wanted. Most did not return. Obviously, the set-aside made no sense except insofar as the United States did not want any worker feeling that he had a right to remain.

The important and telling legal point was that the accords between the United States and Mexico, from 1943 on, were not with the braceros. The latter were third parties to the contract for labor. The United

States and Mexico had agreed to deposit the 10 percent set-aside of the salaries in the Wells Fargo bank in San Francisco. The braceros were not part of this agreement, except insofar as the funds were supposed to be returned to them upon their departure. It is not clear if the accounts were individual, like the immigration and work papers, or simply 10 percent of the total owed the guest workers. In fact, the moneys went into the Mexican government's account with Wells Fargo. The money then supposedly went to the Bank of Mexico and then to the Mexican Agricultural Credit Bank. The deposits were terminated in 1946, even though the agreement was not ended until a year later and braceros were still employed for another decade or more. In 1948, a second bracero program was introduced, once again treating the braceros as third parties. The United States was in charge of the program. Once again the U.S. employers withheld 10 percent of the agreed-upon salary, to be returned directly to each worker when the term of the contract was completed. The checks had to be endorsed by the INS in the United States when the worker crossed back over the border to Mexico.

The suit was filed in March of 2001 by Ramirez Cruz for himself and others against the United States, Mexico, and the various banks that handled the set-asides of salary. All of the suits were transferred to the Northern District of California where the common issues related to all the plaintiffs were adjudicated in a consolidated case. It was not a class action suit, however, as no effort was made to inform and join all the surviving braceros or to give any of them a chance to opt out of the suit (for more on class action, see chapter 8 below). All of the defendants moved to dismiss the case on procedural grounds, without a full trial. The record thus offers the judge's decision on the merits of the motions to dismiss.

The suit against the United States fell immediately because no one could sue the United States without its permission. While a variety of federal statutes conferred such permission in special cases, the braceros, and the braceros' case, did not fit any of these exceptions. Thus this claim was summarily dismissed.

Judge Breyer also dismissed the claims against the Mexican banks because they were agencies of the Mexican government, and sovereign governments have immunity from suits by their own citizens, or at least that was true of suits against the United States by citizens, unless the United States gave permission for the suit to proceed. Since World War

II, Congress has widened the grounds for such suits, but Mexico had not. As a result of judicial deference to the political branches, primarily the executive, foreign sovereigns enjoyed nearly complete immunity from suit in the United States prior to 1952. The claims against the Mexican banks were dismissed.

Next came the suit against Wells Fargo. That suit rested on a series of claims. The first was that Wells Fargo had breached a contract with the braceros. It allegedly had failed to forward the wages deposited with it to the Mexican banks. But the braceros had no contractual relations with Wells Fargo, even as third parties to the contract between the United States and Wells Fargo. They could have claimed that they were still the intended beneficiaries of the latter contract. Judge Breyer was required to turn to California law to settle that question. Under the federal judiciary acts, federal courts are required to use state laws to settle civil suits in the states where the federal court sits. California law required third parties to file suits of this kind before the end of the contract period. Whether that was 1947, 1961, or even 1964, Cruz had failed to meet the deadline. What was more, under California banking law, the bank was not obliged to pay anything to a third party, even when the deposit, as was the case here, was intended for the benefit of a third party (the braceros). "In barring such a cause of action, the law recognizes that the bank/depositor relationship is entered for the sole benefit of the depositor, not third-parties." Once again, the bank was absolved of any obligation to the braceros, even if it did not forward the deposits to the Mexican banks. "Given the unique context of the banking relationship, the Court refuses to undertake traditional third-party beneficiary analysis. Plaintiffs have no cause of action for breach of any contract that Wells Fargo may have entered with the United States or Mexico."

Counsel for the braceros still had a few arrows in their quiver. They argued that even if Wells Fargo did not have a contract with the guest workers, it had a "fiduciary duty" to protect their interest. Again the bank had an answer. There was no evidence that such a duty existed in this case—an easy argument to make at this stage of the trial, because the plaintiff had not had the chance to introduce supporting evidence. The court agreed. "Plaintiffs have not pled facts that would give rise to a fiduciary relationship, and the Court need not accept their conclusory allegation that such a relationship existed." Judge Breyer once again stated that the "plaintiffs had no formal relationship whatsoever with Wells Fargo," fiduciary or contractual. It was the United States that had the relationship with Wells Fargo, and he had already dismissed the guest worker suit against the United States.

Perhaps an argument resting in equity could snatch victory from the jaws of defeat? The braceros' counsel argued that the deposit of funds with the bank constituted an implied trusteeship. Trusteeships were a very old English form of legal relationship, wherein property was given to a trustee to manage for the benefit of one or more beneficiaries. The chancellor ensured that trustees did not waste or use for themselves the property in the trust. "Once the trust is declared, the remedy is delivery of the [property] by the trustee to the beneficiary." The trust was implied— that is, it was not formally created—but "here plaintiffs have alleged that the United States was responsible for transferring funds to Wells Fargo, that Wells Fargo was never intended to take a beneficial interest in the transferred funds, and that Wells Fargo was to transfer those funds for the ultimate interest of plaintiffs."

But again the court could find no evidence that Wells Fargo was meant to serve as a trustee, in part because the plaintiff did not have a chance to produce evidence (once again bearing in mind that this was a hearing on a motion to dismiss all the complaints, not a trial on the evidence). "The complaint however, does not allege, nor could it, that Wells Fargo was meant to hold the funds in trust for the plaintiffs. Without such an intent, plaintiffs cause of action for a resulting trust fails." To be sure, a trust may result without specific intent, but "the complaint does not allege that either the United States or Wells Fargo anticipated that Wells Fargo would hold any funds in trust for the benefit of plaintiffs." On the contrary, the court found that Wells Fargo was merely a conduit to facilitate the transfer of funds from the United States to Mexico. Wells Fargo never even had responsibility for affirmatively transferring funds, "much less for holding them in trust."

A last, almost desperate attempt by counsel for the plaintiffs alleged that Wells Fargo was unjustly enriched by not paying the 10 percent set-aside back to the guest workers. Unjust enrichment, we recall, was the basis for the court awarding partial payment to Britton. Counsel for the braceros recited that "it is black letter law that a person unjustly enriched can be required to pay restitution under the law." Judge Breyer disagreed.

"Unjust enrichment involves a benefit conferred on defendant by plaintiff." The braceros did not work for Wells Fargo. Thus Wells Fargo was not in any way enriched by the braceros. This assumed that Wells Fargo did not convert the funds to its own use, for example by loaning them out at interest, or by simply keeping them. This is called "conversion." But because Breyer was dismissing the case, the plaintiff could not begin the "discovery" of documentary evidence in Wells Fargo's possession that would established what it actually did with the funds. (At the time, and for years afterward, Wells Fargo was engaged in fraudulent practices in its mortgage and insurance divisions which the bank, when investigated by the federal government, finally conceded. Whether these extended back in time to the bank's handling of the braceros' back pay remains uncertain.)

Judge Breyer conceded that his "Court does not doubt that many braceros never received Savings Fund withholdings to which they were entitled. The Court is sympathetic to the braceros situation. However, just as a court's power to correct injustice is derived from the law, a court's power is circumscribed by the law as well." Domestic farm labor has won many victories at the bargaining table and in court, as well as in statute law. They are still not covered by child labor laws, maximum hours laws, or collective bargaining laws. The guest workers' conditions have improved since they were first set to labor in U.S. fields. A minefield of regulations supposedly protecting them cannot save them from being sent home, however. In *Cruz*, plaintiffs had no control over the labor relationship once they entered it. Others—the U.S. government, the Mexican government, the banks, and U.S. growers—controlled it. The workers had no honor under the law, for they were not really persons under the law. Like slave labor, the only object that the law considered was the braceros' labor they performed, and the only rights the law recognized were the rights of the United States, Mexico, the banks, and the employers.

To pay back what the braceros were owed would open the federal coffers to those who had no standing in law. The braceros were not just foreign citizens; they were foreign citizens of the lowest caste. Litigation offered them the chance to gain honor, but in the end, they had no rights, to paraphrase Chief Justice Roger Taney's description of African Americans in *Dred Scott v. Sandford* (1857), that any court had to enforce. The braceros were not free labor.

—‍ɯ‍—

Through litigation, free labor had won back pay, the right to unionize, and reimbursement for injuries on the job. Friendly legislation followed litigation. Recourse to the courts validated the dignity of the worker. Workers' litigation had raised the value of work itself, along with the status of the laboring classes. But litigation had its limits. Where the law did not confer the right to bring a suit, to organize, or to strike, the worker was at the mercy of more powerful economic and political forces. Capital, in its search for cheap labor, had always minimized the value of work and workers. The tug of war between labor and capital in the courts continues. As the French economic theorist Thomas Piketty has explained, the decrease in maldistribution of wealth that marked the rise of labor in the years after World War II has been reversed in recent years. Fewer and fewer individuals and corporate institutions control a larger and larger share of the national income. Those left out include many who labor in our fields.

Part II

Litigation Defends Democracy

THE CIVIL WAR WAS A TEST of the litigation nation—would a law-abiding people survive the carnage? Would people once again sue rather than slay for vindication of their honor? The Civil War changed nothing and everything about litigation in America. Three amendments to the Constitution followed the defeat of the Confederacy, ending slavery; defining citizenship as national rather than based on residency in a state and requiring states to provide equal protection and due process for all American citizens; and, finally, denying to any state the authority to restrict the franchise on the basis of race. Reconstruction was a great experiment in legal reformation of a nation torn apart by slavery, but the war had not destroyed racism in the North or in the South, and Reconstruction would not achieve its legal aims until nearly another century had passed.

Nevertheless, in the face of what might have been the chaos of covert guerilla war, litigation defended democracy. Reconstruction opened the doors of the courts to new litigants—former bondsmen—and to new laws called "civil rights." Even at the height of the Jim Crow regime of racial injustice from the postwar period through the 1950s, black litigants in the South were able to bring suits against whites and win in court.

Litigation reknit the previously warring sections. New legislation by the same Radical Republican majority in Congress that imposed occupation of the former Confederate states was welcomed in the South and brought many ordinary white people to the federal courts seeking relief for debts incurred during the Civil War. Industrialization, technological advances, and a revolution in legal practice (the rise of the law schools and the large legal firms) made litigation more complex and introduced new ideas like mass products liability and revised old ideas like equity.

But litigants and their lawyers still brought and won cases against bigger adversaries. Business in federal and state courts boomed. More and more acts of Congress brought more and more Americans to the courts to vindicate rights and regulations that did not exist prior to 1865. Lawyers and their clients soon recognized that the litigation nation had not only survived the civil strife; it defended American democracy in new and potent ways.

For, what did many of these cases have in common? They were brought by ordinary men and women to assert their right to participate in the economic and social life of the restored Union. They were shareholders, farmers and laborers, and financiers and the suckers they fleeced. Litigation was as close to the great leveler in the new democracy as one could find. When great economic downturns descended on the land, the dispossessed again went to court to stave off foreclosure of homes and loss of jobs. After two world wars, blacks and whites joined in litigation to topple the barriers of racial segregation. In products liability cases, the courts were once again the place where ordinary people harmed by the products they bought and trusted could present their claims to restitution.

5

Stock Swindles and Swindlers

IN 1881, THEN HARVARD LAW School professor Oliver
Wendell Holmes Jr. wrote that the law was not for the good man, but
for the bad man. This nugget of early legal realism made perfect sense in
the so-called Gilded Age of American entrepreneurship and law. From
the end of the Civil War to the beginning of the twentieth century, the
nation and its courts were treated to arrogant swindles and swindlers by
the Gilded Age robber barons and their minions. Never had so many
had so much stolen by so few. The worst of this piratical crew were the
railroad moguls, whose wealth was matched only by their avariciousness
and unscrupulous practices.

It was an era of combinations and collusion, of "tunneling" (self-dealing) by shareholders and board members of major corporations, and of
octopus-like monopolies that sought to control the means of production
and distribution of goods and services. Supposedly the heyday of free
market competition, it was anything but free, and its foremost entrepreneurs sought to crush their competition. Avarice was hardly new in this
Gilded Age, but never before had it been so brazenly displayed.

—∞—

After the Civil War, the nation's foremost business enterprise was railroading. The rails had helped win the war for the Union. In the 1870s,
southern cotton and sugar were still major staple exports, northern
wheat was a close second, and all three rode the rails to seaports on the
Atlantic and Gulf coasts. Smaller railroads carried garden vegetables
from local farmers' markets to the cities. The railroads surpassed the

nation's rivers and canals in freight tonnage and passenger conveyance. Railroads supported the timber industry, the coal industry, the steel industry, and the machine tool industry, without which there could be no tracks, no fuel, and no locomotives and rolling stock.

The 1876 Centennial Exhibition in Philadelphia's Machinery Hall included a Baldwin locomotive, the most advanced steam engine of its kind and a symbol of the railroads' achievement. Pennsylvania's two great rail combines, the Reading and the Pennsylvania, put on special trains to accommodate visitors to the exposition, bringing travelers all the way from Chicago and Boston to the Centennial depot next to the exhibition grounds. In effect, the rail lines had made themselves into an essential partner of the Centennial.

In the East, the two leading lines were the Pennsylvania and the New York Central. In the West, the transcontinentals linked the prairie with the Pacific Coast and made fortunes for nouveau riche speculators like Collis P. Huntington and Leland Stanford. Across the Middle West and South, smaller lines like the Chicago, Danville, and Vincennes; the Chicago, Burlington, and Quincy; the Illinois Central; and the Mississippi Central connected to the major rails, creating a web of transportation and the opportunity for great fortunes (and spectacular failures). The "Katy," the Missouri, Kansas, and Texas Railroad, linked midwestern wheat to southern markets.

Mansions of former Union generals, now executives or board members of the rail lines, lined the Susquehanna River shoreline in Harrisburg, Philadelphia, Pennsylvania's Rittenhouse Square, and Fifth Avenue in New York City. Southern corporate lawyering was built on the wide shoulders of the southern rail development, and lawyering for the railroad companies in federal court "guaranteed income" and garnered "prestige." In this, leaders of the (white) southern bar were much like leaders of the northern bar, railroad fees were lucrative, and railroad lawyers milked the lines just as the lines milked their customers.

Not everyone who got in on the deal was so cynical. Charles Francis Adams, president of the Union Pacific in 1884, was the grandson of President John Adams and the son of President John Quincy Adams. One cannot think that his illustrious and highly moralistic forebears would have entirely approved of his choice of occupation, although he strove for efficiency and profit without corruption and waste. He slammed the railroads for corruption, promised to replace it with efficiency and discipline, and then joined in the taking.

But Adams was not one of the real losers, and there were millions of them. The Indians, whose land was taken for the right-of-way; the workers who cleared and laid the track; the miners who dug the coal that fueled the locomotives; and the farmers who needed the railroads to bring wheat to market all paid a price for the progress of the revolution in transportation costs. On balance, the reduced cost of durable consumer goods, food, and fuel to even the poor was weighed in the scales of history against the obscene display of wealth of a few and the oppression of the rail workers, while members of Congress and state legislatures who paved the right-of-way enjoyed the kickbacks. The legal losers were the stock and bond holders who had invested in the railroads in more or less good faith and found their dollars disappearing along with their hopes of profit.

—␣—

Rail bond and stock holders were vital to the railroads because the enterprise required continual infusions of capital. In fact, the railroads were as important for national fiscal life as they were for national commercial life because the stocks and bonds circulated as a kind of currency. Banks and other institutions along with individuals invested in railroad company bonds, speculating on endless expansion and ever-growing profits. Domestic and foreign investment poured into the rail companies' coffers. The federal government was a major contributor as well, giving to the rail barons huge swaths of land for right-of-way through federal land reserves. In and out of the financial markets, skillful and unscrupulous operators like Jay Gould made and lost millions of their own and others' money in railroad stock speculation.

Like Horatio Alger's characters, so popular in the early years of the Gilded Age, the rail moguls had to have luck and pluck to succeed. For instance, Jay Gould came from the lower middle class in New York, and during the Civil War he built a small fortune speculating in railroad stock. The prize was control of the Erie Railroad, and when it went under, Gould managed to stay afloat as its president. A life raft came in the form of support from the New York City Democratic Party bosses.

Called the "Tammany Hall" Ring for their place of business, led by New York state senator William "Boss" Tweed, the ring managed kickbacks and corruption in the city.

Joined with Gould in his schemes was James "Diamond Jim" Fisk. Vermont's Fisk was born poor, never finished elementary school, and worked at odd jobs until he caught on as a linen salesman. The Civil War gave him a chance to exercise his gift of gab, and at its end he was a bond broker and railroad booster for the Erie. There he fell in with Gould, the two men a slightly better dressed and scarcely more legitimate version of Butch Cassidy and the Sundance Kid.

Their rival was Cornelius Vanderbilt, older and even more ambitious, but like his younger colleagues, a poor son of a Staten Island family who left school at age eleven and never looked back. His first venture was a ferry service between Staten Island and Manhattan, and then he joined with Thomas Gibbons to run a steamboat company. From steamboats on the Hudson, Vanderbilt branched out to water traffic up and down the East Coast, then to California when the Gold Rush began, then to railroads connecting the hinterlands to the ports. Hawkeyed and never averse to risk, he became one of the richest men in America by the end of the war. His New York Central was a rival of the Erie, and that pitted him against Gould and Fisk.

Vanderbilt, Fisk, and Gould went head to head for a time, Gould preventing Vanderbilt from taking over the Erie by issuing "watered" stock—a kind of counterfeit (illegal under New York law) that Vanderbilt had to buy or lose the chance to control the Erie. When the Erie went under for a second time, Gould grabbed for the Union Pacific Railroad and became its president. Fisk divided his attention between the Erie and a young woman, and he died shortly thereafter at the hands of a rival for her affections.

In the meantime, the financiers' schemes periodically fell apart, bringing down the nation's economy with them. In the winter of 1872–1873, for example, the cascading effect of the failure of the Fisk-Gould stock scam for the Erie led to a four-year-long depression. The crisis triggered union strikes in the cities of the North, culminating in the Great Railroad Strike of 1877. Southern economic Reconstruction built on the frail alliance of Republican businessmen and southern entrepreneurs cracked and failed. But the railroaders' financial scheming could not be stopped.

In *Heath v. Erie Railroad Company* (1871), stockholders tried to intervene in the Gould/Fisk versus Vanderbilt war. The case is noteworthy not just for the result but for the counsel employed by the two sides. For the Erie shareholders, William Evarts and Ebenezer Hoar presented the argument that Gould and Fisk could not just print more stock, in effect devaluing the stock the investors already held. Evarts was arguably the leading New York City corporate counsel and had been retained by Lincoln's administration during the Civil War to argue cases before the Supreme Court. Hoar was a Massachusetts Republican who served, briefly, as the first attorney general of the United States to head the Department of Justice (created in 1870). Representing the Erie were two of the leading Democratic lawyers from New York City, law reformer David Dudley Field, whose "code" of pleading became the procedural standard for the state in 1848 and later the whole country, and former Supreme Court justice Benjamin R. Curtis. No more impressive collection of legal counsel had ever been assembled to argue before the federal circuit court since Daniel Webster brought the Supreme Court bench to tears with a four-hour oral argument in the Dartmouth College case of 1819 (he won, defending the college's charter against state interference). On the bench sat a leading figure in the federal judiciary, and perhaps the foremost authority on railroad finance in federal judicial service—Samuel Blatchford. He would shortly join the members of the Supreme Court.

Blatchford had no trouble reaching the issue. Evarts and Hoar alleged "that Gould, Fisk and Lane, holding such offices of trust and confidence under the company, misused, in breach of their trust, and for their own profit, powers actually confided to them by the corporation, and usurped powers not granted to them by the corporation, and, in breach of their duty, used such powers for their own profit." Field and Curtis responded that the stockholders had not exhausted all means to protect their interests through the corporation itself, but instead precipitously rushed to court to seek an injunction against the board of the railroad. Blatchford turned to the general rules for equity and found that "where there has been a waste or misapplication of the corporate funds, by the officers or agents of the company, a suit in equity may be brought by, and in the name of, the corporation, to compel them to account for such waste or misapplication, directors being regarded as trustees of the stockholders, and subject to the obligations and disabilities incidental to that relation."

After a recital of cases on point, Blatchford concluded that the issuing of stock without the permission of the present holders was a fraud, and the suit they brought to compel the board of directors to cease and desist had merit. He did not issue the injunction, however, leaving it to the parties to try to settle the matter in the shadow of the courthouse.

Shareholders thought in terms of the older ideal of the corporation, a fiduciary (financial agent) for the stockholders. Gould, Fisk, and their allies had a newer idea of corporate conduct—fast and loose, with the benefits going to the board of directors. *Heath* was one of many suits in which the stockholders used the courts to force corporate executives to adhere to the older custom, litigation that often failed as the companies simply went belly-up.

—⁓—

As rails expanded their routes and purchased more rolling stock after recovery from the crash of 1873, success brought its own problems. Eastern companies competing for the same routes and lines in the Midwest having trouble with connections to the southern railways, all overbuilt and oversubsidized expansion. One answer was the acquisition of rival firms and their rights-of-way. No rail firm was more aggressive in this than the Pennsylvania Railroad, the largest in the country. But too much expansion squeezed the capital reserves of larger lines like the Pennsy and its great rivals, the Reading Railroad, the New York Central, and the Baltimore and Ohio. Curbs on railroad price fixing and gouging that state governments and the federal Interstate Commerce Commission (ICC) imposed after 1887 made a precarious situation even more perilous for the rail lines. When the crash of 1893 cost the companies freight revenues, they faced bankruptcy. The suits brought by shareholders to recover what they could from the ailing rail lines were among the most contested and the most important pieces of civil litigation in the Gilded Age. In these, counsel for shareholders, creditors, financiers, and the railroad's own lawyers appeared in court to argue over divvying up the remaining assets.

Private suits piled up in the federal district courts from the most aggrieved litigants, the shareholders. (After the passage of the Evarts Act in 1891, the district courts were the major trial courts of the federal system. The old circuit courts remained in place until 1911, but the new circuit courts the act created were appellate tribunals rather than trial courts.) *Van Siclen v. Bartol* (1899) from the Eastern District of Pennsylvania Circuit (federal) Court was one of these stockholder suits, and it demonstrated all the characteristics of the railroad receivership cases. Financial "three-card monte" (the card game that only the dealer and his "shill" can win), with mortgages, second mortgages, doubtful receiverships (receivers were managers of bankrupt firms), and fast dealing, makes the head spin for those not used to following such shenanigans. Other ploys were the creation of dummy companies to siphon off profits and secret rebates to board members and friends of the company directors.

Fortunately for later students of the case, Judge John Bayard McPherson, newly appointed to the district court bench, was a graduate of Princeton University who had practiced law for nearly thirty years in Harrisburg, Pennsylvania, the state capital and center of the eastern railroad system. As a district attorney and later a county court judge, he knew all about the Erie, Reading, and Pennsy tactics. Added to this, he was an instructor of law at the University of Pennsylvania Law School for a decade. President McKinley, who named him to the post, was lobbied by railroad executives and lawyers to elevate McPherson, a lifelong Republican, to the federal bench. But he proved no friend to sharpsters.

McPherson's summary of the case was sure-handed: "In this proceeding the plaintiff seeks to enforce a liability growing out of an alleged breach of duty on the part of the defendants while acting as a reorganization committee in behalf of certain bondholders of the Chattanooga Union Railway Company, and also to compel an accounting for money of the plaintiff, contributed in aid of the reorganization, part of which is averred to be still in the defendants' hands." The rail line was a connecting line in Chattanooga, Tennessee, necessary to bring together various larger lines that serviced the city, but more important, it was an investment opportunity. The line needed capital, and found it by gaining a second mortgage, just like a piece of real estate. To pay back the mortgage, the company issued bonds, although its first mortgage principal was still outstanding. It really did not matter, as the bonds, like the mortgage, were a type of circulating medium—the sort of paper that capitalized all the rail companies. "Other outstanding bonds of the same issue increased the aggregate to $100,000, and the company's property was further incumbered by a first mortgage of $100,000 and a third mortgage of $400,000."

Not surprisingly, "towards the end of 1891 the company passed into the hands of a receiver, and from this time forward no interest was paid on its bonds." The receiver was supposed to handle the bankruptcy to protect the interests of the shareholders. Now the creditors—the bond-holders and others—circled the company like sharks around a sinking ship. The defendants were trustees of the company and also owners of some of the bonds, a conflict of interest of a sort as the trustees were supposed to be looking out for the other bondholders' rights. Instead, "some months after the insolvency of the company became manifest, [the trust-ees] took steps to protect their interest in the property." Things got worse for the company and its bondholders when the country stumbled into the recession of 1893. The trustees scrambled to protect their holdings. The plaintiff in the suit, unaware of the self-dealing of the trustees, took no part in their shenanigans.

In 1894, the trustees, reconfigured as a committee, launched a new campaign to save the company. The plan involved a new mortgage and a new issue of bonds, to solicit enough funds to pay what the company owed and to keep it operating. The plan also included authorization for the trustees to buy bonds for themselves "for such sum as they might see fit to bid. As one means of raising the money for this purpose, the com-mittee were empowered to sell the bonds of the new company on such terms as they might deem wise." This was an invitation to self-dealing. "They were also given the power to make contracts for merging, leasing, or operating the new company. The committee were to be reimbursed for their expenses, and were to receive a reasonable compensation for their services." Who would decide what the compensation was?—the committee itself.

The plan was a pure rip-off of what was left of the company assets, with the ingenious device of having the existing bondholders paying for the new bonds. "The committee shall be the sole judge when and whether a sufficient amount of bonds have been deposited to make the plan operative, and shall have power, if they deem it advisable, to aban-don it." The fox was not only in the henhouse; the fox was the legal owner of the chicken farm until such time as the fox had eaten all the chickens. The committee even provided for the exigency of a lawsuit against its members by indemnifying themselves in advance: "The committee shall not be personally liable in any case for the acts of each other, nor for their own except in cases of willful malfeasance or gross negligence, nor shall they personally be liable for the acts of their agents or employees."

The judge conceded that the "plaintiff assented to the foregoing plan, not realizing all its details, deposited his bonds with the trust company, receiving the usual certificate therefor, and paid $1,000 in cash. Of the other second mortgage bonds, $57,000 came into the agreement, making $67,000 in all." Before he could save himself, the committee moved to sell the right-of-way and the rolling stock to the Southern Railway Company, controlling the Alabama Great Southern Railroad Company. Negotiations for that sale, which might have saved the plaintiff's investment, seemed to fall through, but by the summer of 1895, the Union Railway Company of Chattanooga became part of the Southern Railway system. The defendants' investment was saved. Other bondholders had a limited time to act to redeem their own investment with the cash the Southern had provided. The plaintiff had only a few weeks to make his claim but missed that notice (it apparently got lost in the mails).

Behind the consolidation of routes hard hit by the 1893 depression was the giant figure of J. P. Morgan. Morgan was a New York City financier and banker who saw the importance of the Memphis-to-Norfolk route and how the spiraling out of that route to the Deep South, the coast, and the connection of the southern lines to Kansas City and Cincinnati in the Midwest could control rail service to one-third of the nation. Earlier in the decade, Morgan was the moneyman behind the creation of General Electric Company (Thomas A. Edison's firm) and, subsequently, U.S. Steel (Andrew Carnegie's giant) and International Harvester. It was he who funded the Southern Railways octopus. The first president of the line, Samuel Spencer, was a former Confederate cavalryman and later an engineer and one of the luminaries of the "New South" business world. Van Siclen was no patsy, as the extent of his investment suggests, but against men like these, Van Siclen had little chance of prevailing.

What should the plaintiff do to recover? "Under these circumstances, the plaintiff seeks to hold the defendants liable for willful malfeasance or gross negligence," but Judge McPherson's hands were tied. "I am unable to find the evidence to sustain so serious a charge. The defendants were trustees for the plaintiff and other bondholders, but the agreement under which they were acting protected them from the ordinary liability of a trustee. A large discretion was confided to them, as is no doubt necessary in such cases, and they were expressly relieved from liability unless they should be guilty of 'willful malfeasance or gross negligence.'" In fact, they were only guilty of the sort of conduct that the masters of the rails engaged in every day. The reorganization plan was clear, and they had no particular motive to defraud the plaintiff—only a general plan to protect their own interests. There was no smoking gun, only artillery fired from a distance. If the plaintiff happened to be in range of the shell, it was his own fault. "Fraud is not to be conjectured; and in the present case I not only see no proof of corrupt dealing, but I am satisfied that the defendants acted in good faith throughout. . . . I think the defendants made some mistakes, but it would not be fair to judge them by the light which can now be thrown backward upon a difficult and trying situation." Perhaps the Southern Railway Company's "dexterous management" of the purchase of the Chattanooga company could be faulted, but that was how the railways did business. Let the investor beware.

—⚶—

In the last decade of the century, the rail boom continued, for railroads still carried the coal, steel, wheat, and cotton that was making the nation a global leader in industry and agriculture. Without the relatively cheap cost of transportation the lines provided, national economic growth would stall. But the Gilded Age robber barons of the rails now had to face new sheriffs—popular political movements that demanded accountability and imposed regulations. Farmer parties like the Grange and the Populists of the 1880s and 1890s, loose coalitions of rural reformers seeking monetary among other reforms, and, later, city-dwelling professionals in the Progressive movement of the 1890s (advocates of greater government regulation of the economy) wanted to end the corruption and curb the monopolistic tendencies of the rail owners.

Farmers and cattlemen developed a particularly strong love-hate relationship with the rail lines. Dependent on the lines to bring their cereal crops and livestock to market, they were furious at the way rail barons manipulated haulage rates. The growers turned to state legislatures to regulate the costs of shipping, and then to the federal government. The

Interstate Commerce Commission, created by Congress in 1887, had the power, for a time, to set rates, but the federal courts intervened. Congress had stepped too far into the free market (and the rail barons had bought up enough support) to end the experiment in federal regulation for the next three decades.

Despite the failure to curb the worst abuses of railroad operators' finance, Congress addressed railroad attempts to monopolize certain routes, particularly those in the wheat- and corn-growing regions. The Sherman Antitrust Act of 1890 aimed at the great combinations of corporations that had effectually monopolized industry in restraint of free trade. Corporations like Standard Oil practiced both vertical and horizontal integration of their operations. In the former, the supply chain from raw materials to sales was absorbed within the company. In the latter, competing companies were brought under the same management through acquisition, merger, or simply driving the competition from the market.

By contrast, the statute reflected a very old idea—the inherent value of free market competition—in a time when markets were increasingly controlled by oligopolistic producers. While these may or may not have been more efficient than a marketplace of many smaller businesses, the act had a strong moral component. Competition was good; unfair or conspiratorial efforts to restrict competition were bad. A movement to repeal the law the year after it went into effect failed, not because of insufficient lobbying efforts (the trusts spared no expense to buy the vote), but because the old ideology of free trade was so deeply entrenched in American voters' minds.

The Sherman Act gave a powerful weapon to the federal government to combat the trusts. The key provision, section 4, enabled U.S. attorneys to bring lawsuits in federal court both to "prevent and restrain such violations of this act." These suits came before a district judge and could be appealed, after 1891, to the courts of appeals. Acting in the public interest, the federal government became the prosecutor of monopolists, though under the act individuals and companies could bring their own suits. The discretion given to the district attorneys was immense, but it was exercised with great caution. Over the course of Sherman Act antitrust jurisprudence (1890–1914), relatively few cases came to trial. Of the twenty-one suits brought between 1890 and 1900, half resulted in court-ordered injunctions against the defendants. The law's mechanisms did not act as a particularly effective deterrent, however, as manufacturers, railway owners, and mine owners continued to form monopolies. On one side of the rapidly shifting political climate was the free trade/free labor ideology that had survived the Civil War. On the other side was a new way of doing big business, with interlocking directorates of corporations and various forms of integration of production and sales.

One of these monopolies was designed to control rail service and pricing across the upper tier of the wheat-growing plains. In 1904, the owner of the Great Northern Railroad secured controlling interest in two competing lines serving the farm country, the Chicago, Burlington, and Quincy and the Northern Pacific, in a "holding company" called the Northern Securities Company. It was not what it seemed, a financial plan, but a monopoly for control of the right-of-way. That year, the Theodore Roosevelt administration ordered the Department of Justice to file a suit against the holding company under the Sherman Act. The circuit court for the Circuit of Minnesota in which the federal attorney had brought the suit issued an injunction dissolving the trust. When the case came to the high court in *Northern Securities Co. v. U.S.* (1904), the Court's members sharply divided on the application of the act, demonstrating the two sides of the phase change.

Justices John Marshall Harlan, Henry Billings Brown, Joseph McKenna, and William R. Day agreed that the combination was an entity "in restraint of trade," and that was "enough to bring it under the condemnation of the act." Clearly, the holding company engaged in interstate trade, and regulation of that was explicitly given to Congress in Article I of the Constitution. The majority brushed away objections based on "liberty of contract" (derived from the Due Process Clause of the Fourteenth Amendment) and the notion that the activity was intrastate rather than interstate (and so protected from congressional regulation by earlier Supreme Court decisions). Justice David J. Brewer, in a concurrence, added that corporations like Northern Securities were persons under the law and, like all individuals, were free to "manage their own property." This was the old doctrine of free labor to which Brewer still clung, but here the company was actually an instrument of several companies solely to restrain trade. Thus, it actually prevented free labor from operating. That was a stretch, particularly for Brewer, but not for Harlan, who believed wholeheartedly in the old doctrine.

Harlan wrote the majority decision. He clung to the free soil, free men, free trade culture of the pre–Civil War era (ironic in light of his prewar slaveholding). The Sherman Act reflected those attitudes as well. Harlan rehearsed the facts of the combination to show how it restrained trade. "Let us see what are the facts disclosed by the record." The facts were revealed by the government's efforts to lift the corporate veil. Behind that veil was a picture by now familiar of overextension, ruinous competition, and the bankruptcy of the Northern Pacific's parent company. Its assets were already in the hands of bankruptcy receivers, and the shareholders had agreed to a "virtual consolidation," giving control of the Northern Pacific to the Great Northern. That was illegal under Minnesota state law. Undeterred, the Great Northern in 1901 purchased controlling interest in the Chicago, Burlington, and Quincy, paid for with bonds for the Great Northern and Northern Pacific, with resulting control over rail lines from Chicago to the Pacific. This combination, the Great Northern, created a holding corporation called the Northern Securities Company under the laws of New Jersey, a compliant state (along with Delaware) for such holding companies.

Thus three rail lines in dire straits created a company whose stock was supposed to be valuable because it was now a monopoly of the northern route. As a business maneuver it was worthy of the best of the bad old days (in fact, famous banker J. P. Morgan was a lender in more ways than one to the scheme). The total stock was to be $400 million, underwritten by J. P. Morgan's bank. There was nothing more in the coffers of the new holding company than the $30,000 needed to get the registration in New Jersey and the promise to pay off on the bonds in the future.

This was a kiss and a wave, Harlan implied, to scam investors. For the new company "does not have and never had any capital to warrant such an operation." The real payoff to those who ventured to buy the new bonds would be complete control of the haulage rates for the high plains wheat and beef trade. "The Government charges that, if the combination was held not to be in violation of the act of Congress, then all efforts of the National Government to preserve to the people the benefits of free competition among carriers engaged in interstate commerce will be wholly unavailing, and all transcontinental lines, indeed the entire railway systems of the country, may be absorbed, merged and consolidated, thus placing the public at the absolute mercy of the holding corporation." Harlan decried the evil motives of the board of the Great Northern. "The stock-holders . . . will see to it that no competition is tolerated. They will take care that no persons are chosen directors of the holding company who will permit competition between the constituent companies." Harlan noted in passing, with some dyspepsia, that the Court had exempted intrastate manufacturing from the Sherman Act in *U.S. v. E.C. Knight* (1895), a case in which he had dissented. Now the Court had to exercise "the full and free exercise of all National powers and the security of all rights entrusted by the Constitution to its care. The strong arm of the National Government may be put forth to brush away all obstructions to the freedom of interstate commerce."

Harlan held up the language of a Pennsylvania Supreme Court opinion on a similar railroad case in the coal country as a model for the high court in the Northern Securities case:

> When competition is left free, individual error or folly will generally find a correction in the conduct of others. But here is a combination of all the companies operating . . . and controlling their entire productions. They have combined together to govern the supply and the price of coal in all the markets from the Hudson to the Mississippi rivers, and from Pennsylvania to the Lakes. This combination has a power in its confederated form which no individual action can confer. The public interest must succumb to it, for it has left no competition free to correct its baleful influence. When the supply of coal is suspended, the demand for it becomes importunate, and prices must rise, or if the supply goes forward, the prices fixed by the confederates must accompany it. The domestic hearth, the furnaces of the iron master and the fires of the paralyzed and hungry mouths are stinted.

Finally, Harlan gave New Jersey a free pass:

> It is proper to say in passing that nothing in the record tends to show that the State of New Jersey had any reason to suspect that those who took advantage of its liberal incorporation laws had in view, when organizing the Securities Company, to destroy competition between two great railway carriers engaged in interstate commerce in distant States of the Union. The purpose of the combination was concealed under very general words that gave no clue whatever to the real purposes of those who brought about the organization of the Securities Company. If the certificate of the incorporation of that company had expressly stated

that the object of the company was to destroy competition between competing, parallel lines of interstate carriers, all would have seen, at the outset, that the scheme was in hostility to the national authority, and that there was a purpose to violate or evade the act of Congress.

Harlan's opinion confirmed the supremacy of the federal government in matters explicitly delegated to the Congress, as regulation of interstate commerce was. Justice White, who had served the Confederacy and preferred states' rights to federal supremacy as a guiding principle, dissented. He too clung to an even older model of governance, the ideal of states' rights that permitted slavery to flourish in one part of the country when it was illegal in the rest. This model was even older than the federal government. "It cannot be denied that the sum of all just governmental power was enjoyed by the States and the people before the Constitution of the United States was formed. None of that power was abridged by that instrument except as restrained by constitutional safeguards, and hence none was lost by the adoption of the Constitution. The Constitution, whilst distributing the preexisting authority, preserved it all." There was no limit to the act if it applied to Northern Securities. Justices Rufus Peckham and Oliver Wendell Holmes Jr. joined in the dissent.

White's rationale was that the new company was chartered in New Jersey; hence its operations were not interstate—they were wholly within a single state. This was, of course, something of a fiction, but fictions of this sort were nothing new in the doctrine of states' rights. The stock was owned by the Northern Securities Company, and nothing in the Sherman Act or in the powers of Congress forbade one company from owning the stock of other companies. The fact that the companies might be engaged in interstate commerce did not mean that the ownership of their stock was itself interstate commerce. This power was not delegated to Congress and so could not be exercised in the present case. The opposite "would result that it would be in the power of Congress to abrogate every such railroad charter granted by the States from the beginning if Congress deemed that the rights conferred by such state charters tended to restrain commerce between the States or to create a monopoly concerning the same." Too much power for Congress was bad for the country, White thought.

White would not lift the veil of a corporate charter to see what was behind it. "It has been decided by this court that, as the Anti-Trust Act forbids any restraint, it therefore embraces even reasonable contracts or agreements. If, then, the ownership of the stock of the two railroads by the Northern Securities Company is repugnant to the act, it follows that ownership, whether by the individual or another corporation, would be equally within the prohibitions of the act." So, not only did the act go too far; it did not go far enough, as it only dismembered the holding company, not the underlying combination of the rail lines.

White's target was not just the circuit court's decision, or even the majority opinion; it was the very idea that the federal government had the authority to intervene in business activities. "It may not be doubted that, from the foundation of the government, at all events to the time of the adoption of the Anti-Trust Act of 1890, there was an entire absence of any legislation by Congress even suggesting that it was deemed by anyone that power was possessed by Congress to control the ownership of stock in railroad or other corporations, because such corporations engaged in interstate commerce." He offered a review of the history of rails to prove his point. Charles Francis Adams would have been delighted. "Without stopping to recite details on the subject, I content myself with merely mentioning a few of the instances where great systems of railroad have been formed by the unification of the management of competitive roads, by consolidation or otherwise, often by statutory authority. These instances embrace the Boston and Maine system, the New York, New Haven and Hartford, the New York Central, the Reading, and the Pennsylvania systems."

Prior decisions of the Court that Harlan brushed away White reintroduced. "The decisions of this court, to my mind, leave no room for doubt on the subject. As I have already shown, the very definition of the power to regulate commerce, as announced in *Gibbons v. Ogden*, excludes the conception that it extends to stock ownership." There followed, in White's turgid and pedantic style, a list of cases, some on point, others more distant, to shore up his argument. The fact that many of them came from a period before the Civil War, with its immense increase in federal power, and before the Reconstruction Amendments and the Civil Rights Acts, which White found repugnant but which further added to federal power, did not divert him from his objective. Nor did he hesitate to quote his own opinions in later cases.

Oliver Wendell Holmes Jr. had just arrived on the high court bench from the center chair of the Massachusetts Supreme Judicial Court. He had earlier been a member of the Harvard Law School faculty, prior to that a Civil War veteran, and still earlier a student at Harvard College. He had written a study of the common law in 1881 and given lectures at Harvard in 1896 that brought him notice as a realist and critic of legal formalities. President Roosevelt assumed that Holmes would be a trust-buster on the Court but was sadly mistaken. He never forgave Holmes. Oddly, like Roosevelt, Holmes was a modernist, but his version of modernity did not include federal intervention in the market. He did not base his aversion to intervention on states' rights, but on a realistic view of the inevitability of bigness. Holmes wrote, "I am unable to agree with the judgment of the majority of the court, and although I think it useless and undesirable, as a rule, to express dissent, I feel bound to do so in this case, and to give my reasons for it." There followed a series of phrases that, as in the past and in future, would elevate Holmes to the pantheon of great legal writers. "Great cases, like hard cases, make bad law. For great cases are called great not by reason of their real importance in shaping the law of the future, but because of some accident of immediate overwhelming interest which appeals to the feelings and distorts the judgment. These immediate interests exercise a kind of hydraulic pressure which makes what previously was clear seem doubtful, and before which even well settled principles of law will bend." The Court had overreached itself in this case, by trying to fix "the meaning of some not very difficult words."

Holmes judged that the majority of the Court had found implications in the text of the act that were not there. "The question to be decided is whether, under the act . . . it is unlawful, at any stage of the process, if several men unite to form a corporation for the purpose of buying more than half the stock of each of two competing interstate railroad companies, if they form the corporation, and the corporation buys the stock. I will suppose further that every step is taken, from the beginning, with the single intent of ending competition between the companies." Nothing in any of these steps fit the terms of a criminal statute, which, after all, was what the Sherman Act was.

Secondly, the statute was of a very sweeping and general character, too sweeping for Holmes. "It hits 'every' contract or combination of the prohibited sort, great or small, and 'every' person who shall monopolize or attempt to monopolize, in the sense of the act, 'any part' of the trade or commerce among the several States. There is a natural inclination to assume that it was directed against certain great combinations, and to read it in that light. It does not say so." Third, "the statute must be construed in such a way as not merely to save its constitutionality but, so far as is consistent with a fair interpretation, not to raise grave doubts on that score." But even if it were read heroically, "Congress might regulate not only commerce but instruments of commerce or contracts the bearing of which upon commerce would be only indirect." The mere fact that a group of men agreed to pool their stocks would not justify the imposition of the criminal sanctions in the act. Such would not constitute "combinations or conspiracies in restraint of trade . . . to keep strangers to the agreement out of the business." Nor could the act be read to require "that all existing competitions shall be maintained."

What was left—well, a monopoly. But again, "according to popular speech, every concern monopolizes whatever business it does, and if that business is trade between two States, it monopolizes a part of the trade among the States. Of course, the statute does not forbid that. It does not mean that all business must cease. A single railroad down a narrow valley or through a mountain gorge monopolizes all the railroad transportation through that valley or gorge. Indeed, every railroad monopolizes, in a popular sense, the trade of some area." The law made no distinctions between the size of monopolies, though were one to read the debates in Congress it would become clear that large monopolies were its targets, while small ones could pass without fear of indictment. "I think the whole argument to the contrary rests on a popular, instead of an accurate and legal, conception of what the word 'monopolize' in the statute means."

Holmes closed, "In view of my interpretation of the statute, I do not go further into the question of the power of Congress. That has been dealt with by my brother White, and I concur in the main with his views. I am happy to know that only a minority of my brethren adopt an interpretation of the law which in my opinion would make eternal the *bellum omnium contra omnes* and disintegrate society so far as it could into individual atoms." In effect, Holmes was criticizing Harlan's free labor argument and passing by Harlan's federalism argument. The irony was that White, in gray, would have shot Holmes, in blue, dead if the two had come upon one another in battle, but Harlan, who led a battalion of federal troops, would have succored the wounded Holmes on the field where White had left him. White clung to a very old ideal of a limited constitution. Holmes saw the world very differently. The law makes interesting bedfellows.

—∭—

The twentieth century had not been good for the major rail lines. Mismanagement and the rise of the trucking industry cut deeply into freight income. Auto and air transportation severely limited long-distance passenger trade. The intercity and suburban commuter lines and the freight traffic of the East Coast rail lines were still viable and, more important, were vital to commerce in the "corridor" between Boston and Washington, DC, even if the railroad companies themselves were no longer profitable. Over the course of the 1960s, the Interstate Commerce Commission presided over a series of rail mergers designed to save the eastern coastal lines. The first to be merged were the Chesapeake and Ohio and the Baltimore and Ohio, whose principal carrying trade was coal. The Penn Central, largest of all, had filed for bankruptcy protection in 1970 under chapter 11 of the Bankruptcy Act of 1898 and 1938. This provided for protection of some assets, while the bankruptcy court arranged for the sale of other assets to pay off creditors. The Penn Central would stay in business during the reorganization. By the opening of the new decade, the commission was ready to deal with the remaining lines. Three lines left out of the scheme filed suit. They would be driven out of business, bankrupted, by the new combination. In effect, they argued, it was a government-sponsored oligopoly of the sort outlawed by post–Gilded Age antitrust legislation.

In an earlier case, *Baltimore & Ohio R. Co. v. United States* (1967), regarding the same issues, a skeptical Justice William O. Douglas described the backstairs, backhanded way that these reorganizations took place:

> The eastern [railroad consolidation] story begins with the [Interstate Commerce] Commission's approval of the merger between the Norfolk & Western and the Virginian in 1958, two successful and competitive coal roads. By that merger, the New York Central lost its access to the Pocahontas coal territory and it lost a friendly connection which more or less had always been considered a Central road. Thus, the Virginian, apparently not "attainable" by the Central was now placed in a position to enhance the competitive power of the Pennsylvania (which

controlled the Norfolk & Western). This merger, plus the announced intention of the Chesapeake & Ohio to acquire control of the Baltimore & Ohio, sharpened the Central's interest in its competitive survival against the massive Pennsylvania system, which was well entrenched in the rich Pocahontas coal fields and in the Tidewater ports. The Central tried to outpoint the C & O in getting control of the B & O, but it lost out, largely because it couldn't convince Swiss bankers of any financial advantage in the merger. Then the Central negotiated with the C & O for a three-way merger between the respective companies, which the Central's president Perlman believed would provide a balanced, competitive system with the Pennsylvania. At the same time, Mr. Perlman was stating that a B & O-C & O union would seriously hurt the Central. In the meantime, the Norfolk & Western had filed for merger with the Nickel Plate, for a leasing of the Wabash, and for the purchase of the Pennsylvania's Sandusky line. This was apparently the last straw for the Central. It had been outmaneuvered, and thus did the only thing left it could do—agree to merge with the Pennsylvania. That merger was "attainable," and is now the crucial determinant of most rail reorganizations.

In the *Regional Rail Reorganization Act Cases* (1974), the Supreme Court surveyed the Rail Act of 1973's actions to save the railways. Congress had stepped in periodically to save the rails, but in prior years, there was more than a sniff of corruption. Indeed, the first right-of-way grants to the Central and Union Pacific were facilitated with gifts of stock. Now the project was hedged around with administrative rules rather than partisan lobbying, but the rules were still subject to interpretation. There would be winners (or at least survivors) and losers just as in the 1870s and the 1890s. Reorganizations were no longer managed by the likes of J. P. Morgan and his cronies, however, but by a calculation of "the public interest." Any of the railways' stockholders who thought they had been unfairly treated could appeal to a special court. That court's decision would be final.

In effect, Congress had delegated to the special court an administrative job. Courts of bankruptcy and other special topics routinely acted like administrative agencies. Thus the law of the Rail Act of 1973 had circled back to the kinds of decisions the original ICC of 1887 was supposed to impose on the rail lines. But 1974 was different from 1887. The old ideal of an entirely free market was giving way to a "government corporation, the United States Railway Association (USRA), which is directed to formulate a 'Final System Plan' (Plan) by July 26, 1975, for restructuring the railroads into a 'financially self-sustaining rail service system.'" The plan was also to be submitted to the special court for approval. What could go wrong? "If the Special Court finds the conveyance not fair and equitable," the Supreme Court would find the entire mess back in its own lap. In the meantime, "railroads may discontinue service and abandon properties not designated for transfer under the Plan, but, until the Plan becomes effective, may only discontinue service or abandon any line with USRA consent and absent reasonable state opposition."

The last line was a time bomb. Rails that were going under had to keep treading water if the new government corporation, called Conrail, or the states in which they did business objected. As one might have guessed, the reorganization did not go according to plan. Congress might propose, but it was left to the Supreme Court to dispose, for "parties with interests in Penn Central Transportation Co. (Penn Central) brought suits attacking the constitutionality of the Rail Act, contending that the Act violates the Fifth Amendment by taking Penn Central property without just compensation." Sounds familiar, right? While rejecting the "takings" issue as premature in view of a number of decisional steps required before the final conveyance, the district court held that the claim of a managed erosion of Penn Central's property was not imaginary. The district court also rejected the statutory provisions for Penn Central bringing a suit under the Rail Act. They violated the Fifth Amendment, taking without compensation. In short, Congress's plan to end endless litigation regarding the rail lines by combining and managing them had led to more litigation under an entirely different act of Congress.

The Supreme Court reversed the district court and allowed the reorganization of the Rail Act to proceed. But not before the majority of the court (Douglas dissenting) labored through its own rendition of the entire legislative and subsequent judicial proceedings. Justice William Brennan sounded the alarm if the Rail Act were discarded: "A rail transportation crisis seriously threatening the national welfare was precipitated when eight major railroads in the northeast and midwest region of the country entered reorganization proceedings under . . . the Bankruptcy Act. After interim measures proved to be insufficient, Congress concluded that solution of the crisis required reorganization of the railroads, stripped of excess facilities, into a single, viable system operated by a private, for-profit corporation." So, Congress had not created a national rail system, of the sort common in Europe and Asia, but had created a privately run, publicly financed corporation, a hybrid. To ensure profitability, or at least viability, Congress permitted the new plan to dispose of the underperforming lines. The act would have the effect of taking lines away from some of the eight companies, in the name of the public interest. Sounds like a simple Fifth Amendment question; that is, would the act provide due process compensation to the shareholders of the affected railroad companies if the taking were in the public domain? The act created a special court to hear and decide what that compensation would be. Its determinations would be final. A fund of $500 million was created to repay stockholders the lost value of the stocks under eminent domain.

The act also created the U.S. Rail Authority to manage the new national line. Was it socialism? Or was it another agency subject to "capture" by the very individuals and groups whose interests it was supposed to manage in the public interest? The answer was in the plan: "The Final System Plan must provide for transfer of designated rail properties by the railroads in reorganization to a private state-incorporated corporation, Consolidated Rail Corporation (Conrail)." Who would then win and who lose by the transfer of power? Who would decide those questions? The special court next determines whether the conveyances of the rail properties to Conrail "are in the public interest and are fair and equitable to the estate of each railroad in reorganization in accordance with the standard of fairness and equity applicable to the approval of a plan of reorganization."

The ideal of administrative neutrality was introduced in American law late in the nineteenth century with the introduction of independent regulatory agencies like the ICC (1887). Under the Progressives, the number and scope of federal administrative agencies was expanded to include the regulation of food and drugs, among other subjects. The civil service system, introduced in the Pendleton Civil Service Reform Act of 1883, replaced presidential patronage appointments with bureaucratic tests, job descriptions, and pay scales. These civil servants would staff the new independent regulatory agencies, although their boards or directors would still be presidential appointees confirmed by the Senate. The entire scheme of a fourth branch of the federal government based on the agencies grew enormously during the New Deal to include the Securities and Exchange Commission, the National Labor Relations Board, the Social

Security System, and other agencies. That process continued into the period of the Rail Act of 1973 with agencies concerned with the environment, workplace safety, and consumer protection. The Administrative Procedure Act of 1946 provided that decisions of the agencies could be appealed to the federal courts. In the later part of the twentieth century, Presidents Richard M. Nixon, Ronald Reagan, Bill Clinton, and George W. Bush called for greater executive control of the agencies, something of a throwback to the pre-agency period of presidential patronage.

The provisions of the Rail Act in miniature reflected something of the history of the administrative state. But a transfer of private ownership from the existing eight lines to one new private line inevitably would lead to challenge in court, just as earlier, partial reorganization plans regarding the Chesapeake and Ohio and the Baltimore and Ohio had led Congress to act in the first place. Congress knew this and provided that the affected lines could not discontinue service. The line most directly and unfavorably affected, Penn Central, rushed to the federal district court arguing that the Rail Act was an unconstitutional taking of their property. They knew that the promised just compensation under the act would fall far short of what they valued their property to be worth. Worse was the likely discontinuance of their more profitable lines. Justice Brennan and the majority were not convinced, but if petitioners wanted to pursue a remedy, they could take their cause to the federal courts of claims. For the present, "We are persuaded that the legislative history supports the conclusion that Congress intended that financial obligations" of the USRA and Conrail under the Rail Act "be limited to the express terms of the Act." In other words, too bad.

Brennan relied in part on the findings of the special court the act created. In its opinion, Judge Henry Friendly of the Court of Appeals of the Second Circuit, serving on the new court by appointment, was one of the most admired federal judges of his time. Brennan reported, "The Special Court, speaking through Judge Friendly, comprehensively canvassed both issues, and, in a thorough opinion, concluded that the Rail Act does not bar any necessary resort to the [federal courts] . . . and that the remedy is adequate. Our independent examination of the issues brings us to the same conclusion, substantially for the reasons stated by Judge Friendly." Judge Friendly and Justice Brennan were both Harvard Law graduates, Friendly having set records for his high grades. Brennan knew and respected Friendly, in part because in private practice Friendly had long represented transportation companies and knew the problems and prospects of those entities in great detail, and in part because Friendly's opinions on the bench were not especially elegant, but they were thorough and evidenced the judge's mastery of detail. Another feature of his opinions was his deference to the aims of legislatures, here Congress's purposes in framing the Rail Act. It is rare for the high court to give such frank name recognition to the author of an inferior appellate court opinion. In effect, Brennan was reminding everyone that a Friendly opinion was something special.

Justice William O. Douglas was a Yale Law School graduate and had served as the head of the Securities and Exchange Commission during the New Deal. He had little patience for the insider deals that the rail moguls had made then, or their role in the new legislation. He certainly did not defer to Friendly, although Douglas often sided with Brennan on constitutional issues. In 1974, Douglas had suffered the last of a series of severely debilitating strokes, and he attended court in a wheelchair. But his mental acuity was not diminished, nor was his suspicion of big business and his willingness to allow for regulation by the federal government. There were limits, however. "We are urged to bow to the pressure of events and expedite in the public interest the reorganization of these six rail carriers. An emergency often gives Congress the occasion to act. But I know of no emergency that permits it to disregard the Just Compensation Clause of the Fifth Amendment or the uniformity requirement of the Bankruptcy Clause of the Constitution. I fear that the 'hydraulic pressure' generated by this case will have a serious impact on a historic area of the law, jealously protected over the centuries by courts of equity in the interests of justice."

A new phase change peeked out of the dissent in the *Railroad Reorganization Cases* (1974). Justice Douglas was hardly naive when it came to business misconduct, but he bridled at the idea that there were no longer any standards for fiscal probity or public good in what had become a public transportation utility. He had been part of the regulation revolution of the New Deal, but behind the introduction of the Securities and Exchange Commission and its fellow agencies was a moral ideal that business should be regulated in the public interest. The consolidation of the East Coast rail lines was entirely in their interest. No one spoke of honor or dignity, as these values had long since been discarded by the business schools. But ethical conduct was still a required course in the

MBA programs, and the majority seemed indifferent to it. The robber barons had lost their wealth and their control of the rails, but perhaps the ethos of the robber barons had won in the courts.

—⁓—

As for stock swindles and swindlers, nothing matched the Enron endgame. The Texas firm's rise in the late 1990s was nothing short of amazing. Enron was an energy middleman trading in oil and gas futures and selling stock, as well as buying stock. The firm acted like a brokerage, although its corporate charter did not encompass that kind of activity. By 2001, the company's accounts showed huge losses in the trading game, which Enron was concealing. Its subsidiary business ventures, particularly the broadband cable enterprise, were the chief culprit, but the losses were everywhere, covered by loans that Enron could not repay. Even the core business, the selling of oil and gas, was troubled, as the return was fixed by contract, but the cost was outrunning the income. Everything about the looming crash of the company was being hidden from the shareholders. The chief officers, Ken Lay, Jeff Skilling, and Andy Fastow, were not really teammates but rivals and out of touch with the crisis, or so they later said when federal investigators came calling. Still, Skilling and Fastow made out like bandits just before the reckoning in 2001.

At the height of its success in 2000, Enron's assets were overvalued, the debt was kept off the company books, and the firm's answer to the impending crisis was to offer new bundles of stock to an unaware public. The losses were not just in failed business ventures; they were in failed accounting transactions, the new version of the stock swindle that caught the Chattanooga railroad bondholders short. The only structural member holding up the jerry-rigged structure was the marketing of more and more Enron stock—a tactic worthy of the Jay Goulds of the Gilded Age. When the building crashed, it crashed on the shareholders to the tune of $38 billion. On December 2, 2000, Enron filed for bankruptcy, and the parade of investigators, court cases, denials, and trials began. Lawyers, among others sorting through the debris, came away with $1.2 billion in fees for the cleanup. Everyone still denied responsibility. To accept it would be to commit professional suicide. Honor no longer mattered, for none of the denials were credible.

6

Divorce

NOTHING IN AMERICAN LAW CHANGED more from the founding of the country to the present day than divorce and the litigation it spawned. From an insignificant number of cases and an infinitesimal annual rate of divorce at the beginning of the nineteenth century to hundreds of thousands of cases each year in the twenty-first century, divorce has become only a little less common than marriage. From a requirement of accusations of the most grievous nature to no-fault proceedings, divorce litigation has evolved alongside Americans' changing way of life. Today divorce law is a major part of the general category of "family law" or "domestic relations law," a course offered at every law school and a significant part of the practice of single-practitioner and small partnership law firms.

—⁂—

In the eighteenth century, divorce was a minor part of the subject of "baron and feme" in English common law. In this body of law, derived from medieval notions of gender, man and wife were considered one person. With a few exceptions, the wife had no legal identity or property of her own. Her personality was merged into her husband's. This was called coverture, and it persisted into the first years of the nineteenth century.

Divorce was not really a viable option in early America. Well into the antebellum period, many states would only grant a divorce by public legislative decree upon one married party's petition. Reform came slowly in the period 1820–1850, with Pennsylvania leading the way. State legislatures passed general divorce laws that allowed "private" (court-granted) divorces. Even then, the grounds for divorce were limited in most jurisdictions to adultery and desertion, and divorce actions did not include provisions for joint property or custody of children. Judges routinely lamented having to intervene in the breakup of marriages, and many couples effected the equivalent of a divorce by simply separating, often moving to different states. Such moves might be accompanied by new unions, though these were no more legal than the separations. Divorce as a matter of fact thus was far more common than divorce by law. Nevertheless, two-thirds of "actual" (legal) divorces were sought by women, and by 1900, there were over fifty thousand divorce decrees each year, a startling increase over the beginning of the previous century.

Throughout the nineteenth century and well into the twentieth, federal courts and Congress regarded divorce as a state legislative and judicial matter. In other kinds of lawsuits involving residents of different states, one of the parties might, if the "diversity" of residence is complete and the financial stake is large enough, "remove" the suit into a federal court. The provision written in the Judicial Act of 1789 and retained to this day says "all suits." In 1890, the Supreme Court decided that federal courts lacked the power to issue divorce, alimony, or child custody decrees, despite the fact that some of these kinds of cases involved diversity of residence. In fact, divorce law is one of the last bastions of "states' rights" jurisprudence in America. The result is a crazy quilt of divorce law precedents and some prickly problems in divorce litigation.

Although Progressive Era divorce law was a matter of state action and varied considerably across the country, in general, a divorce was still hard to obtain. One party had to prove desertion or adultery by the other party. Old ideas of the authority of the husband in the marriage, tied to his responsibility for providing for wife and children, thus persisted, as did the equally hoary conception of coverture. In a time when few women could vote and fewer still held public office, such notions seemed to reflect reality. But the reality was changing, and so would the shape of litigation.

—ɯ—

New York law in this Progressive Era, from 1900 to 1929, was among the most reformed of any state. Statutes protected the rights of children, workers, and immigrants. But the legislature did not reform the divorce law. The courts, whose judges were elected, quietly began to fill the gap. It was easier to get an annulment in New York than in its neighboring states (decried by conservatives as a type of "trial marriage"). The state allowed divorce by separation, with those who could simply moving to a nearby state and the remaining resident filing for divorce on the basis of desertion. Adultery was still the only grounds for a complete divorce, but an industry grew up around this cause of action as well. While "hasty" remarriage was delayed in some states (a waiting period of up to two years in Alabama, Wisconsin, and Tennessee) or barred if the party seeking to remarry was guilty of adultery (in Maryland and Louisiana), New York did not impose such restrictions. The parties that wanted a divorce simply arranged for evidence of adultery to arise, often by simply going to a hotel with a cooperative third party and having an investigator document the delict. In this, the courts of New York were responding to the larger changes in the social environment. Urbanization played a role, as divorce was more common in the metropolis than in the hinterland—and New York was more citified than most of the country.

While jurists writing about divorce and judges hearing cases agreed that marriage was a special institution deserving of preservation, the facts of marriage and separation in the late nineteenth and early twentieth centuries increasingly challenged the elite male assumptions. Society, for good or evil, was becoming more a gathering of individuals rather than collectivities. Membership in unions, fraternal organizations, and even charitable institutions was increasingly voluntary. Women in particular were stretching the older conventions of subordination by going to college, beginning careers, and living apart from men.

As Hendrik Hartog explains in *Man and Wife in America*, nineteenth-century men and women more often separated (or hid from one another) than sought a divorce. Some states gave their imprimatur to such arrangements by subsequently awarding one of the parties a legal end to the marriage. New York was not one of those states. "The state's continuing refusal to liberalize its divorce laws" well into the new century "produced many cases" in which older values, held by one party in the divorce action, came into conflict with the other party's adoption of new values.

Haddock v. Haddock (1906) was the most important of these, going all the way to the U.S. Supreme Court. In it, Justice White reviewed the divorce law of the various states at length, such length that in his dissent

Justice Oliver Wendell Holmes Jr. could be heard mocking his senior colleague. The tangled web of separation, desertion, foreign (out-of-state) divorce, and issues of "comity" (one state agreeing to enforce the decision of another state's courts) in White's opinion in *Haddock* looked back to earlier views of the marriage bond. Holmes looked ahead to a time when divorce (counting second and third divorces) would almost be easier and more frequent than first marriages.

The case came from New York and was argued at the Supreme Court in October 1905, the decision coming in the spring of 1906. It would have occasioned little interest save for the exhausting review of divorce law in the majority opinion. Evidently, Justice Edward Douglass White of Louisiana thought that this was the time to demonstrate his knowledge of every state's law on the subject, and thus an appropriate case for the historian to examine the state of law at the turn of the century.

The appellant, a husband who lost the judgment in the New York courts and owed alimony, argued that the New York courts should have taken notice of a divorce decree entered in Ohio. This was a "full faith and credit" claim, based on Article IV, section 1, of the Constitution: "Full Faith and Credit shall be given in each State to the public Acts, Records, and judicial Proceedings of every other State." In New York, the wife filed against the husband, arguing that he had deserted her. The husband responded that he had obtained a legal divorce in Connecticut, where he resided. But Connecticut did not have jurisdiction over the wife, as she had never resided there. The divorce degree was enforceable in his state, but not in hers. Why then should the New York decree, including alimony, be enforceable against him, if New York did not have jurisdiction over him? In fact, he was served the decree papers when he set foot in New York to contest them! It was a puzzlement of great importance, if one liked such puzzles, which White did and Holmes did not.

Divorce law was about as far away from the great political issues of the day as one could get. Progressives and conservatives battled in Congress over reforms like the Food and Drug Act and the regulation of railroad rates, Theodore Roosevelt's tussles with isolationists over foreign policy, and his criticism of the majority of the Supreme Court for overturning Progressive legislation. Yet in the American legal system, the penumbras—the shadows—of one kind of litigation could fall over many other subjects, even one as obscure as divorce. If the Court in *Haddock* bowed to the sovereignty of each state, was the decision an omen that the Court would not accede to President Roosevelt's aggressive nationalism? If the Court imposed a uniform national regime on divorce law, was it hinting that sweeping national reforms would pass muster when they too were challenged? The answer might not lie in the substantive matter of the case at all but in the Court's interpretation of the Full Faith and Credit Clause of Article IV, section 1. It stated that "Full Faith and Credit shall be given in each State to the public Acts, Records, and judicial Proceedings of every other State." But did this apply to the power of the states over the divorce of citizens of other states?

The Haddocks were married for thirty years before the wife sought to end the marriage because her husband had left her right after they were married. He responded that the marriage was based on a fraud and was never consummated. Justice White, a conservative Louisianan who had, as a youth, served in the Confederate forces and later strongly supported Jim Crow, wrote the majority opinion. He was not a great supporter of federal power, in this or other cases. "The Federal question is, Did the court below violate the Constitution of the United States by refusing to give to the decree of divorce rendered in the State of Connecticut the faith and credit to which it was entitled?" White relied on a procedural rather than a substantive rule, and that rule was not in the text of the Full Faith and Credit Clause but in a precedent the Court had established for a state's jurisdiction. The rule, in *Pennoyer v. Neff*, was prudential; that is, it was invented by the Court.

The rule protected the state's sovereignty in diversity cases. "Neff, who was a resident of a State other than Oregon, owned a tract of land in Oregon. Mitchell, a resident of Oregon, brought a suit in a court of that State upon a money demand against Neff. The Oregon statutes required, in the case of personal action against a non-resident, a publication of notice, calling upon the defendant to appear and defend, and also required the mailing to such defendant at his last known place of residence of a copy of the summons and complaint." Neff lived somewhere in the neighboring state of California, which should have made the case one of diversity under the Judiciary Act of 1789. Pennoyer told the court that Neff did not appear to defend himself, and Neff won the suit by default. Neff now awakened to his plight and brought a suit in diversity in the Circuit Court of the United States for the District of Oregon (at the time a trial court, not a court of appeals) to recover the property, and the question presented was the validity in Oregon of the judgment there rendered against Neff.

After the most elaborate consideration, it was expressly decided that the judgment rendered in Oregon under the circumstances stated was void for want of jurisdiction and was repugnant to the Due Process Clause of the Constitution of the United States. In short, the federal court held that Oregon's long-arm procedure did not reach someone who lived out of state. White disagreed with respect to marriage. The federal overturning of the Oregon ruling in *Pennoyer* was about property, not persons. What about marriage, over which "the inherent power which all governments must possess over the marriage relation, its formation and dissolution, as regards their own citizens" was at issue? White had a definitive answer: a state's divorce law was binding on citizens of that state, no matter what the laws of another state might say. Nothing in the Constitution of the United States could change that. But the Constitution was the supreme law of the land, and the judgments of state courts were all subject to the federal Constitution. At least that was the understanding of the framers of the Constitution and of the Fourteenth Amendment. White then went on to cite line and verse from other cases of abandonment and crossed jurisdictional lines from state statutes and case law.

Hidden in all the precedents was White's view that abandonment was immoral and violated marital obligation. "Where the domicil of matrimony was in a particular State, and the husband abandons his wife and goes into another State in order to avoid his marital obligation, such other State to which the husband has wrongfully fled does not, in the nature of things, become a new domicil of matrimony." No man (note the gendered terminology) was going to benefit because he left his wife and went to another state whose laws would gain him the divorce he could not get in the state where he married. The husband could not gain through law what he had sought to gain through leaving his obligations behind by crossing state lines. Marriage, unlike disputes over property by citizens of different states, was special, and its dissolution, like its creation, demanded attention to the moral value of marriage from all in the legal system—legislatures, judges and justices, and state and federal governments. One can also see in White's opinion vestiges of the chivalric notion of southern male duty to the otherwise helpless wife.

White's colleague Justice Oliver Wendell Holmes Jr. was the first of what would later be called realists in their jurisprudence. His service in the Union army during the Civil War, during which he was wounded three times and his life nearly despaired of, and his experience as a law professor and judge on the Massachusetts Supreme Judicial Court gave weight to his conclusion that the life of the law was not logic; it was experience. White's heavy-handed, repetitive, and Victorian moralist view of marriage made little sense to Holmes; no more than did White's tedious recitation of every state's case law on divorce.

Holmes, joined by Justices John Marshall Harlan, Josiah Brewer, and Henry Billings Brown, dissented. Holmes wrote for them, "I do not suppose that civilization will come to an end whichever way this case is decided." What worried him most was that White's decision "is likely to cause considerable disaster to innocent persons and to bastardize children hitherto supposed to be the offspring of lawful marriage." Once more, hidden within what appeared to be a very conventional procedural essay was the recognition that the nature of marriage, and in particular of women's place in it, had changed, and law, to be effective, must change too.

The morality or immorality of the parties captured in the decrees of the two states was material to the Supreme Court's decision. But not to Holmes. For Holmes it was the woman's fate that mattered, not the man's honor. "I therefore pass such arguments without discussion, although they seem to me easy to answer. Granting the divorce does not depend upon the fact of her desertion, but continues even if her husband's cruelty has driven her out of the State and she has acquired a separate domicile elsewhere upon the principles which we all agree are recognized by this court." It did not matter who deserted whom. "I can see no ground for giving a less effect to the decree when the husband changes his domicile after the separation has taken place. The question whether such a decree should have a less effect is the only question open, and the issue is narrowed to that." The immorality attached to the party who deserted was a kind of fiction that only law relied on to decide cases. "It is unnecessary to add more cases. The only reason which I have heard suggested for holding the decree not binding as to the fact that he was deserted." But no one asks anymore that "the domicile of the wife accompanies him wherever he goes. . . . Of course this is a pure fiction, and fiction always is a poor ground for changing substantial rights." The reality was that women fled across state lines as often as men, and the outcome of the case should protect "the rights of the wife in the matrimonial domicil when the husband deserts."

Holmes the realist then spoke: "There is no question that a husband may establish a new domicil for himself, even if he has deserted his wife. Yet in these days of equality I do not suppose that it would be doubted that the jurisdiction of the court of the matrimonial domicil to grant a divorce for the desertion remained for her, as it would for him in the converse case." Were not cases being decided for the wife in similar situations? That was the brave new world of marriage. The wife was no longer her husband's possession, nor did her rights emanate from him, nor were her rights subordinate to his. "I suppose that the notion that a wife can have a separate domicile from her husband is a modern idea." If the courts established equality of this sort, then a woman's matrimonial status was the same in the state to which she traveled as the state from which she came. Holmes, a realist, had little time for distinctions that did not make a difference. "I have heard it suggested that the difference is one of degree. I am the last man in the world to quarrel with a distinction simply because it is one of degree. Most distinctions, in my opinion, are of that sort, and are none the worse for it."

The issues litigated so thoroughly in *Haddock* were typical of divorce suits. The majority of the Court employed, largely by citing older state precedent, the moral nature of divorce. Holmes and his brethren in dissent cited the newer idea of the equality of the parties in such cases, although one can read a kind of grudging admission of women's equality in the tone of Holmes's dissent. But as divorce was still only a small cloud on the horizon of male supremacy in the law, Holmes was not unduly concerned with the impact of women's equality on the whole of the law, or indeed on society as a whole.

Then something happened. The rate of divorce, for the first time, changed dramatically. Change in divorce rates was not itself unheard of. After the Civil War, divorce rates grew from two per thousand married women in 1870 to five per thousand married women in 1915. From 1916 to 1920, however, that rate leaped to thirteen per thousand married women, an increase of 300 percent. After that, the rate once more leveled off until the World War II era. At work behind the new numbers was a series of shifts in social and cultural attitudes. The new divorces were more often sought by women, were related to middle- and upper-class values, and, more speculatively, were evidence of growing feminism. Women were entering college, joining in political rights movements, and demanding moral reforms like Prohibition. Courts were now faced with a new kind of divorce suit, one rooted not so much in older ideas of moral obligation as in newer ideas of individual empowerment and choice.

New York courts were still more conservative on divorce than the rest of the country, but change was coming. The case that indicated a change in the law was *Hubbard v. Hubbard* (1920), itself coming on the cusp of the phase change in values. The first wave of feminism had reached something of a peak. Women had successfully fought for a federal guarantee on the right to vote. The Nineteenth Amendment to the Constitution, passed by Congress in 1919 and ratified a year later, was only the tip of the iceberg. Women's roles in government on the federal level were still a novelty, but women were taking their place in state and local government, in higher education, and in national commerce. Women athletes were no longer anomalies, and women "flappers" dared to raise the hems of their dresses above the knees. Dating was replacing courtship as the road to marriage. There were still limitations on what women could do in the workplace—glass ceilings that would not be broken until many years later—but it was a beginning of a new era of relative equality.

The question in *Hubbard* was whether the wife's divorce from a previous marriage, a fact he did not know, was grounds for the husband to annul his marriage to her subsequently. The two had been married in North Dakota, the husband not knowing that the wife's former spouse was still alive when they married. Were the former marriage still in effect, the husband was entitled to a decree of annulment. As in *Haddock*, the divorce from her first husband was out of state, and her current husband, in *Hubbard* the plaintiff, argued that the out-of-state divorce was not valid in New York. If it were found invalid, then she could not have married him legally because it would have been bigamous. The supreme court (in New York the intermediate court of appeals) had ruled in favor of the defendant (wife), refusing to accede to the annulment. The husband appealed to the court of appeals, the state's highest tribunal.

Frederick Collin read the opinion of a unanimous court. Collin was a liberal Republican appointed to the court by Governor Charles Evans Hughes and served until the end of 1920, when he returned to his law practice in Elmira, New York. Both sides' counsel, as it happened, cited *Haddock*, but to opposite effect. One should note the mobility of the parties, particularly the wife. The court reported that "the plaintiff, the husband, seeks to annul this marriage upon the ground that the defendant was not then legally and validly divorced from her former husband who was then living." Why?—because by annulling rather than acceding to the divorce, the husband did not have any financial responsibilities. Morality did not matter. Paying support did.

What interests the historian of divorce litigation is the backstory. "Each of the plaintiff and defendant was at the time of the marriage, and for several years last theretofore had been, a resident of and domiciled in the state of Massachusetts." In 1874, however, the future Mrs. Hubbard and John A. Murphy were living in Philadelphia, Pennsylvania, and were married there. Then they separated. She moved to Massachusetts, where she met Mr. Hubbard. Mr. Murphy moved to New York, where he lived until his death in 1912. On August 11, 1892, Mrs. Murphy sought and gained a decree of divorce from Mr. Murphy on the grounds of desertion. Actually, she had departed Philadelphia first, but such separations were a necessity for a fault-based divorce action. Presumably it was consensual, for the time a typical "scripted" fault necessary for a divorce action. "Murphy was not served in that proceeding with any process within the state of Massachusetts, did not appear in the proceeding and made default therein. The court duly ordered, and pursuant there was, constructive service of process upon him. November 4, 1893, the court rendered a decree absolutely divorcing the defendant from John A. Murphy."

End of story, or not? Surely she was then free to marry Mr. Hubbard and become Mrs. Hubbard. "It is this divorce which the plaintiff here alleges was invalid. In 1900 the plaintiff became and in 1902, prior to the commencement of this action, the defendant became, and each since becoming has been, a resident of the state of New York." Now, New York did not have to accept the Massachusetts divorce decree as valid. "While the decree divorcing the defendant from her former husband may adjudge her marital status within the state of Massachusetts as to the husband and the world at large, the courts of the state of New York, untrammeled by the constitutional clause [of full faith and credit], may give it within the confines of their jurisdiction the efficacy and effect they deem rightful and salutary in view of the public policy of the state."

Why not? Was not this a perfect example of the "comity" required by the Full Faith and Credit Clause of the Constitution? New York, unlike its neighboring states, had only one grounds for "absolute" divorce, adultery. The law went back to the early statehood period, in 1787, and was written in the New York state legislature by Alexander Hamilton, a notorious womanizer. It did not apply to Massachusetts, which had modernized its divorce law to some extent. Thus, if the defendant were living in New York, she could not have argued that she had been abandoned and successfully brought the divorce action.

The courts of New York did not view divorce as simply a matter of contract, falling under the Full Faith and Credit Clause. "The policy of this state is not embodied in any legislative enactment or is not a rule of universal law. It exists to promote the permanency of the marriage contracts and the morality of the citizens of the state." Divorce was special, rooted in the morality of a society rather than its legal rules. "Whether or not the operation of a foreign decree [i.e., Massachusetts] of divorce in a given case will contravene the policy or wrong or injure citizens of the state is exclusively for its courts to determine. They are the final judges of the occasions on which the exercise of comity will or will not make for justice or morality."

Hubbard stands as one of the last bastions of the state's guardianship of morality. That morality was no longer rooted in the subordination of the wife to the husband, however, and this is how *Hubbard* represents the phase change. Divorce reflected the morality of the entire community. A state filled with married people was a more moral society than one filled with divorced people. Marriage was a public good as well as a private good, and the state's divorce law was there to protect marriage, not to speed its dissolution, whatever the private problems the couple might have. As a matter of law, New York did not find for the plaintiff, but the court added that "the moral or legal principles adopted by the state will not be weakened or deteriorated by refusal to declare unlawful and void the marriage between the parties. This conclusion makes unnecessary a discussion of the other claims of the plaintiff." The judgment of the trial court was affirmed. The marriage was not annulled and would be ended by a divorce and financial settlement.

Hubbard was, like *Haddock*, a marker in the evolution of divorce law, and with that, a somewhat pale reflection of changing American middle-class attitudes toward domestic relations. If *Hubbard* did not change the impact of contested divorces on American culture, it showed that the changes in marriage from a private good to a public good in the 1920s was not accepted everywhere—at least not in New York's highest court.

Would the public good be promoted by the protection of interracial marriage? Or was it, like adultery, an affront to social harmony? Interracial marriage was not a major subject of divorce law in the 1920s. Many southern states, including every former member of the late Confederacy, specifically outlawed the marriage of men and women of different racial identities, although often enough the state could not determine the racial composition of either party. Nevertheless, for these sixteen states, the ruling case was *Pace v. Alabama* (1883), in which the U.S. Supreme Court, in a decision by Justice Stephen J. Field, found that Alabama's law criminalizing interracial marriage did not violate the Equal Protection Clause of the Fourteenth Amendment. Field wrote, "Indeed, the offense against which this latter section is aimed cannot be committed without involving the persons of both races in the same punishment. Whatever discrimination is made in the punishment prescribed in the two sections is directed against the offense designated and not against the person of any particular color or race. The punishment of each offending person, whether white or black, is the same." Field's devious defense of racialist marriage law (he was himself an adulterer) held sway until *Loving v. Virginia* (1967) ended the regime of state-imposed racial purity in marriage. New York never had a law barring interracial marriage, but the Kip Rhinelander–Alice Jones divorce trial, involving class, gender, and race, tested whether there was a way for some married partners and their lawyers to employ domestic law to do what the state refused to do.

A marriage based on trickery or misrepresentation, like a contract based on similar devices, could be challenged in New York courts. In *Rhinelander v. Rhinelander*, the family of the husband argued that the marriage was based on a racial lie and so should be annulled. Leonard "Kip" Rhinelander was the scion of a rich but unlucky New York family, losing his mother and two of his siblings before he reached adulthood. In 1924, he married the family's domestic, Alice Jones, a mixed-race immigrant from England. A socially awkward young man, Kip nevertheless pursued the attachment avidly, despite opposition from his family and Alice Jones's father. The marriage, kept secret for a time, soon became fodder for the national tabloids. Kip was reluctantly convinced to sign an annulment, but Alice refused to assent. The basis of the annulment was that Kip supposedly did not realize that Alice was part West Indian and that she had concealed the fact from him.

In her defense at trial, Alice's counsel offered evidence of premarital sex in which it would have been impossible for Kip to have missed her mixed-race ancestry. An all-white, all-male jury found for Alice. Counsel for the Rhinelander family appealed, citing as error the trial court judge's instructions to the jury regarding Alice's failure to testify. The supreme court, the first layer of appeals, found no ground to overturn the jury verdict. The court of appeals agreed. Rhinelander left New York for Nevada, where he obtained a divorce, but New York did not regard that divorce as binding on Alice, who remained in Westchester. After years of negotiation resulting in a yearly annuity and a lump-sum payment, she agreed to a formal settlement and renunciation of the marriage.

At trial, all but one of the judges of the supreme court reasoned, "In affirming the judgment in this case, we think our views should be stated with reference to the alleged error in the charge of the trial court concerning the failure of the defendant to take the stand and deny certain statements which plaintiff testified the defendant had made to him to the effect that she was not of colored blood." In other words, plaintiff now swore that Alice told him that she was not of mixed parentage. Alice did not take the stand to confute those statements. "Appellant's [Kip's] contention upon this point is that, as the defendant was in court throughout the trial, and capable of testifying and did not testify, the evidence of the plaintiff as to personal transactions with her and statements made by her should have been taken by the jury most strongly against her and accepted by them as true." Again, in other words, her silence should have been read as proof that she had hidden her racial identity from him. If she had testified under oath to an untruth, she would have perjured herself. In effect, this was the very old and much hated "ex officio" argument. If you stay silent, you admit what the other party has alleged. If you testify, you risk a charge of perjury.

In earlier cases, the precedent had been that failure to testify could be mentioned in a judge's instructions to the jury. Judges had told juries that they could weigh failure to testify as shedding light on the facts, although no hard-and-fast rule applied. Counsel in a civil case was not obliged to put their client on the stand, but a jury could, within the bounds of its duty to weigh the evidence, include in this calculation the absence of testimony. The court of appeals in *Rhinelander* dodged the issue.

> An examination of the portion of the [judge's] charge [to the jury in *Rhinelander*] referred to shows that it was not definite or specific. No reference was made by the court to the particular statements which plaintiff had testified the defendant had made to him which she might have denied if untrue. . . . Appellant's counsel, however, made no request of the court to charge upon the subject, but merely excepted to the charge of the court that no presumption arose against the defendant from her failure to testify in her own behalf or to call her father. In our opinion, this exception was insufficient to raise the point of error now presented by the appellant. We think, under the circumstances, that, if the appellant desired a charge of the court upon the subject as now contended for, it was the duty of counsel to point out the alleged error and request a charge as desired.

In any case, there was no proof that Alice had said she was white. "There was no conclusive presumption that these statements had been in fact made by the defendant to the plaintiff, because the defendant did not deny that she made such statements."

Judge Edward Lazansky dissented. He wanted "to grant a new trial upon the ground that it was error for the court to charge the jury, in effect, that no presumption grew out of the failure of defendant to testify. . . . This error became really serious in light of the statement in the summation of defendant's counsel—improper and prejudicial to the plaintiff—that he assumed the responsibility for defendant's absence from the witness stand." For Lazansky, the real issue of the case was the interracial marriage. By not allowing Alice to testify, her counsel did not allow the jury (recall—all white, all male) to weigh the credibility of her testimony. Race mattered. If she were a fortune hunter, having her testify, and face cross-examination, would have exposed her. Even if she and her counsel were perfectly within her rights not to have her take the stand, the judge's instruction to the jury that they were not to weigh that decision seemed to Lazansky to deny the jury the chance to see her as a predator. In effect, he wanted to bring fault back into the jury's mind and the trial.

Why did he dissent? The court of appeals unanimously affirmed the Lazansky court's opinion. Of both benches, he alone thought that there was more here than a mere technical point. One can only speculate. His parents were immigrants who arrived in New York City, the great gateway to the brave new world, four years before he was born. His father was an artisan and was disappointed that Edward decided on a career in law rather than the family business. Lazansky attended Columbia College and then Columbia Law School, something of a unique achievement at a time when Jewish admission to colleges were either limited by quotas or barred by prejudice. The route to success in law lay in politics, and Lazansky was soon a recognizable figure in Brooklyn Democratic circles. Elected to the supreme court and later appointed by Governor Al Smith to the court of appeals, Lazansky was one of the first Jewish judges on the high bench in the state, along with such notables as future Supreme Court Benjamin Cardozo (also a Columbia College and Columbia Law School grad). Lazansky retired in 1942 and returned to private practice and charitable works. He died in 1955.

So what did he see that his brethren did not? Did race matter to a member of what was classed as a racial minority at that time? Was he wont to look behind formalities of pleadings to seek the morality of the actors? Did he retain an Old World view of marriage—odd when Jewish marriage was a contract rather than a sacrament.

There was only one other Lazansky opinion in an annulment suit, *Applegate v. Applegate*, in the supreme court term of 1922. The husband asked from the court an annulment because his wife's first marriage had not been legally ended. But the couple believed that they were free to marry when they entered into matrimony, and they continued to act as husband and wife after Mrs. Applegate's first husband died. Lazansky wrote, "I would have no difficulty whatsoever in following [a precedent for common-law marriage] and hold that from January 1, 1908, this plaintiff and defendant were husband and wife by reason of a common-law marriage. Surely if out of certain facts where there is no express promise or other words of agreement an ordinary contract may be implied in fact, surely where parties have recognized each other in such a holy relationship the law should not be timid in holding that a contract of marriage was implied."

After an exhaustive review of precedents, Lazansky concluded, "Although it appears that these parties lived together after the removal of the disabilities as husband and wife, upon the basis of their original ceremonial marriage, it seems to be that there can be no valid objection in holding that since they intended to be husband and wife after the removal of the disability they were such. If the marriage cannot be implied out of the facts, then it may be implied in law. I, therefore, direct judgment for the defendant dismissing the complaint, with costs." Marriage must be based on the consent of both parties to live as husband and wife. By 1926, when *Rhinelander* arrived at the New York courts, that consent no longer existed, if it had ever truly existed. Whether love and obedience, much less submission was required, certainly consent was essential, so Lazansky reasoned.

—⁂—

For Lazansky, *Rhinelander* should have turned on the fraud at the heart of a predatory seduction that undermined genuine consent from the outset, but the law in the state was moving beyond the old rules for weighing the legitimacy of marriage on private moral grounds. Still, the only grounds in New York when both parties were domiciled in the state remained adultery. Then, in the 1960s, something new and, well, maybe not so wonderful happened to divorce law: no-fault divorces. It was an age of not quite free love, but one in which men and women were reexamining the basis of cohabitation.

In 1963, with divorce rates rising after a period of relative stability (the baby boomers), California legislators held hearings, and then Governor Edmund G. Brown Jr. formed a commission to revise domestic law. Law professor Herma Kay Hill drafted its report calling for no-fault divorce: neither party would have to allege wrongdoing on the other party's part. The resulting 1969 act was meant to replace the old law with an action for "dissolution of marriage." If the marriage had already fallen apart and was clearly at an end, why add insult to injury? The proceeding would be faster, cheaper, and would not require the parties to do more than separate themselves, already a part of most divorces. In 1970, New York followed suit. An earlier reform, in 1965, had added mental or physical cruelty as grounds for divorce, but by 1970 the law included "living apart" for a period of time, in effect no-fault. That is, neither party had to assert or prove fault in the other party's actions to trigger the divorce. Simple failure of the marriage was sufficient. Soon the idea spread through other states, with support from national commissions, and by

1989, all but Arkansas had adopted one or another version of no-fault. The essence was irreconcilable differences, in itself a slippery idea, but in fact something that both parties could simply assert in court. New York finally capitulated in 2010 and adopted no-fault (irretrievable breakdown of the marriage for at least six months) divorce along with categories of domestic abuse, adultery, abandonment, and imprisonment of one of the parties. The party filing for divorce had to be a resident of the state. The other party could have departed the state.

The idea of fault had not disappeared, of course, especially in New York, because in most divorce cases one party thought the other had failed in its duties. This was an example of the old phase change phenomenon. One party expected a traditional marriage, with the husband providing and the wife as the inferior partner, where the other party wanted equality or interchangeability of duties and rewards. The contest played out in disputes over the distribution of couples' assets, the custody of children, child support, alimony, and the responsibility for legal fees. Feminism and traditionalism thus went to war in some divorces, but not all of them, for in many marriages initial expectations simply gave way as the parties grew apart in interests. The rise of the two–professional career family (the two-worker family was as old as marriage itself) put new stresses on marital life, including jobs in different places. Child-rearing practices had changed as well, as families moved away from multigenerational caregivers and substituted institutional child care.

There is no reason that no-fault options should have led to fewer divorces, although some advocates of marriage have accused it of fostering a culture of divorce. In fact the surge in divorce rates in the 1960s began before the introduction of no-fault. But raw numbers seem to indicate that the divorce rate per one thousand married women increased from 9.2 in 1960 to 21.7 in 1985. However, this rate declined to 17 percent in 2016, and the trend is down. This did not affect the percentage of the population that was married (in 1960 about 68 percent and in 1987 about 63 percent) but suggested that many were in second or third marriages (a pretty steady rate of 24 percent of all marriages were second or more).

No-fault simply removed some of the cost of contested divorces, the distress and anger associated with long, drawn out contests of blame throwing, and the undermining of the legal system by collusive submissions of adultery and perjury. If in fact no-fault reflected the same fundamental changes in social values, including nonmarital partnerships, same-sex couplings, and multiple-adult households, rather than being a fomenter or abettor of these new forms of group association, one should expect the number of divorces to rise in no-fault regimes. Like the law of sex itself, society was moving away from the idea that the state could mandate or monitor adult sex. It had happened in barring states from criminalizing birth control, in *Griswold v. Connecticut* (1966) and *Eisenstadt v. Baird* (1972); it had happened in same-sex intercourse in *Lawrence v. Texas* (2003); and it had happened in same-sex marriage in *U.S. v. Windsor* (2013), *Hollingsworth v. Perry* (2013), and *Obergefell v. Hodges* (2015).

The result, however, was somewhat ironic, insofar as custody disputes and bitterness did not evaporate. Dispute over property held in joint increased. Some scholars have suggested that the animosity that led to the divorce simply shifted to a later period in the process, that is, from bringing the suit to settling it. Instead of blaming the other party as a reason for ending the marriage, blaming the other party became grounds for efforts to gain custodial care of the children or a favorable division of the marital property. According to surveys of divorce lawyers, there is just as much bitterness in the later stages of the divorce as there ever had been. False allegations of mistreatment of children or misappropriation of property (or at least contested evidence on these matters) remains a feature of many no-fault divorces.

A final charge against the no-fault divorce paradigm is that it has left mothers who gained custody with a kind of impoverishment, losing a portion of the post-marital income because the grounds for alimony (abuse, adultery, etc.) had vanished. Even those men who fully complied with court-ordered alimony and child support retained a substantial portion of their pre-divorce income, while former wives, particularly those who had been married for more than ten years and had given up careers to rear children and manage households, suffered a precipitous decline in both income and standard of living. Of course, one could argue that such statistics should not have been based on what the couple earned, which in effect added individual earnings twice (once to each partner), but on what each partner would have been earning had there never been a marriage. Still, in practical terms it meant that the custodial parent suffered a disproportionate loss of income. Insofar as a breakup begins in dishonor—abandonment, adultery, or verbal, psychological, or physical abuse—it ends in financial indignity.

Consider then when a same-sex marriage ends in divorce. The same rules apply: lawyers represent one side or the other of the couple, and as long as the couple were married in New York and remain in the state, divorce begins and ends in the same fashion. The great phase change ushering in same-sex marriage simply overlapped older phase changes in the roles of men and women in domesticity and the workplace.

The no-fault revolution had reset the terms of the relationship. Traditional family values still mattered, but in a world in which same-sex marriage had become legal, and the numbers of married couples were declining, a new phase change had appeared. No-fault divorce embodied that shift. Marriage was no longer the norm; the norm was coupling. When that failed, the parties severed the domestic tie with far greater facility than formal divorce. A brave new world of sex without obligation was emerging. Its consequences have yet to make themselves fully apparent.

Perhaps the cutting edge of that uncertainty is same-sex marriage divorce. When custody of children is the issue, nothing was certain. The same federalism that had made divorce itself a mélange of varying state laws applied to custody of children either adopted in the course of a same-sex marriage, the result of a full-term pregnancy of one of the female members of a same-sex marriage, or a child brought into a same-sex marriage by one of the partners, either from a previous marriage or from an unwed pregnancy. Where the state of residence of the couple allowed, both were the legal parents of the child or children and had parents' rights under the law. Where both parents legally adopted the child or children, or the nonbiological parent obtained adoptive rights, the child or children legally belonged to both parents. Where the nonbiological mother had none of these protections of her rights to the child, evidence that she was the custodial parent, had paid substantial or even entire costs of the upbringing of the child, or had an established emotional relationship with the child did not confer legal rights to parenthood. In states where no second parent gains these rights, there can be no claim to shared custody, visitation, or other contact. In states where case law or statute confers some portion of these rights, both parties may have to assert their case in court. A nightmare awaits in some of these cases, as contested custody in same-sex marriages is no less fraught than in heterosexual unions. The more things change, the more they are the same.

7

Civil Rights and Wrongs

JIM CROW WORE MANY FACES, none of them attractive. Before the Civil War, he was a white man in a minstrel show who bootblacked his face so he could sing dirty songs and tell lewd jokes. After the war, he was the symbol of race hate that allowed whites to denigrate blacks. But above all, Jim Crow connoted a legal regime that demoted people of color to second-class citizenship—the back of the bus, the substandard schoolhouse, and the "colored" part of town with unpaved streets and no running water. Under Jim Crow laws, people of color could not be seated in segregated restaurants, spend the night in hotels on main streets, or go to "white" hospitals.

Efforts by alliances of white reformers and black activists like the National Association for the Advancement of Colored People (NAACP) in the first years of the twentieth century to convince Congress to pass laws against lynching and to ensure equal treatment in employment regularly failed. Presidents Franklin Delano Roosevelt and, even more, Harry S. Truman took steps to desegregate federal facilities, but these reforms were strongly resisted by members of their own Democratic Party and did not go beyond the federal shipyard and military base gates.

There was one place of redress left—the courts. It would not be easy to overthrow so deeply entrenched and so strongly defended a regime, however. Few black people in the South could afford lawyers; white jurors were unlikely to find favorable verdicts in cases that directly challenged Jim Crow; the threat of violence always hung over the heads of anti-discrimination plaintiffs; and allies in the southern bar were hard to find. Little points of light glowed in the darkness—a handful of remarkable lawyers who took on the state legal establishments and decisions by the federal courts that ended the all-white primary, the grandfather clauses for voting, the restrictive housing covenant, and the peonage that Alabama imposed on its poorest black farmworkers.

From New York City and Washington, DC, the lawyers of the Legal Defense Fund (LDF) of the NAACP and the students and faculty of Howard University's law school joined with local NAACP lawyers to manage civil rights suits. During Reconstruction, universal manumission of slaves by the Thirteenth Amendment and congressional legislation on behalf of the newly freed men and women opened the door to civil rights suits. Civil rights acts in the 1950s and 1960s enabled further litigation. For much of the first half of the twentieth century, however, civil rights suits were limited in their impact. Brave plaintiffs, often facing local white violence, chipped away at the wall of separation. Local NAACP chapters, aided by the LDF in New York City and Washington, DC, worked within the confines of the "separate but equal" formula of *Plessy v. Ferguson* (1896) and its progeny. Progress, if one can call it that, was slow, and hope, never failing, was still unfulfilled.

Honor takes many forms, and the plaintiffs' willingness to offend powerful local employers and authorities by challenging Jim Crow was surely as much about black honor in the twentieth century as one southern gentleman challenging another to a duel in the antebellum South. The stories of those plaintiffs' struggle against Jim Crow are heartening and heartbreaking, in the course of which the rise of civil rights litigation became the face of the litigation nation.

—⁂—

After World War II, a war fought in part for civil rights around the world, begetting a United Nations Charter that decried racism, a change in cultural values swept over much of the country. In the majority of the nation, it was no longer acceptable to claim that racial separation was good for both races. But in the Deep South, white racial prejudice and Jim Crow laws went hand in hand. The confrontation between the postwar liberality of the North and the mentality of the Lost Cause in the South resulted in a surge of litigation. These civil rights cases are among the best known and, for most Americans, the most honorable in all of litigation history. Because an intransigent white southern resistance often led appellants and appellees to the steps of the U.S. Supreme Court, historians know more about the parties, counsel, and bench in these cases than in any other of the topics we have covered in this book.

—⚏—

In 1946, Heman Sweatt, a thirty-eight-year-old postman in Houston, Texas, decided that he wanted to become a lawyer. He held a BA from Wiley College, a blacks-only school in his home state, but had been admitted and finished the first year of medical school at the University of Michigan in Ann Arbor. He returned to Texas to marry, teach school, and dare to challenge racial segregation in the University of Texas Law School in Austin, the state capital.

Historian Gary Lavergne recounted what happened next. The law school admitted all applicants, regardless of preparation, but state law and the state's constitution forbade any of its educational institutions from integrating. The state made a beginning in complying with the *Plessy v. Ferguson* mandate for equal facilities, but little had come of the effort when Sweatt sought entrance to the school in Austin. The local NAACP chapter came to Sweatt's aid, and local attorney W. J. Durham filed suit in the Texas circuit court for Travis County seeking an injunction to compel the law school to admit Sweatt. Students at the university and in the law school urged admission as well. The LDF in the form of Thurgood Marshall and his associates joined Durham to make Sweatt's case.

Thurgood Marshall grew up in Jim Crow Baltimore, his father a railroad dining car waiter and his mother a teacher in a segregated elementary school. Marshall worked as a bellhop to put himself through college at Lincoln University in Pennsylvania and Howard University Law School, both black schools, because Maryland denied blacks admission to its premier undergraduate and graduate institutions. He had won a number of equalization cases implicitly accepting the "separate but equal" rule but had not yet launched a frontal attack on *Plessy*.

Sweatt lost at a May 16, 1946, hearing in the circuit court for Travis County, counsel for the university simply citing Texas law. Sweatt had gone out of state for medical school; he could go out of state to gain a legal education. Judge Roy C. Archer agreed that the rejection of Sweatt was simply a matter of Texas law. He gave the state six months to provide for a segregated alternative law school.

In the fall of 1946, with Marshall orchestrating publicity, the case was already a cause célèbre in the state. Despite a plea by the dean of the law school, Charles McCormick, that the state change its mind and admit Sweatt, the color line held. What was more, little progress was made on Judge Archer's ruling. Attorney General Grover Sellers, counsel for the state, told the county court that everyone had to obey Texas law. The fault lay in the black colleges for not providing a law school for their students. Sellers had made up his mind about the case even before it was filed. A one-term attorney general, he would run for governor in 1946, lose, accept a post on the state bench, and return between sessions to his cattle ranch. He thought separation of the races was a "wise" policy. In short, the trial court once again wholly and without qualification adopted the position of the defendants.

Sweatt appealed to a higher Texas court of appeals but could not have hoped for victory. Southern state institutions of higher learning and professional training were not overawed by the LDF blitz. Instead, they marshaled their own battalion of lawyers. These included the states' attorneys general and their assistants, some specially hired, like Jack Greenberg was for the LDF, to battle in segregation cases. Although Texas attorney general Price Daniel signed the brief for the state in the state court of appeals, it was assistant attorney general Joseph Greenhill whom Daniel hired and assigned the drudge work of research and writing. A 1939 graduate of the University of Texas Law School, Greenhill had been working as a brief researcher for the state supreme court when the post came along. It paid more and he was comfortable working with Daniel. Greenhill would later go on to a distinguished career on the state supreme court, an elective post. The two men were thus what one could, in justice, regard as the best products of Texas legal training and political reputation.

Greenhill recalled, "There was not any preconceived racism on my part. I had a job and I could do it or I could quit. My job was to represent the University of Texas, A & M [the other state university system] and school districts. At that time the Constitution of Texas required separation of the races and supposedly equal facilities." Greenhill had already met Marshall in court, and bested him in "several cases," as he recalled, but the law school case was the only one that Marshall and his team appealed. Greenhill knew that there was no separate law school, much less an equal one. The legislature responded to the lawsuit; they wanted "an instant equal separate school." Following the instructions of the legislature to create a law school for blacks in Austin, "we bought up all the law books you could buy . . . we bought all we could" and put them in a "three story building across the alley from the state capitol," Greenhill recalled, but it did not matter. "There wasn't any way we could lose that case in Austin."

The decision of the Civil Division Court of Appeals showed that Greenhill's work was persuasive. Delivering the opinion for a unanimous court was Chief Justice James Wooten McClendon. The chief justice was born in Georgia in 1873, on the eve of the "redemption" of the state by Democrats opposed to Reconstruction. He moved to Texas a young man and earned his law degree at the then still new law school in Austin. After practicing law, he was named to the court in 1923, three years later moving his wife into a French medieval-style mansion in Austin and serving as the court's chief justice at the time of his retirement in 1949. McClendon was a distinguished jurist, named to the American Law Institute and the National Conference of Judicial Councils among other prestigious offices. *Sweatt* was his last great case. He died in 1972.

McClendon made clear from the outset that the crucial question of fact was stipulated by both sides—Sweatt was black. There was no question of him passing for white, like Homer Plessy. "Admittedly, he possessed every essential qualification for admission, except that of race, upon which ground alone his application was denied, under Sec. 7 of art. 7 of the Texas Constitution . . . which reads: 'Separate schools shall be provided for the white and colored children, and impartial provision shall be made for both.'" Did this violate the Equal Protection Clause of the federal Constitution? No—not according to *Plessy*. "The gist of these decisions is embodied in . . . *Plessy v. Ferguson*," from which McClendon quoted at length. Marshall argued, in vain, that "it is impossible to have the equality required by the Fourteenth Amendment in a public school system which relegates citizens of a disadvantaged racial minority group to separate schools." McClendon realized the full implications of Marshall's plea: "Implicit in these quotations is the assertion that race segregation in public schools, at least in the higher and professional fields, inherently is discriminatory within the meaning of the Fourteenth Amendment, and cannot be made otherwise." But he denied Sweatt the remedy he wanted and substituted the hope that Texas would soon have a separate but equal law school for blacks—soon. The ruling of the trial court was affirmed.

Durham was the local attorney who had served in the trenches, defending people of color in all manner of causes. Like so many of the local black attorneys, he was a bulwark of the NAACP. To him, Sweatt had turned. He had presented the case to the local court, but as the stakes mounted and the LDF turned to the Supreme Court, Durham stepped aside for the national office men. They were not from Texas. But they had paid their dues in the civil rights cause. If there was glory in the eventual victory, history will have to ensure that William Durham gets his share.

Both sides presented their case in oral argument before the U.S. Supreme Court on April 3, 1950, Greenhill at the appellee's table with Price Daniel, Marshall across the aisle with Robert L. Carter, the cream of the LDF team. Durham did not participate in the oral argument. Oral argument followed the lines of the state case, with the clear exception that Marshall had now won the battle within the LDF and the NAACP to attack segregation directly. The absence of equality in the black and white schools was no longer the question. There could be no equality in segregation, hence equal protection of the law could never be satisfied, so long as a state mandated separate schools. Separate but equal was impossible, and that was that. The Supreme Court ordered Texas to admit Sweatt to its law school.

—⁂—

In the same year, 1950, as Sweatt won his case, black parents in Clarendon County, South Carolina, brought their case against Jim Crow to the courts. Journalist Richard Kluger told their story. Clarendon County was poor, and in it, poor blacks had far worse public school accommodations than their poor white neighbors. Joseph Albert DeLaine was one of these black parents, and his child had to attend what looked like a schoolhouse from the nineteenth century. There were buses for the white children— thirty of them—but none for the black children. Could they not be bused to the far better white school, he complained to the head of the school board, R. W. Elliott, whose sawmill was one of the few commercial establishments in the county. DeLaine was mixed race, and Elliott was white. Elliott reportedly replied that there was no money for black children.

Before the case was done, DeLaine and his family were fired from their jobs, their house was burned down, and they were threatened with death. Such was the climate in the Jim Crow South. For Jim Crow not only dictated a regime of state-mandated separation of the races; it enforced that regime with almost casually inflicted violence, the occasional lynching or bombing of black civil rights workers, and an arrogant disdain for public opinion in the rest of the country and the world. Let us handle our local affairs, white supremacist leaders proclaimed, running for office by competing with one another in their outspoken racism.

But plaintiffs like DeLaine and his neighbor Harry Briggs persisted. They found support in the NAACP and the LDF. In what came to be called "the school cases," local NAACP counsel and the LDF openly challenged the rule in *Plessy* that the Fourteenth Amendment was satisfied by states' "separate but equal" public facilities. Everyone knew that the rule was a myth, for rarely were the facilities provided for black people even close to equal to those provided for white people. Whether water fountains in train stations or books in public schools, the difference was obvious. It was the result of an intention to demean as well as inattention to decency.

Still, there were obstacles to litigating against the "separate but equal" formula in the public elementary schools. It had been in place for over half a century. State courts were very unlikely to overturn state constitutions or state statutes that codified segregation. States' rights ideology was alive and well in these state courts. Federal courts were only slightly more amenable to voiding state law on federal grounds. When the LDF sought federal court injunctive relief against the state of South Carolina's mandated separation of the races, federal civil procedure required the impaneling of a three-judge court. One or more of those judges might be willing to rule in favor of the plaintiffs. Even if the panel upheld the state law, appeal from the three-judge panel went directly to the U.S. Supreme Court, and that is exactly where the LDF, led by Thurgood Marshall, wanted to go.

The three-judge district court that heard and decided *Briggs v. Elliott* (1951), with an opinion by circuit judge John Parker, found that the facilities for black students in South Carolina's rural Clarendon County schools were not equal, but the reason was not discrimination so much as the economic deficiencies of the Clarendon County region. The LDF's

Marshall, along with Robert Carter, Spottiswood Robinson, and local attorney Harold R. Boulware of Columbia, South Carolina, led the plaintiff's case, relying on the expert witness testimony that Marshall had helped pioneer in the graduate school cases. Professor Kenneth Clark, for example, repeated his black dolls/white dolls test with children from the Clarendon district and found that the black children once again thought the white dolls were good and the black dolls were bad.

On the other side of the aisle, Robert McCormick Figg, a longtime Charleston, South Carolina, politician, representing the state alongside its attorney general, T. C. Callison, insisted that the outside academic experts were not qualified to speak to the conditions or the attitudes of a rural South Carolina county. Instead, the court should listen to the county's former school superintendent, E. R. Crow, currently the director of the South Carolina Educational Finance Commission. Marshall cross-examined, seeking to know whether the state would actually close its public schools rather than desegregate them. Would the government refuse to obey an order to desegregate if such were issued? No answer. Marshall won the day, but not the case.

Judge Parker, joined by district judge George Bell Timmerman, did not order desegregation. Parker was a distinguished jurist, having served on the Fourth Circuit Court of Appeals from 1925 to 1958, the last ten years of which he was its chief judge, and been nominated for a seat on the Supreme Court in 1930. There is some evidence that President Eisenhower had considered Parker for the center seat of the high court when Chief Justice Vinson died. A born and bred North Carolinian, he did not hide his sympathy for the defeated South in the Civil War. Parker had also given a speech in which he defended the "grandfather clauses" exemptions from literacy tests for voting if an individual's ancestor had voted, effectually subjecting would-be black voters (whose ancestors were slaves) to franchise restrictions white voters did not face. He added that he thought it unlikely that the mass of African American voters could ever fulfill the obligations of republican citizenship.

Parker's opinion rested upon local knowledge, a set of supposed facts that he shared with men like Elliott. "The defendants contend, however, that the district is one of the rural school districts which has not kept pace with urban districts in providing educational facilities for the children of either race, and that the inequalities have resulted from limited resources." Governor James F. Byrnes and the state legislature had promised in future to make up the difference, although no positive steps had been taken. Nevertheless, as equity presumed good faith on the part of the defendant state (petitioners sought injunctive relief), Parker continued, "how this shall be done is a matter for the school authorities and not for the court, so long as it is done in good faith and equality of facilities is afforded."

Harry Briggs had asked the federal courts to provide appropriate injunctive relief. Parker replied that "one of the great virtues of our constitutional system is that, while the federal government protects the fundamental rights of the individual, it leaves to the several states the solution of local problems. . . . Local self government in local matters is essential to the peace and happiness of the people in the several communities." He did, however, order the state to equalize facilities in Clarendon County. A few years earlier, the LDF might have counted this as a victory. When, six months later, the state reported tentative financial steps toward compliance, Judge Parker was content that the state had fulfilled its constitutional obligations: "There can be no doubt that as a result of the program in which defendants are engaged the educational facilities and opportunities afforded Negroes within the district will, by the beginning of the next school year in September 1952, be made equal to those afforded white persons."

None of this persuaded the dissenter on the panel, district judge J. Waties Waring. He was educated in Charleston, the descendant of Confederate leaders, a son of the South deeply wedded to its traditions. He practiced law in Charleston for nearly forty years before Franklin D. Roosevelt named him to the Eastern District court in 1942. By the time the case came to the district court, he had become frustrated by the injustice of separate and invariably unequal laws. After listening to Thurgood Marshall argue the case for the petitioners, Waring grew impatient with Judge Parker's temporizing, and his dissent hinted what everyone in the courtroom and on the bench knew or should have known: South Carolina had no more intention of equalizing its educational facilities for the two races than it did of abolishing segregation itself. "If this method of judicial evasion be adopted, these very infant plaintiffs now pupils in Clarendon County will probably be bringing lawsuits for their children and grandchildren decades or rather generations hence in an effort to get for their descendants what are today denied to them." In effect, he was accusing his brethren of conspiring with the state government to deny the petitioners their long-overdue rights. Waring did not agree with Parker when the state reported its plan for equalization, writing to Parker that he would not sign off on anything short of the end of segregated schools. For his courage, Waring was ostracized by polite society and threatened by racist terrorists, ultimately leaving the court and the city for northern climes.

In the meantime, plaintiffs appealed to the Supreme Court. Although when the Supreme Court rendered its opinion, *Brown v. Board of Education of Topeka, Kansas* was the lead case for the three others coming from South Carolina, Virginia, and Delaware, in many ways *Briggs* was still the most important of the five cases, in part because it was the first of the school cases heard by the Supreme Court, and in part because the state of South Carolina was the most adamant of all the appellees. After two hearings at the high court, petitioners won a unanimous decision: Jim Crow could not haunt the halls of public schools again. But the Court did not give the black families want they wanted—genuine, immediate relief. Instead, the district courts were instructed to work with local school boards with "all deliberate speed," a formula that led to decades of delay.

Marshall's effort was the culmination of the courage of the plaintiffs in Clarendon, the contributions of historians and social scientists on the LDF team, the work of the many lawyers of the LDF, and, finally, Chief Justice Earl Warren's persuasion of all his brethren to join in his historic opinion for the Court in *Brown*. Davis's arguments were unpersuasive. Warren: "We conclude that, in the field of public education, the doctrine of 'separate but equal' has no place. Separate educational facilities are inherently unequal. Therefore, we hold that the plaintiffs and others similarly situated for whom the actions have been brought are, by reason of the segregation complained of, deprived of the equal protection of the laws guaranteed by the Fourteenth Amendment. This disposition makes unnecessary any discussion whether such segregation also violates the Due Process Clause of the Fourteenth Amendment."

—⁂—

Martin Luther King Jr.'s 1963 invocation of a dream in which sons of the former slaves and sons of the former masters would sit down at the same table as equals would have made a fitting conclusion to the struggle for desegregation. But if that table was a lunch counter in southern cities, the sons of the slaves would not have been served. Restaurants, motels, and other public accommodations were not available to persons of color. The product was the right to sit at a luncheon counter and be served. The liability was the denial of accommodation.

The Civil Rights Act of 1875 had anti-discrimination provisions that applied to public accommodations, including amusement parks, theaters, and swimming pools. In the *Civil Rights Cases* (1883), the Supreme Court struck down this part of the act because Congress did not have the authority to bar discrimination in privately owned and operated public accommodations under the Fourteenth Amendment, because it only applied to "state action." Justice John Marshall Harlan dissented, claiming that the Constitution was color-blind, and the authors of the Fourteenth Amendment, on which the Civil Rights Act was based, intended it to end racist discrimination in public spaces. During and after World War II, students in Washington, DC, Chicago, and then in North Carolina and throughout the South began a campaign of "sit-ins" at restaurants. Cases arising from chain restaurant owners' refusal to serve these peaceful patrons led to some of the most important civil rights victories for the students, people of color, the LDF, the NAACP, and the nation.

Bruce Boynton was a student at Howard University Law School when he was denied a seat in the whites-only section of a Richmond, Virginia, bus terminal counter. When he refused to leave, the manager called the police, and Boynton was arrested, fined, and brought suit in federal court. In *Boynton v. Virginia* (1960), a majority of the Supreme Court reversed his conviction. William H. Burton, a black member of the city council of Willington, Delaware, tried to eat at a privately owned restaurant attached to the city parking lot. When he was refused service, he asked the state's courts for relief. The state supreme court refused his appeal. The restaurant was a private enterprise and thus supposedly exempt from Fourteenth Amendment anti-discrimination requirements. He took his case to the Supreme Court. In *Burton v. Wilmington Parking Authority* (1961), the Court's majority reversed the state court's finding.

Christopher Schmidt tells the story of the student sit-ins that changed the face of public accommodations in the South. On February 1, 1960, Ezell Blair Jr., a student at North Carolina A & T State University, a black college, led three of his classmates to the lunch counter at the Greensboro, North Carolina, Woolworth's. Under the Jim Crow regime, blacks could go to the back door of restaurants and order food to go, but they could not sit in the restaurants and expect to be served. The four simply wanted to be served. They were frustrated by the go-slow of the school cases' decrees and had decided on a direct-action approach.

Greensboro became the model for student sit-ins at lunch counters throughout the South. In the North, students picketed Woolworth's and other stores that denied southern black students service. Opponents of this grassroots civil rights movement, including the KKK, tried to intimidate the students, and cities passed ordinances making it a crime to criminally trespass at the lunch counters. In 1963, cases from Greenville, South Carolina; Durham, North Carolina; and Birmingham, Alabama, in which students who had braved bigoted violence and local white intransigence to sit at lunch counters were denied service, came to the U.S. Supreme Court. The LDF brought suit in federal courts against the segregation ordinances under which owners and managers denied the students service. The LDF's Jack Greenberg argued that the students had a constitutional right to eat in public restaurants. The owners claimed that these were private places, and they could turn away whomever they chose and refuse to serve whomever they chose. In a controversial 1963 split decision, *Peterson v. City of Greenville* (1963), the majority of the U.S. Supreme Court ruled that the denial of service was unconstitutional, because owners and managers had relied on ordinances passed by the states and municipalities (agencies of the state).

The sit-ins debate continued in *Bell v. Maryland* (1964), a case coming from a Baltimore sit-in. In this case, the sit-ins were not only refused service; they were arrested for trespassing. At trial they were convicted of misdemeanor trespass. Now there was a "case or controversy," and the U.S. Supreme Court, which heard the matter on appeal, could not dodge the central issue: did the perpetrator of a civil rights violation have to be a state or the agent of a state for the Fourteenth Amendment's Equal Protection Clause to apply? Nothing in the case involved the state of Maryland except the arrest and trial of the sit-ins. There was no law that forbade the restaurant owner to serve them. He simply wanted them to leave, and when they did not, he got a warrant for their arrest.

Justice Hugo Black, an Alabaman who had strongly opposed state segregation, drew the line at federal intervention in a dispute over private citizens' use of private property. For a time he was joined by a majority of his brethren. The arrests and convictions would stand. Chief Justice Earl Warren and Justices William Brennan and William O. Douglas furiously disagreed. The Court, they feared, was taking a backward step from *Brown v. Board of Education*, and they convinced Justices Tom Clark and Potter Stewart that they should not agree with Black. Justice Goldberg was already on Warren's side. In the meantime, the Civil Rights Act of 1964 had passed the House of Representatives and was facing a southern filibuster in the Senate. Its section 2 would have barred discrimination in public accommodations. President Lyndon Johnson was pressing Congress hard to pass the act.

The final decision of the Court in *Bell* came down in June, a victory for the sit-ins, but on the technicality that Maryland had, in the time between the 1960 arrest and the Supreme Court's opinion, passed antidiscrimination laws barring public facilities from refusing to serve people on the basis of race. Nevertheless, civil rights law advanced because twelve sit-ins at the lunch counter demanded to have their rights litigated in courts of law.

In the meantime, the fate of the Civil Rights Act of 1964 public accommodations provision (Title II) itself hung in the balance, as opponents swarmed to file suits against the provision. The Atlanta business community seemed poised to accept the act's provisions and move on, but two business owners had other plans. The first was Lester Maddox's Pickrick chicken restaurant. Maddox would carry his often obstreperous opposition to integration into election to the governor's office. The second was Moreton Rolleston Jr.'s client, the Heart of Atlanta Motel. His argument was that the law improperly applied to the motel, a wholly local business with no interstate connections. He went further in his filing, alleging that the law effectually enslaved the owners of the motel, forcing them, in violation of the Thirteenth Amendment, to serve Negro patrons. The suit seeking an injunction against the federal law went to a three-judge federal panel in the old Court of Appeals for the Fifth Circuit, where chief circuit judge Elbert Tuttle, a longtime friend of desegregation, was joined by district judge Frank Hooper, whose view of race relations was far more cautious than Tuttle's, and newly appointed district judge Lewis R. Morgan. Tuttle was an Eisenhower appointee whose Republican Party affiliation was largely derived from his opposition to the southern Democrats' segregationist policies. Hooper was an Atlanta-born-and-bred Democrat who had already ordered the integration of the city's schools. Morgan was a small-town politician who grew into his judicial role under Presidents Kennedy and Johnson and eventually replaced Tuttle on the court of appeals.

The Pickrick case was heard alongside the Heart of Atlanta suit on different grounds, a criminal charge against Maddox in his own person (i.e., not against the restaurant) for violently refusing access to black would-be patrons. (He was passing out axe handles to whites to use to enforce his edict.) In what may have been one of the most expeditious hearings of so contentious cases, the panel unanimously dismissed the *Heart of Atlanta* suit and instead enjoined the motel from refusing service to blacks, and it upheld the federal case against Maddox.

The U.S. Supreme Court expedited the appeal of *Heart of Atlanta* shortly before the end of the year. The decision was unanimous, with two concurrences. It gave the Court an opportunity to review civil rights jurisprudence. Archibald Cox, solicitor general of the United States, and Burke Marshall, deputy attorney general, both of whom had played major roles in formulating federal policy on civil rights, argued for the United States. Note that the LDF did not play a role in pleading the case. This was thus a major shift from grassroots-driven cases like the desegregation of the schools and the sit-ins to a top-down civil rights initiative. Advocacy of civil rights had, in this case, passed from the hands of the aggrieved to the hands of those in power.

The owner of the motel appealed from the three-judge panel's dismissal of his claim. Rolleston, for the owner, argued that "the prohibition of racial discrimination in places of public accommodation affecting commerce exceeded Congress's powers under the *Commerce Clause* and violated other parts of the Constitution." He was not alone. James W. Kynes, attorney general of Florida, and Fred M. Burns and Joseph C. Jacobs, assistant attorneys general, for the State of Florida, and Robert Y. Button, attorney general of Virginia, and Frederick T. Gray, special assistant attorney general, for the Commonwealth of Virginia, filed friends of the court briefs urging it to reverse the ruling of the three-judge panel. The sectional nature of the case was even more apparent when the attorneys general of California, Massachusetts, and New York filed briefs urging the Court to affirm the decision of the lower court.

Justice Tom Clark wrote for his brethren. Clark was something of a convert to civil rights advocacy. Initially hesitant to tell local school boards how to run their schools, he became one of Chief Justice Warren's most trusted allies in later years. Here he answered Rolleston's argument that the motel was not involved in interstate commerce. "The motel is located on Courtland Street, two blocks from downtown Peachtree Street. It is readily accessible to interstate highways 75 and 85 and state highways 23 and 41. [The motel ownership] solicits patronage from outside the State of Georgia through various national advertising media, including magazines of national circulation; it maintains over 50 billboards and highway signs within the State, soliciting patronage for the motel; it accepts convention trade from outside Georgia and approximately 75% of its registered guests are from out of State." That settled the interstate commerce question.

The discrimination question was similarly easy to describe. "Prior to passage of the Act the motel had followed a practice of refusing to rent rooms to Negroes, and it alleged that it intended to continue to do so. In an effort to perpetuate that policy this suit was filed." In other words, Heart of Atlanta wanted no part of the civil rights public accommodations provision and had no intention of obeying the law unless forced to do so. It contended, nonetheless, that as a private operation it should have the right to choose whom it would serve. This was the same argument that defendants made in the sit-in cases. Rolleston must have realized that it was a losing argument by this time, but he and his clients wanted to state, through the litigation, their commitment to a segregated society and white southerners' right to discriminate against their black neighbors.

The arguments defendants made adopted those in the sit-in cases. Congress was imposing a kind of servitude on the motel when it required that they rent rooms to all who could pay, a "taking" of their property and their liberty. The reliance on the Thirteenth Amendment in defendants' response was a cruel inversion of the historical purpose and the plain meaning of the text, and surely a legal version of passive-aggressiveness. For Rolleston and his clients, the Civil War had not ended, and they regarded Title II of the act as an example of continuing northern aggression against the white South. The inclusion of the amendment in the Rolleston's pleading suggests that the appeal was more than a chance to undo the legislation. It was an opportunity to restate the honor of the white South. The world had changed, but Rolleston's client, like Lester Maddox and those who voted for him, had not. Litigation was a way to restate those older traditions of forced separation and denigration of one race by another.

Clark, whose Texas boyhood surely included personal acquaintance with Jim Crow, regarded the Thirteenth Amendment argument in particular with scorn, "because it is entirely frivolous to say that an amendment directed to the abolition of human bondage and the removal of widespread disabilities associated with slavery places discrimination in public accommodations beyond the reach of both federal and state law." He realized as well that Rolleston and his client must have intended the appeal to be a symbolic gesture of defiance, for they had offered no evidence in support of their claims.

Justice Clark supplied that want with a thorough review of the history leading up to the 1964 act. At the conclusion of his summary, he reminded the packed courtroom that the act was a bipartisan one, with support from Democrats and Republicans. It had been on the administration's agenda when President John F. Kennedy was assassinated, and President Lyndon Johnson had pressed Congress to expedite it. There were extended hearings, and in the Senate the vote was further extended by a southern filibuster. Title II as passed required that "all persons shall be entitled to the full and equal enjoyment of the goods, services, facilities, privileges, advantages, and accommodations of any place of public accommodation, as defined in this section, without discrimination or segregation on the ground of race, color, religion, or national origin." Hotels, motels, and other establishments that served the public were specifically mentioned in the act. Private clubs were excepted under certain conditions.

Clark knew that in the *Civil Rights Cases* (1883) the Supreme Court had struck down similar provisions for public accommodation. "We think that decision inapposite, and without precedential value in determining the constitutionality of the present Act. Unlike Title II of the present legislation, the 1875 Act broadly proscribed discrimination in 'inns, public conveyances on land or water, theaters, and other places of public amusement,' without limiting the categories of affected businesses to those impinging upon interstate commerce." The foundation of the 1875 act was the Fourteenth Amendment's final clause, giving Congress the authority to enforce the Amendment through legislation. Section 2 of the 1964 act was not based on the Fourteenth Amendment, however, but on Congress's power, under Article I, to regulate interstate commerce. That power was recognized and upheld by the Supreme Court long before 1883 and undergirded the 1964 bill's provisions on public accommodations when these were debated in Congress. There was no question in his mind, or his brethren's, that denial of services to interstate travelers based on racial discrimination was a proper subject for congressional remediation.

Justice Hugo Black, who had strong reservations about joining the majority in the sit-in cases, here concurred with the judgment of the Court. He could have remained silent, but he felt that he needed to distinguish these cases from the sit-ins, in which he had dissented. "It requires no novel or strained interpretation of the Commerce Clause to sustain Title II as applied in either of these cases," a somewhat veiled reference to what he deemed the Court's strained majority opinion in *Bell*. Here the facts were different from the sit-in cases, for "the facilities and instrumentalities used to carry on this commerce, such as railroads, truck lines, ships, rivers, and even highways are also subject to congressional regulation, so far as is necessary to keep interstate traffic upon fair and equal terms." Even local establishments could be regulated if "their activities burden the flow of commerce among the States."

Finally, "there can be no doubt that the operations of both the motel and the restaurant here fall squarely within the measure Congress chose to adopt in the Act and deemed adequate to show a constitutionally prohibitable adverse effect on commerce." Of course, "the choice of policy is . . . within the exclusive power of Congress; but whether particular operations affect interstate commerce sufficiently to come under the constitutional power of Congress to regulate them is ultimately a judicial rather than a legislative question, and can be settled finally only by this Court." Black could not close without a final defense of his views in the sit-in cases, however. "I recognize that every remote, possible, speculative effect on commerce should not be accepted as an adequate constitutional ground to uproot and throw into the discard all our traditional distinctions between what is purely local, and therefore controlled by state laws, and what affects the national interest and is therefore subject to control by federal laws."

Justice William O. Douglas, whose liberality in the sit-in cases had set him against his former ally, Justice Black, also concurred. His concurrence was an attempt to show the likeness of the present case to the sit-in cases. He did not see why the Commerce Clause should be the sole basis for Title II. Instead, it was "my belief that the right of people to be free of state action that discriminates against them because of race . . . occupies a more protected position in our constitutional system than does the movement of cattle, fruit, steel and coal across state lines" under the Commerce Clause. He would have preferred to see the Court rest its affirmance of the three-judge panel's ruling on the Fourteenth Amendment itself, "for the [Amendment] deals with the constitutional status of the individual not with the impact on commerce of local activities or vice versa." Just to make sure that everyone got the message, he continued, "My opinion last Term in *Bell v. Maryland*, makes clear my position that the right to be free of discriminatory treatment (based on race) in places of public accommodation—whether intrastate or interstate—is a right guaranteed against state action by the Fourteenth Amendment and that state enforcement of the kind of trespass laws which Maryland had in that case was state action within the meaning of the Amendment."

A final concurrence was filed by Justice Arthur Goldberg. Goldberg was a labor lawyer and secretary of labor before he joined the court. He was perhaps its most liberal member on the subject of race before Thurgood Marshall was named to its bench in 1967 by President Lyndon Johnson. Goldberg took a holistic view of the act rather than a narrow view of Title II, and he interpreted the latter in light of his statement that "the primary purpose of the Civil Rights Act of 1964, however, as the Court recognizes, and as I would underscore, is the vindication of human dignity and not mere economics." He agreed with Douglas that section 1 of the Fourteenth Amendment "guarantees to all Americans the constitutional right 'to be treated as equal members of the community with respect to public accommodations,'" and Congress and the Court under that section had the authority to bar discrimination in public accommodations. "The challenged Act is just such a law and, in my view, Congress clearly had authority under both § 5 of the Fourteenth Amendment and the Commerce Clause to enact the Civil Rights Act of 1964."

—〰—

The object of the civil rights suit is usually some kind of court order, an injunction, compelling the defendant to do or not do something. This was true of the suits to end state-mandated segregation of schools, public facilities, and public offices, but a new trend has appeared in the past few decades: jury trials with monetary awards for violations of civil rights laws. In 2008, the Department of Justice reported that the number of civil rights cases filed in U.S. district courts increased from 18,922 in 1990 to 43,278 in 1997. Civil rights filings stabilized in the late 1990s and early 2000s and subsequently declined. From 2003 through 2006, civil rights filings in federal district courts decreased by almost 20 percent. Leading the way were suits over employment discrimination. During this period of growth followed by stabilization in civil rights litigation, the percentage of civil rights claims concluded by trial declined from 8 percent in 1990 to 3 percent in 2006. At the same time, civil rights cases in U.S. district courts declined from a high of 17 percent of all federal civil cases in 1998 to 13 percent in 2006.

From 1990 through 2006, about nine out of ten civil rights filings involved disputes between private parties. The percentage of plaintiffs who won at trial between 1990 and 2006 remained steady at about a third, and from 2000 through 2006, the median damage award for plaintiffs who won in civil rights trials ranged from $114,000 to $154,500. The combined 2000 through 2006 median jury award was $146,125; the median bench award was $71,500. Not every complaint ended in court. Many were resolved by administrative agencies like the Department of Education. It handled more than ten thousand complaints a year, almost half of which presently concern students with disabilities. Discrimination on the basis of sex is another significant component of these Department of Education civil rights complaints.

While the petitioners' suits are girded by the Thirteenth, Fourteenth, and Fifteenth Amendments and the Civil Rights Acts of 1866 through

1994, at their core they are still about honor. Slaves could not have honor because they were not people, much less citizens, under slave law. They were commodities, property, in the stream of commerce. Such things cannot feel injuries although they can be damaged. The owner or renter, not the slave, sues the person who caused the damage for the cost of replacement or remedy. Today, the victim of discrimination feels the injury precisely because he or she is a person, and all persons have honor. Civil rights suits can be brought in state or federal court, as most states have civil rights provisions in their constitutions and statutes.

8

Product Liability and Mass Tort Litigation

A TORT IS A HARM TO A PERSON or property which the law considers actionable. Tort suits can be found in the very first American courts. We have already encountered some of them in chapter 1—defamation. The remedy may be a damage payment or some form of court order to do, or not do, something. The defendant must have, or have had, some duty or obligation to the plaintiff that the defendant violated for the case to move forward. Far more important in the twentieth-century story of litigation are tort suits arising from defective products because manufactured products, particularly mass-produced products, are widely purchased and often have defects. These may have caused harm because they were defectively produced, because the seller or the manufacturer had been negligent in inspecting them, because there was a defect in their design, or because of some other act or failure to act.

Two major shifts in law, both driven by striking changes in the way Americans lived, marked twentieth-century tort litigation. The first was the return of "strict liability." The second was the introduction of the mass tort "class action." In nineteenth-century America, when a consumer bought something, s/he most often saw the maker face-to-face. If there was a problem, the buyer and the seller worked it out. The lawsuit was an uncommon last resort. The early twentieth century ushered in a time of mass consumption of manufactured goods. Purchasers of these products rarely met the manufacturers. The only contact the consumer of a product had was with the merchant or seller. Under existing law, if there was a defect in the product, the buyer could sue the seller, but not the manufacturer, because the buyer had no contact (called in law "privity") with the manufacturer. The exception to this rule was a product that was inherently dangerous, like a firearm or a boiler. If these were negligently made and the resulting harm to the buyer was foreseeable, the buyer could sue the maker.

In a society in which machine-made products, medical devices, and foods are all mass marketed, with resulting distance between the maker and the buyer, so-called strict liability of the manufacturers for harms their products caused made common sense. But the law is not about common sense. It does not change from within, a machine making itself pure. Instead, it is litigation that forces change on the law to make law conform to the felt needs of the day. This is what happened with the rise of strict liability in tort lawsuits.

Mass tort litigation required a different kind of procedure from the simple strict liability suit. In the latter, strict liability extended the reach of the suit horizontally, to include the manufacturer along with the seller. In the former, the suit extended vertically, to include all those who suffered the same damage as the plaintiff. This kind of suit has a name—class action—and it is as old as equity jurisprudence itself. In the classic English common-law suit, each plaintiff files for himself or herself an action for each count or harm. In the class action suit, the plaintiff represents a class of all those similarly affected. The rise of the modern class action suit, like the rise of strict liability, resulted from demands of people harmed by products they had bought, used properly, and found defective.

The class action mass tort suit reflected the mass marketing of products. Advertisements promised results, and thousands if not millions of consumers relied on these promises. Law protected the advertiser, a middleman, from all but deliberate lies. Exaggerations and hype were permissible, so long as the product was not incorrectly described or its use mischaracterized. But some products had hidden defects, and these were not shielded from tort suits. The problem for the courts was how to manage thousands of lawsuits against the same manufacturer having common fact patterns. The class action suit was one answer.

—⚜—

As the twentieth century opened, the doctrine of negligence stood astride the law of tort like a colossus. The plaintiff had to prove that the manufacture of a particular product s/he had purchased had been negligently handled to win a lawsuit. The harm was one that a rational man could have foreseen. That made sense in an era when individual craftsmen made and sold goods, but less sense when machines were mass-produced by other machines. Still, the courts resisted tinkering with the doctrine of negligence, creating a dike holding back a flood of defective products cases. Like the cracks in a dike, a single case, a single scholarly commentary, a single judge willing to depart from precedent might break down the dike and let the waters flow.

The first of those cracks in the dike came in *McPherson v. Buick* (1916), a New York case. Court of appeals judge Benjamin Cardozo wrote that the manufacturer was also liable for faults (in this case a faulty tire) when the manufacturing process was flawed. This was the harbinger of a new standard of care. "If the nature of a thing is such that it is reasonably certain to place life and limb in peril when negligently made, it is then a thing of danger. Its nature gives warning of the consequence to be expected. If to the element of danger there is added knowledge that the thing will be used by persons other than the purchaser, and used without new tests, then, irrespective of contract, the manufacturer of this thing of danger is under a duty to make it carefully." The victim had to show that she had used the item in the proper way and that the defendant manufacturer had been negligent in producing the faulty item. Even a warranty warning to the buyer did not save the manufacturer from liability.

More cracks in the dike appeared at opposite ends of the country, as two judges, one in California and one in New Jersey, confronted very similar cases of harm without proof of a manufacturer's negligence. Roger Traynor was a New Deal liberal who taught law at the University of California and served briefly as the state's deputy attorney general when Earl Warren was the state's attorney general. Traynor went on to the state's highest court in 1940 and served there with distinction for thirty years, in 1964 becoming chief justice. His law review pieces and his opinions were highly original, gaining praise from some and harsh criticism from others.

Traynor's first assay at strict liability appeared in *Escola v. Coca-Cola Bottling Co* (1944). Gladys Escola worked in a restaurant, and when shelving bottles of Coca-Cola she had the misfortune of having one of the bottles explode in her hand. Her injuries were serious and she sued the bottler. She was fortunate that her lawyer was Melvin Belli, later celebrated as the king of torts, and he won a jury verdict on the grounds that the bottler was negligent and she wasn't. On appeal, the California Supreme Court sustained the jury verdict, based on the old doctrine of negligence, presuming that the bottler had been negligent in producing the bottle. Judge Traynor concurred, but on a different doctrine. "Even if there is no negligence, however, public policy demands that responsibility be fixed wherever it will most effectively reduce the hazards to life and health inherent in defective products that reach the market." Traynor's reference to public policy took Cardozo's more conventional reasoning and applied it more generally. "It is evident that the manufacturer can anticipate some hazards and guard against the recurrence of others, as the public cannot. Those who suffer injury from defective products are unprepared to meet its consequences." Traynor found that the victim was helpless against the mistake of the manufacturer. "The cost of an injury and the loss of time or health may be an overwhelming misfortune to the person injured, and a needless one, for the risk of injury can be insured by the manufacturer and distributed among the public as a cost of doing business. It is to the public interest to discourage the marketing of products having defects that are a menace to the public."

Traynor's conclusion was just as striking as his reasoning. It wholly shifted the burden in such cases onto the shoulders of the defendant. "If such products nevertheless find their way into the market, it is to the public interest to place the responsibility for whatever injury they may cause upon the manufacturer, who, even if he is not negligent in the manufacture of the product, is responsible for its reaching the market."

A case from one state's supreme court cannot be compelling in another state, but it can be persuasive. Judge Traynor was no doubt watching when another case raised very similar issues to *Escola*. It came from New Jersey. It involved a Plymouth sold to Claus Henningsen and his wife, Helen, by Bloomfield Motors in New Jersey. While Helen was driving, the steering failed and she hit a wall, injuring herself. She sued both the dealership and the manufacturer, although she could not show negligence in either of them and a car was not an inherently dangerous product. The state supreme court nevertheless allowed the suit, *Henningsen v. Bloomfield Motors* (1960), to proceed. The bill of sale had been a typical "boilerplate" contract, with many clauses in tiny print that absolved the dealership of defects traced to the factory and the factory of negligence by the dealership. The Henningsens, like most buyers, did not read the entire document and may not have been able to understand its clever evasions of liability even had they read it. In addition, the dealership had not serviced the car prior to giving it to the Henningsens, despite their standing promise to inspect and prepare all cars they sold before giving them to the buyers.

The trial court, instructed by the presiding judge in the old rules of negligent liability, refused to award damages to the Henningsens, although they did win under the old doctrine of warranty of merchantability—that the seller offered the goods with the promise that they were free of defects. Chrysler appealed, because like many large corporations selling consumer goods, it had distanced itself from the warranty offered by retailers of its cars.

Justice John J. Francis wrote the opinion for a unanimous New Jersey Supreme Court sustaining the strict liability count that the trial judge threw out. New Jersey is a state crisscrossed by highways and studded with car dealerships. Francis grew up and practiced law in North Jersey, where traffic and accidents go hand in hand. He was appointed to the high court by Democratic governor Robert B. Meyner and served from 1957 until his retirement in 1973. Like Prosser, Francis sprinkled his opinion with case law, references to legal treatises, and other scholarly pieces. He knew that he was making law, and he obviously relished the task. A longtime Democrat, he had no hesitation taking on a major corporation and protecting the rights of ordinary consumers.

Francis pilloried the automaker's attempt to avoid responsibility. "[Chrysler] ceased selling products to the consuming public through their own employees and making contracts of sale in their own names. Instead, a [franchise] system of independent dealers was established; their products were sold to dealers who in turn dealt with the buying public, ostensibly solely in their own personal capacity as sellers." This was supposed to insulate Chrysler from liability when the dealership failed to inspect the cars before turning them over to the buyers. It did not work. The court found that the promises made by warranties were "illusory" and the manufacturers knew it. "Under modern conditions the ordinary layman, on responding to the importuning of colorful advertising, has neither the opportunity nor the capacity to inspect or to determine the fitness of an automobile for use; he must rely on the manufacturer who has control of its construction, and to some degree on the dealer who, to the limited extent called for by the manufacturer's instructions, inspects and services it before delivery. In such a marketing milieu, his remedies and those of persons who properly claim through him should not depend 'upon the intricacies of the law of sales.'"

Another way of putting the warranty questions was that in modern mass products liability cases, the buyer and the seller/manufacturer did not stand on equal footing. "The conflicting interests of the buyer and seller must be evaluated realistically and justly, giving due weight to . . . the mass production methods of manufacture and distribution to the public, and the bargaining position occupied by the ordinary consumer in such an economy." The court adopted that realistic approach by holding both the dealership and the Chrysler Corporation to a strict liability standard. But what permitted a New Jersey Supreme Court to change the standard of care so forcefully and thoroughly? The court explained itself by relying on what is an old friend for readers of this book: equity. "Practically all judges are 'chancellors' and cannot fail to be influenced by any equitable doctrines that are available. . . . There is sufficient flexibility in the concepts of fraud, duress, misrepresentation and undue influence, not to mention differences in economic bargaining power to enable the courts to avoid enforcement of unconscionable provisions in long printed standardized contracts." (It is only fair to mention here that New Jersey's court of chancery was one of the oldest and the busiest in the country.)

As the accident happened to Helen Henningsen and she was not the buyer of the car, Bloomfield and Chrysler argued that they had no legal obligation to her. The court was not impressed. "In the present matter, the basic contractual relationship is between Claus Henningsen, Chrysler, and Bloomfield Motors, Inc. The precise issue presented is whether Mrs. Henningsen, who is not a party to their respective warranties, may claim under them." Was this the escape hatch for the manufacturer and the dealer? No. "We are convinced that the cause of justice in this area of the law can be served only by recognizing that she is such a person who, in the reasonable contemplation of the parties to the warranty, might be expected to become a user of the automobile."

Across the country Judge Traynor took note of *Henningsen*. Although a New Jersey high court ruling had no force in California, Traynor would cite it along with his own concurrence in *Escola* when later writing for the state supreme court in *Greenman v. Yuba Power Company*

(1963). Traynor began with the facts, the first element in almost all appellate court opinions. "Plaintiff brought this action for damages against the retailer and the manufacturer of a Shopsmith, a combination power tool that could be used as a saw, drill, and wood lathe." Greenman saw a demonstration at the retailer and read a brochure that Yuba Power prepared. He wanted one for his workshop at home, and his wife gave him one for Christmas. "In 1957 he bought the necessary attachments to use the Shopsmith as a lathe for turning a large piece of wood he wished to make into a chalice. After he had worked on the piece of wood several times without difficulty, it suddenly flew out of the machine and struck him on the forehead, inflicting serious injuries." Nearly a year later, he filed his suit against both the retailers and the manufacturer. The basis for his claim was breach of warranty (the power tool was not supposed to loosen the wood) and negligence (the manufacturer had not paid proper attention to the safety features).

At trial, the jury found for Greenman against the manufacturer. Traynor, writing for the court, upheld that verdict but again found a basis in the suit to extend what was fast becoming the rule of strict liability for products put on the market. "To impose strict liability on the manufacturer under the circumstances of this case, it was not necessary for plaintiff to establish an express warranty. . . . A manufacturer is strictly liable in tort when an article he places on the market, knowing that it is to be used without inspection for defects, proves to have a defect that causes injury to a human being." Here, as in Francis's opinion in *Henningsen*, the justification for the imposition of strict liability lay not in the law but in public policy. "The purpose of such liability is to insure that the costs of injuries resulting from defective products are borne by the manufacturers that put such products on the market rather than by the injured persons who are powerless to protect themselves."

A fourth crack in the old structure of tort law appeared in a very different place. Law in America has many sources—constitutions, rulings of courts of appeal, statutes, and, more and more, the work of legal scholars. The American Law Institute (ALI), the brainchild of University of Pennsylvania Law School dean William Draper Lewis in 1923, brought together judges, lawyers, and law professors to "restate" the law, foster uniformity in state laws, and, quietly, to reform outmoded law. Lewis's successors, Herbert Goodrich and Herbert

Wechsler, carried on in this tradition. The research of legal historian N. E. H. Hull demonstrated this latter purpose by delving into the private correspondence of the directors of the institute with the "reporters," the primary authors, of the various restatements of the law. One of the works of the members, the *Restatement of Torts, Second*, volume 2, published in 1965, featured the doctrine of strict liability in section 402a, and thereupon hangs the third part of our tale.

The reporter of this volume was law professor William L. Prosser, and he had a personal stake in the acceptance of strict liability for defective products. In support of his sweeping decision, Justice Francis cited Prosser's *Law of Torts* (1955 edition) eight times. In two 1960s articles, Prosser advocated the replacement of negligence with strict liability. His favorite case citation—Justice Francis's opinion in *Henningsen*. For Justice Francis, like Judge Traynor, and Prosser himself recognized that the law must reflect the real world. According to legal scholar G. Edward White, whose influential study of tort law in America focused on the post–World War II period, a heightened sense of realism pervaded much academic and judicial thinking in this period. So-called legal realism was an academic jurisprudence, or legal philosophy, that advocated a contextual view of law. In other words, advocates of legal realism thought that the law should take into account social and economic realities. Realists believed that a new sense of the "purpose" of tort law must result. White summarized their views: "Injured people should be compensated, the argument ran, because their injuries affected society at large." Tort suits, rather than insurance or liability limiting contracts, were the best way to ensure that compensation was available not just to the injured party who sued, but to all similarly harmed.

Prosser could write clear, compelling, and even dramatic prose. In his two articles, "Assault on the Citadel" in the *Yale Law Journal* in 1960 and "Fall of the Citadel" in a 1966 issue of the *Minnesota Law Review*, he announced the arrival of strict liability. In the 1960 essay, he predicted that the "absurd and outrageous consequences" of "negligent liability"— that there was no liability without proof of negligence—would soon fall before the assault of strict liability. In the 1966 piece, he celebrated the fall of the citadel (his metaphor for the old doctrine of negligence). In addition, his treatise (or "hornbook" as legal textbooks were called) on torts changed over the course of four editions from the mid-1930s to 1971, two years before he died, and the direction of the changes was clear—the tort victim was helpless in the face of outrageous conduct by manufacturers. Strict liability alone would repay the plaintiffs for the harm they suffered. Traynor's and Francis's opinions were also featured in the later editions of the hornbook. The cracks in the old doctrine had now widened, and the trickle of cases for strict liability had become a flood.

—ɯ—

Ironically, part of this flood was lawsuits involving products that were intended to protect people from harm. These included asbestos, commonly used as a fire retardant; Agent Orange, a defoliant; and intrauterine devices used to prevent conception. The victims of the side effects of these mass-produced and mass-purveyed products ran into the hundreds of thousands. When they took advantage of the strict liability formula for bringing suit—there was no question of negligence, only of harm—courts were overwhelmed. The flood tide of cases loosed by the rise of strict liability threatened to sink the state and federal courts.

The answer, potentially at least, lay in the procedure known as the "class action suit." When many people sued for products liability when the same manufacturer's product had caused similar injuries to them, just as when students were segregated by state law, courts could bundle the cases into a "class action" suit. *Escola*, *Henningsen*, and *Greenman* were not class action suits. Contrariwise, like the school desegregation cases and the sit-ins, many civil rights cases were class action suits. That is, the complaint and the remedy sought applied to all persons in the same situation, though only one or a few named plaintiffs appeared on the legal filings. The next round of mass products litigation were class actions. In these, plaintiffs could ask for certification of their case as a class action, and judges had discretion to certify or not certify the case, depending on a series of variables discussed below.

Complex class action suits involving products liability differed greatly from civil rights class action litigation. The civil rights class action plaintiffs wanted an injunction to end discrimination. By contrast, the plaintiffs in products liability cases wanted monetary awards to repair the damage that the defendant's products had caused. That distinction made the products liability class action harder to resolve. Presumably, everyone in the civil rights class faced the same harm and could benefit from the same relief. Did everyone in the products liability class suffer the same harm? In the civil rights cases, the cause of the harm was, again presumably, the same. Was the same true of all the members of the products liability class? These were the kinds of questions that would, to coin a phrase, cross the judges' eyes.

Specifically, when did the rights or fact situation of one or more of the parties in the products liability class not conform to the others? When did the remedy sought for the whole class not fit the harm to particular members of the class? How were parties (and potential parties) to the class action to be notified? How were parties able to "opt out" of the class and bring their own suit? The federal rules of civil procedure governed all these matters, but successive rules revision committees that tried to iron out these wrinkles never seemed finished. Individual judges at hearings offered suggestions, the advisory committee proposed amendments, and Congress approved four categorical requirements for certifying class action suits. Bypass the next four paragraphs if you do not enjoy legal procedure.

The first requirement of certification of a class was "numerosity"—the size of the potential class. Federal courts would be deluged if thousands of claims were filed when a single class action could adequately and fairly accommodate all the claimants. Second, commonality of claims, including common facts and legal theories under which the litigation was begun, had to be established. Third, the claims or defenses of any one member of the class named in the action had to be typical of the others in the class that the named litigant supposedly represented. The same was true of the named defendant. Finally, the class members had to have adequate legal representation. All of these bore on the certification of a class, apart from the remedy segment of the litigation.

The class action lawsuit had the benefit of (potentially) affording some reward to injured parties who could afford to hire counsel or wait for trial, or would lose when the better-financed defendant was able to sway a jury. These "negative value" plaintiffs (because the award at the end of a successful suit did not match the cost of the suit) would benefit from being bundled with other similarly situated plaintiffs. To some critics, it seemed that the attorneys were the real beneficiaries of such suits, because their return for victory exceeded any individual plaintiff's award. On the other hand, counsel had considerable risk in investing time and money (think of the TV advertising for clients), paying expert witnesses, and working the suit. If the attorney lost, the result could be catastrophic. What was more, such class action suits seemed to deny a windfall to individual plaintiffs with good cases, able counsel, and the financial ability to wait out a case. The argument can be gussied up with high-sounding language against constraining "an individual ability to direct the course of his interaction with the judicial process" that infringes "on an individual's process-based autonomy interest."

One answer to the potential mismanagement of the plaintiff's cause by inept or corrupt counsel is judicial management of class actions. This became a regular part of class action litigation when the underlying claim was products liability, as the Dalkon Shield case demonstrated. The Dalkon Shield was an intrauterine device designed to prevent conception. A. R. Robins, a major pharmaceutical firm, had bought the birth control device from Dalkon and at first marketed it widely and successfully. But women were finding that use of the shield led to uterine infections, bleeding, and infertility. Robins anticipated litigation and was preparing its defense—it was the user's misuse of the product, not a defect in the product itself, that caused the harm. Plaintiffs responded that they had suffered the harm even when they used the device properly, and won. What was more, because Robins had concealed the likelihood of the dangerous side effects, plaintiffs were convincing juries to award punitive damages considerably larger than the costs of medical treatment and emotional harm. Robins began to send letters to doctors warning that infections were a common side effect if the shield was in place for more than a limited period of time and stopped marketing the shield, but the company did not recall the product until 1980. By 1981, litigation costs for the company were mounting steeply.

Most of the lawsuits were diversity cases; that is, the plaintiffs were not domiciled in Virginia, where Robins had its corporate headquarters. The lawsuits thus landed in federal district courts. A district court in California was the first to certify the class action. The Court of Appeals for the Ninth Circuit (which included California) reversed the certification under the theory that each plaintiff had to prove that the device and not some other medical problem had caused her injury. The court of appeals decision did not help Robins. It continued to lose suit after suit. Worse was to come. In the course of a series of federal suits against Robins in Minnesota, plaintiffs' lawyers discovered evidence that the company had not only known about the dangers; it had destroyed internal documents that warned about them. In 1984, ten years after the first suit was filed in a Wichita, Kansas, federal court, with the punitive awards mounting still higher and plaintiffs winning all their cases, Robins sought the consolidation of the cases in one federal jurisdiction, as it happened, in the Northern District of Virginia.

In 1984, Judge Robert Merhige, who had nearly two decades earlier managed the desegregation of the Richmond public schools, found himself managing the Dalkon Shield litigation. His decision in the former case, busing students across school district lines, was highly controversial (and ultimately reversed), but it was matched in boldness by his handling of the Dalkon Shield cases. He sympathized with the defendant's request for certification of all of the cases as a class action but denied the request for res judicata (the issue had already been settled). Still, he worked with all the parties to reach a solution that did not deny plaintiffs adequate recompense while keeping the company afloat, perhaps by refusing to impose punitive damages. In 1985, he arranged a meeting of judges handling the cases, but soon afterward Robins's petition for bankruptcy ended his plan to manage the entirety of the litigation from his courtroom. Things were getting testy. In an exchange in his courtroom, in which one plaintiff's lawyer asked Judge Merhige if he had sought to have all the cases brought to his court, he replied, "I am a judge, not a huckster; I don't advertise for business."

Robins was going underwater, and its insurer, Aetna, had stepped into the arena to battle for its own interests. By 1985, with Aetna and Robins disputing the extent of Aetna's liability in the cases, the Dalkon Shield plaintiffs turned their guns on Aetna. Robins filed for bankruptcy, exposing Aetna to the full fury of the litigation. As the federal courts were managing the manner by which Robins might emerge from bankruptcy, as well as the various suits against Aetna, plaintiffs asked the courts to manage the payouts of damages. Although he knew about the Ninth Circuit's ruling, Judge Merhige certified the suits against Aetna as a class action.

In 1989, fifteen years after the first suits against Robins were filed, the Court of Appeals for the Fourth Circuit upheld the certification of the class action. Judge Donald Russell wrote the opinion. "In summary, we take it as the lessons to be gleaned from the authorities already cited and discussed to be . . . that the 'trend' is once again to give [the federal rules of civil procedure governing the certification of class action suits] a liberal rather than a restrictive construction, adopting a standard of flexibility in application which will in the particular case 'best serve the ends of justice for the affected parties and . . . promote judicial efficiency.'"

Judge Russell's opinion was more than a procedural one. It captured the future of mass products litigation in America. Lawsuits against Agent Orange, Monsanto and other asbestos companies, and other big pharma firms littered the federal courts' dockets. The insurance industry was exposed as well as manufacturers of defective consumer products. Judge Russell said as much: "Aetna was neither the manufacturer nor the vendor of the device; it was the products liability insurance carrier of A. H. Robins Company, Inc. (Robins), the manufacturer and distributor of the device. It is the theory of the plaintiffs that Aetna's conduct, while acting in its role as insurance carrier, was such that it rendered itself liable as a joint tortfeasor with Robins for any injuries sustained by persons using the device." Thus the suit, here appealed, spread a web of liability that reached companies almost too big to fail. But the potential for failure was huge, as the first cases included not only awards to the women for pain and suffering, but also "punitive damages" because Robins had left a product it knew was defective on the market long after it should, according to the jury verdicts, have been taken off the market. Had cases brought by individual plaintiffs been litigated one by one, they would have taken up great space on dockets across the country and destroyed both the pharmaceutical company and its insurer. "Many of the courts referred the multiplicity of suits in their district for consolidated pre-trial proceedings under the direction of the Judicial Panel on Multi-District Litigation in the hope that such action might reduce the difficulties of disposing expeditiously of the mounting Dalkon Shield case burden." This was a Band-Aid for an arterial hemorrhage.

Judge Russell was sympathetic to other judges' attempts to consolidate the cases. For example,

> District Judge Miles Lord of the Minnesota federal district court, to whom had been assigned in the late 1970's and early 1980's a large number of Dalkon Shield cases, determined to try his hand at expediting the disposition of such cases as were before him. He consolidated a

large number of such suits and appointed a lead counsel to handle discovery. He prodded the counsel so appointed to proceed aggressively, and he named two masters to sift through all the material discovered and to prepare a report for counsel and the court based on all material discovered and any developed in their independent investigations.

This step was more effective but still did not lessen the bleeding of judicial resources. "Other courts took another tack in an effort to manage expeditiously and fairly the mass of Dalkon Shield cases. They turned to the class action procedure provided by [federal rules of Civil Procedure]. The great volume of cases which were inundating the court system and the similarity of the issues in all the cases, it was thought, provided a proper basis for class treatment both in the interests of the parties and of the courts."

Nevertheless, Judge Russell reported that some trial courts' judges had balked at this reasoning, believing the defendants to the effect that "the complicated issues of fact . . . must be resolved on an individual basis." Apparently there was no more uniformity of opinion on the bench than there was among the plaintiffs and the defendants. Some judges thought, according to Russell, that "common questions of law and fact do not predominate in this action." In other words, the injuries the women suffered were so various and complex that each case required its own attention to detail.

Like Merhige, Russell was aware that the Court of Appeals for the Ninth Circuit had refused to let the California trial court certify the cases as a class action. As in the strict liability cases, the decisions of one federal circuit did not dictate the rulings in another. Hence Russell, writing for the Court of Appeals for the Fourth Circuit, was not bound to follow the dictates of the Ninth Circuit. Nevertheless, he did take notice of three points the Ninth Circuit opinion had made. The first concerned punitive damages. Juries were (relatively) free to set the level of these awards to plaintiffs for the bad conduct of the defendant, and thus they varied from one case to another. One would assume that the conduct of Robins and Aetna in all the cases on which punitive awards were sought would be the same, but the Court of Appeals for the Ninth Circuit had decided that juries in each case should decide on the amount of the punitive damages. Second, at issue for the Ninth Circuit was whether the plaintiffs had adequate counsel. Robins and Aetna could afford the best lawyers in the country, while the plaintiffs' bar was more varied in its abilities.

Russell dealt with one more obstacle to Merhige's certification order. The class action was a diversity case, which under federal rules required a minimum payout of $10,000 to the successful plaintiff. Otherwise every one of the individual cases belonged in state courts. The named plaintiffs in the suit in Virginia all passed this test. But did the three hundred thousand other unnamed plaintiffs in the class also suffer more than $10,000 worth of actual damages? Judge Russell performed an end run around the issue— appellants had to show "to a legal certainty" that the unnamed members of the class would not meet this threshold. After all, damages in such cases were determined by juries, and who could tell what juries would award?

Judge Russell believed that this case would become the benchmark, the precedent for future cases, and at the outset he needed to make a distinction. "Mass tort suits are generally divided into two classes. . . . The first is concerned with what is designated as the mass accident suit, in which a large number of persons are injured as a result of a single accident. . . . The other is a mass tort action, of which this case is an outstanding example, is one arising out of the sale, on a national or international market to thousands of persons, of an alleged defective product, from the use of which has caused many persons to have suffered injury." The first posed little novelty to the courts, while the second was a genuine test of the role of courts in mass products litigation.

Russell tried to visualize the new reality, the future likelihood of litigation in a densely populated, consumer-driven society, and its impact on the judicial system. "Within recent years, the proliferation in the development and distribution of new products and remedies and the complaints of injuries from the use of these products have brought an accelerating avalanche of mass products liability suits." Because these were diversity suits, they ended up in federal courts, and that "represents what is, as we have already observed, probably the most important and difficult management problem facing the federal court system today."

In other words, the mass products liability suit made the federal courts into administrative agencies and the federal judges into managers of suits. No more the godlike neutral arbitrator, robed and sitting on high, the judge was now a part of the suit, moving its pieces around efficiently. Was this kind of management of cases necessary? Was it fair to litigants? Was it fair to parties to other cases waiting, sometimes for years, on the courts' dockets? Russell reasoned backward from the damage award problem.

"Asbestos litigation [for instance] has resulted in far more expense than in recovery of damages for injured persons. A Rand Corporation study estimated that injured persons receive less than thirty-seven percent of the total amount spent on litigation. Almost two-thirds of the total expenditures are for attorneys' fees and other litigation expenses. . . . When account is also taken of the toll of such cases on the court system itself, it is evident that the proper functioning of the courts and the fair and efficient administration of justice for other litigants" suffered when "clogging of the court system by mass tort actions tried individually" occurred. Class action was the only answer—even if it did not result in perfect justice for any of the parties.

Judge Russell claimed that the "public was crying out" for public and speedy resolution of these cases. That may not be the case—at least not for parties who feel that their case would give them a larger slice of the pie than the award for members of the class. But for the bench and bar, and for the future of mass products litigation, Dalkon Shield seemed to be the future. "Mass torts in modern-day jurisprudence are taking a fresh look at the value of . . . class actions. The economies of time, effort, and expense of the class device cut across categorical tort lines and ought not to be obscured by the narrow application of circumstances or by undue emphasis on traditional interests in one-to-one litigation." Russell then made a remarkable personal admission from the bench. "I was an ex officio member of the Advisory Committee on Civil Rules when [the rule on class actions] was amended, which came out with an Advisory Committee Note saying that mass torts are inappropriate for class certification. I thought then that was true. I am profoundly convinced now that that is untrue. Unless we can use the class action and devices built on the class action, our judicial system is simply not going to be able to cope with the challenge of the mass repetitive wrong that we see in this case and so many others that have been mentioned this morning and afternoon."

Judge Russell's opinion was forty-three pages long, studded with citations of precedent and references to law review articles, treatises on torts, and comments to the federal rules. It was, in effect, a law review piece itself. Writing at the end of nearly two decades of Dalkon Shield litigation, he no doubt felt that he could have something like the last word. He had been a senator and governor of the state of South Carolina, and before that, president of its university. One could find few who had as much experience in all the branches of American governance and academia as he.

But in American litigation, there is no last word. The pendulum swung against permissive certification in the next decade. With *Robins* as precedent, district courts were certifying class actions in mass products torts. Appellate courts reversed, determining that defendants with stronger cases than *Robins* were caving in and settling rather than face certification of a class action. Central to these appellate decisions to decertify cases were tobacco-related suits and asbestos exposure suits. Some of the decisions involved the old tort law element of causation. Did the product actually cause the harm, or was the connection (called proximity) only presumed from the generality of evidence (an example of the "statistical fallacy")? Other decisions involved payouts from a limited fund. None of the reversals slowed the more general advance of managerial judging, however.

A campaign by publicists for large corporate defendants followed the Dalkon Shield cases. It was successful in limiting punitive damage awards in many states. In 2003, Congress gave the courts the power to offer parties the chance to opt out of the class at the settlement stage of litigation, as well as in pre-trial stages. The 2005 Class Action Fairness Act (CAFA) revisited suits that offered little financial benefit to individual members of the class, but windfall rewards to counsel. If the attorneys' fees outweighed the members' return, the court could intervene in the settlement. CAFA also countered shopping by plaintiffs looking for friendly state class action forums by making removal to a federal court on the basis of partial diversity easier for defendants. As a result, courts found themselves engaged in determining "reasonable" attorneys' fees. The resulting formulas for determining compensation resulted in courts having to weigh and rate the performance of counsel, an activity at the very extremities of managerial judging. Whatever one concludes about the purpose of the act (and its critics cite it as shaped by corporate lobbyists), there was a significant increase in class actions filed in federal courts from 2002 to 2007, primarily in consumer fraud and tort cases. Litigants and their lawyers were not deterred by the new regulations.

—☜—

What does the rise of the strict liability and the class action mass tort suit tell us about American culture in the twenty-first century? Perhaps we are entering a long period of declining litigant autonomy, when most victims of mass tort harms will simply have to "lump it," that is, suffer the harm without starting a lawsuit, as many victims of such harms now do. The introduction of widespread insurance plans alongside mandatory class actions certainly reduces the role of the individual litigant, but more and more often such litigants' claims lie in the "negative return zone." In other words, it would cost more to file the suit, pay the lawyer, and invest time and energy in the litigation than the monetary return was worth if one was victorious. Will the result show a declining faith in the civil justice system of adversarial lawyering and "unfettered ability" of traditional litigants?

If history is any guide, the unfettered ability of clients to control the lawsuit is itself a myth. Most clients simply do not have the time and energy to bring lawsuits with small chance of reward. Society has become too big and the system too overloaded to hold out much hope of victory. The size of the defendant corporations—huge, sometimes multinational, entities—also deters suit. But some individuals will file the suit, and some will win, a proof that democratic access to litigation still has the potential to remind us of who we are. What is more, if enough ordinary victims target a giant malfeasor, the litigation costs for the defendant corporation, even if it is well heeled, may force it to negotiate a settlement. Rarely will a court summarily dismiss a properly filed claim, even when the defendant asks for a summary judgment without further hearing. The party with the better lawyer will sometimes win when common sense dictates the opposite result, and the costs in time and money can be heavy to all parties. But public interest lawyers will sometimes take a case "pro bono" (without a fee), and tort lawyers will often take a case on "contingency" (paid only when their party wins, out of the damages the court orders the other party or parties to pay). It is not a perfectly level playing field, but it may be the only field on which the average American can "wager his law." It is in this sense that the courts are often the most democratic of our governmental institutions, and we are truly a litigation nation.

Conclusion

The Value of Litigation in America

In America, litigation is both effect and cause. In times of rapid and significant social and cultural change, litigation rates rise because the gap between older values and newer ones widens. Plaintiffs defending tradition face defendants who have adopted newer ways, or the reverse. Parties in these legal contests not only speak for themselves; they (believe) they speak for the community. Litigation in this sense is not me against you; it is us against them. On some occasions, litigation is not just the effect of change; it is a cause. It spurs the pace of change. Civil rights lawsuits, for example, helped bring down the Jim Crow regime.

If litigation is so important and so prevalent in America, hopefully a conclusion one can draw from the chapters above, why do so many people who have been harmed, for example by malpractice, or by defamation, or by assault, forego the courts? Why do they choose to lump their injuries? It is difficult for the historian who deals with what actually happened—in this case a lawsuit—to explain why something did not happen. One may speculate, of course. People choose not to sue when they don't feel comfortable suing, when they blame themselves, when they think the injury was natural, when they don't want to be further bothered, when they don't want to look litigious, or when they feel weak and unworthy compared to the potential defendant. The litigation rate measures the decision to sue and hints at the decision to lump it.

Even this refinement of the problem does not answer it. When do people overcome their hesitancy and bring the lawsuit? The answer seems to me to be, when they want to tell their story. When plaintiffs believe that their story should be told, they bring the suit. When defendants want their side to be heard, they refuse to settle. It is not merely the prospect of winning or losing that causes potential suitors to launch litigation or defend it. In fact, from the beginning of the colonies in North America to this day, the root of litigation has been wounded honor or personal dignity. We sue for ourselves and for our sense of a larger right and wrong. We defend rather than settle because we feel in the right and because someone needs to stand up for our values. When those values are in a state of flux, litigation rates will rise. When a kind of consensus returns, the rates will stabilize or decline.

With this solution to the why question in mind, one can see that litigation has a private and a public meaning. The private meaning remains much the same as it was at the beginning of our story. Challenged honor or wronged dignity, actual harm or imagined insult all result in litigation. Rates change as shared perceptions of honor and dignity change. The public character of litigation has evolved in a different way, as the role of government and the scope of commerce have evolved. Big government and large-scale consumption have dwarfed the individual in a way almost inconceivable to the first settlers. Thus the temptation of those who study litigation to look at large numbers, over long spans of time, rather than the "anecdotal" case study. By so doing, they may miss the intimate side of litigation and its attendant "litigation fever." By reattaching the private and the public stories, as in the case presented below, one can see the social and cultural context of the numbers.

Faced with a variety of suits from gays, atheists, and women, the Boy Scouts of America (hereafter BSA) initially adopted a scorched-earth legal strategy, defending every suit to the utmost. Most often, they won, but the cost away from the courthouse, including loss of local funding and accommodations, threatened to beggar the institution. So scouting conceded that gays, lesbians, atheists, and girls can now be members and, as adults, lead scout troops. A traditional institution whose oath was fashioned in 1910 gave way to the changing realities of culture and social life in the twenty-first century because of litigation. Before that concession, as both effect and cause, came *Boy Scouts of America v. Dale* (2000).

Where was wronged honor? Everywhere. James Dale, whose long career as a Boy Scout, explorer, and volunteer scout master was summarily ended when he came out as a gay man, defended his honor with the lawsuit. A brave new world had accepted the place of LGBT in America. Dale saw this world in terms of the values of democratic inclusion. A truly democratic law included people who wanted in. He saw the Scouts in this way—an organization that reflected and embodied inclusive democracy.

The upper administration of scouting refused to accede to his pleas for reinstatement because they saw themselves defending older, better values (called "clean living" in the Scout Code). The scouts asserted that they were not covered by New Jersey's anti-discrimination law because they were neither a public accommodation nor a business, and because the Scout Code, as they interpreted it, did not allow gays to be members. This was a version of the freedom of association and freedom of expression rights presumed by courts to lie in the First Amendment. It was a privilege to be part of scouting, which the organization itself rather than society extended. Such organizational or institutional exclusivism epitomized a traditional ideal of society—only those who belonged could belong.

Dale's was a civil rights suit, but not a class action. It nevertheless had the same effect. He did not seek monetary damages. He simply wanted his dignity as a longtime scout and a potential scoutmaster upheld by the courts. As reported in the U.S. Supreme Court dissent by Justice John Paul Stevens, "In a *New York Times interview*, Dale said 'I owe it *to the organization* to point out *to them* how bad and wrong this policy is.' This statement merely demonstrates that Dale wants to use *this litigation—not* his Assistant Scoutmaster position—to make a point, and that he wants to make the point to the BSA organization."

Chief Justice William Rehnquist delivered the opinion for the majority of the Supreme Court in a 5–4 decision for the BSA. "The forced inclusion of an unwanted person in a group infringes the group's freedom of expressive association if the presence of that person affects in a significant way the group's ability to advocate public or private viewpoints." Letting Dale remain a scout would, in the view of the BSA, imply that scouting accepted deviant sexual behavior. If, as Rehnquist believed and the BSA asserted, "the general mission of the Boy Scouts is clear: '[T]o instill values in young people,'" rather than to teach skills associated with surviving in the wilderness, then the code was the key to scouting. "The Boy Scouts seeks to instill these values by having its adult leaders spend time with the youth members, instructing and engaging them in activities like camping, archery, and fishing. During the time spent with the youth members, the scoutmasters and assistant scoutmasters inculcate them with the Boy Scouts' values—both expressly and by example." The activities were not the primary goal of scouting. They merely provided the occasion for the inculcation of certain attitudes.

Presumably, Dale's homosexually adversely affected his fellow scouts. The measure was subjective; that is, it lay not in his conduct as a scout, but in the BSA's fear that he would promote homosexuality among the boys in his care. Rehnquist accepted the subjectivity of "expressive values"; indeed, he made that subjectivity the centerpiece of his opinion. "Given that the Boy Scouts engages in expressive activity, we must determine whether the forced inclusion of Dale as an assistant scoutmaster would significantly affect the Boy Scouts' ability to advocate public or private viewpoints. This inquiry necessarily requires us first to explore, to a limited extent, the nature of the Boy Scouts' view of homosexuality."

The BSA's view of their own code, rather than the New Jersey Supreme Court's view (which Rehnquist's majority opinion overruled), controlled the outcome of the case. "The Scout Oath and Law do not expressly mention sexuality or sexual orientation. And the terms [in it] 'morally straight' and 'clean' are by no means self-defining. Different people would attribute to those terms very different meanings. For example, some people may believe that engaging in homosexual conduct is not at odds with being 'morally straight' and 'clean.' And others may believe that engaging in homosexual conduct is contrary to being 'morally straight' and 'clean.' The Boy Scouts says it falls within the latter category." The next step was again subjective rather than objective. "We must then determine whether Dale's presence as an assistant scoutmaster would significantly burden the Boy Scouts' desire to not 'promote homosexual conduct as a legitimate form of behavior.'" Rehnquist found that it did, because the BSA said that it did.

Chief Justice Rehnquist had adopted a subjective standard, that is, the party's own sense of wrong rather than the "rational person" test. In this, his constitutional jurisprudence was in accord with his own decision in *Meritor* (see the Mechelle Vinson case in the introduction). In sexual harassment, it is the complainant's subjective reading of the workplace, her feeling that it has become hostile, that matters to the court. Rehnquist accorded the same license to the BSA. It was their sense of what could happen, rather than any evidentiary material or proof they produced at trial, much less an objective standard that they could elucidate, that Dale was recruiting gays, or that his being gay had the effect of recruiting gays from the scouts. The subjective, in their mind's eye standard, borrowed from sexual harassment cases, found its way into this one.

Justice John Paul Stevens's dissent, joined by Justices David Souter, Ruth Bader Ginsburg, and Stephen G. Breyer, was disarmingly simple on its face but deeply complex in its implications. Values in America had changed from the time when the BSA code and oath were written. He assayed an objective standard: gays and lesbians were accepted members of the larger community of Americans. The BSA were out of step with those changes, and in expelling Dale, as well as in contesting the anti-discrimination suit, the Scouts were clinging to long out of date and offensive stereotypes of gay and lesbian behavior and views.

Stevens's reading of the Scouts' own texts demonstrated to him (objectively) that nothing in them referred to or barred or even hinted that homosexuality was an evil or was dangerous to the core values of scouting. The "BSA apparently did not consider it to be a serious possibility that a State might one day characterize the Scouts as a 'place of public accommodation' with a duty to open its membership to all qualified individuals." Instead of the subjectivity that he found in the Scouts' defense of its unwritten standards, Stevens wanted objectivity. "BSA's broad religious tolerance combined with its declaration that sexual matters are not its 'proper area' render its views on the issue equivocal at best and incoherent at worst. We have never held, however, that a group can throw together any mixture of contradictory positions and then invoke the right to associate to defend any one of those views. At a minimum, a group seeking to prevail over an antidiscrimination law must adhere to a clear and unequivocal view." Let the BSA come out in its oath and code and condemn gay and lesbian lifestyles—but then, in 2000, many states and municipalities were barring discrimination on those very grounds. The legal team for the Scouts knew this and thus preferred the subjective definition of freedom of association rather than an objective rejection of any but heterosexual males.

Although *Boy Scouts v. Dale* was not about defamation, the language of appellant and appellee was a coded up-to-date version of the very first sexual misconduct defamation cases in the seventeenth-century colonies. Everything had changed; nothing had changed. Everything had changed with the introduction of identity politics. In this newest version of personal honor, one's place in society derived not from the traditional categories of age, wealth, and place of origin, but was assured whatever one's own adoption of gender and ethnicity.

—◆—

Affronts to performed as opposed to biological identity have given rise to a new genre of litigation, denoted by the "hashtag" #MeToo. Gay pride, Black Lives Matter, transgender rights, and above all the effort to use the law to redress prior sexual harassment episodes will likely bring another hike in litigation rates. Every change in social and cultural mores that spurs conflict between the new and the old leads to lawsuits, and that is good thing. For litigation, rather than violence, is what makes the rule of law in America so vital.

Bibliographic Essay

THE SCHOLARLY AND PROFESSIONAL literature on litigation in America is vast, but space allotted for this bibliographic essay is limited. I have included all sources used in this book, along with some suggestions for further reading. Page numbers following the entries below are the sources of specific information in the text, in lieu of notes.

The primary (original, contemporary) sources in the book come from legal documents in manuscript or printed form. One should note that the law cases from the seventeenth and eighteenth century, whether printed or still in handwriting in record books, rarely include more than names, dates, and legal terms. The underlying evidence—the real-life stories of the parties—does not make it into this historical record, although some courthouses and archives retain the "file papers" lawyers gave to clerks and depositions taken out of court. In the end, one has snapshots of what was at stake.

The printed volumes of state and federal appeals courts "reporters'" (court-hired archivists/clerks) introduced at the end of the eighteenth century in the United States reveal somewhat more of the facts of the cases. Even these accounts were limited because the reporters were publishing what counsel submitted to the courts of appeals. The full accounts—what the parties said and the evidence they produced at the trial stage of the case—did not make it into the courts of appeals reports, although sometimes they survived in file papers at the courthouse. When newspapers began to cover trials, a fuller account in real time was preserved. This was true of the second half of the nineteenth century and after, because the papers sent a different kind of reporter, a journalist, to sit in the gallery and take notes. Finally, when recording devices in court became common, the most accurate record of trial court proceedings emerged. Even so, these almost exclusively concerned criminal trials. Civil suits rarely made the media. All of this means that the excerpts of cases in the pages above come primarily from reports of courts of appeals.

On law in America generally, see Peter Charles Hoffer, *A Nation of Laws: America's Imperfect Pursuit of Justice* (Lawrence: University Press of Kansas, 2010), xii–xiii and after; John C. Coffee Jr., *Entrepreneurial Lawyering: Its Rise, Fall, and Future* (Cambridge, MA: Harvard University Press, 2015), 7, 12–13, 59–60; and Lawrence Friedman, *A History of American Law*, 3rd ed. (New York: Simon and Schuster, 2007), as well as the articles in Christopher Tomlins and Michael Grossberg, *Cambridge History of Law in America*, 3 vols. (New York: Cambridge University Press, 2008). On lawyers and styles of lawyering, see Deborah L. Rhode, *Lawyers as Leaders* (New York: Oxford University Press, 2013), 12–22, and Robert D. Dinnerstein, "Client-Centered Counseling: Reappraisal and Refinement," *Arizona Law Review*, 32 (1990): 501–604, quotation on p. 501. On judging, see Richard Posner, *How Judges Think* (Cambridge, MA: Harvard University Press, 2010), 125–26, and Robert M. Cover, "Violence and the Word" *Yale Law Journal*, 95 (1986): 1601–30, quotation on p. 1601.

INTRODUCTION: LITIGATION AND HONOR

Federal case loads from http://www.uscourts.gov/statistics-reports/federal-judicial-caseload-statistics-2017. Although criticism of overloaded state and federal dockets was a staple of American court life going back at least as far as the Gilded Age, the literature on the "litigation explosion" exploded with the publication of Randy M. Mastro, "The Myth of the Litigation Explosion," *Fordham University Law Review*, 60 (1991): 199–216, quotation on p. 199, a response to the media embrace of Walter K. Olson, *The Litigation Explosion: What Happened When America Unleashed the Lawsuit* (New York: Dutton, 1991).

Figures in the text for the Upper Midwest in the nineteenth century are taken from J. Gordon Hylton, "The Wisconsin Lawyer in the Gilded Age: A Demographic Profile," *Wisconsin Law Review*, 1998, 765–76, figures on p. 768. Additional figures for civil litigation in U.S. trial courts appear in "Caseloads, Civil Cases, Private, 1873–1917," Federal Judicial Center, http://www.fjc.gov/history/courts/caseloads-civil-cases-private-1873–2017. Other statistical studies put the United States behind modern European nations; Koen Van Aeken, "Civil Court Litigation and Alternative Dispute Resolution," in *Comparative Law and Society*, ed. David S. Clark (Cheltenham, UK: Elgar, 2012), 221–23; Marc Galanter, "More Lawyers than People: The Global Multiplication of Legal Professionals," in *The Paradox of Professionalism: Lawyers and the Possibility of Justice*, ed. Scott L. Cummings (New York: Cambridge University Press, 2011), 69.

The notion that litigation is a matter of broken cultural understandings and feelings of harmed honor is the centerpiece of Peter Charles Hoffer, *Law and People in Colonial America*, 2nd enlarged ed. (Baltimore, MD: Johns Hopkins University Press, 1998), 76–85, from which the above pages are extracted. On Mechelle Vinson, see Meritor Savings Bank v. Vinson, 477 U.S. 57 (1986). The entire story is told in Augustus B. Cochran III, *Sexual Harassment and the Law: The Mechelle Vinson Case* (Lawrence: University Press of Kansas, 2004).

PART I: LITIGATION DEFINES A NATION

Quotation on revolutionary lawyers comes from Peter Charles Hoffer and Williamjames Hull Hoffer, *The Clamor of Lawyers: The American Revolution and Crisis in the Legal Profession* (Ithaca, NY: Cornell University Press, 2018), 152–53.

CHAPTER 1: DEFAMATION

For background on the first English settlers, see James Horn, *Adapting to a New World: English Society in the Seventeenth-Century Chesapeake* (Chapel Hill: University of North Carolina Press, 1994), 14, 16, and David Grayson Allen, *In English Ways: The Movement of Societies and the Transferal of English Local Law and Custom to Massachusetts Bay in the Seventeenth Century* (Chapel Hill: University of North Carolina Press, 1981), 4.

On defamation in America generally, see Norman L. Rosenberg, *Protecting the Best Men: An Interpretive History of the Law of Libel* (Chapel Hill: University of North Carolina Press, 1986).

For various cases involving defamation in the early colonies, see T. H. Breen, *Imagining the Past: East Hampton Histories* (Reading, MA:

Addison-Wesley, 1989), 114–37; Mary Beth Norton, *Founding Mothers and Fathers: Gendered Power and the Forming of American Society* (New York: Knopf, 1996), 30–34, 84, 211–14; Thomas L. Haskell, "Litigation and Social Status in Seventeenth-Century New Haven," *Journal of Legal Studies*, 7 (1978): 219–42, figures at pp. 229–30; Susan Juster, *Sacred Violence in Early America* (Philadelphia: University of Pennsylvania Press, 2016), 174; Clara Ann Bowler, "Carted Whores and White Shrouded Apologies: Slander in the County Courts of Seventeenth Century Virginia," *Virginia Magazine of History and Biography*, 85 (1977): 411–26; David Konig, *Law and Society in Early Massachusetts* (Chapel Hill: University of North Carolina Press, 1979), 81–82, 96–97, 184; Dale J. Schmitt, "Community and the Spoken Word: A Seventeenth-Century Case," *Journal of American Culture*, 13 (1990): 51–55; and Roger Thompson, "'Holy Watchfulness' and Communal Conformism: The Functions of Defamation in Early New England Communities," *New England Quarterly*, 56 (1983): 504–22.

The literature on witchcraft in the American colonies is vast, but a few of these books especially focus on the social context of accusations. Eunice Cole's case is taken from David D. Hall, *Witch-Hunting in Seventeenth Century New England: A Documentary History 1638–1692* (Boston: Northeastern University Press, 1991), 213–29. Other sources are John Demos, *Entertaining Satan: Witchcraft and the Culture of Early New England*, updated ed. (New York: Oxford University Press, 2004); Richard Godbeer, *The Devil's Dominion: Magic and Religion in Early New England* (New York: Cambridge University Press, 1992); Peter Charles Hoffer, *The Devil's Disciples: The Makers of the Salem Witchcraft Crisis* (Baltimore, MD: Johns Hopkins University Press, 1996); Mary Beth Norton, *In the Devil's Snare: The Salem Witchcraft Crisis of 1692* (New York: Knopf, 2002); and Elizabeth Reis, *Damned Women: Sinners and Witches in Colonial New England* (Ithaca, NY: Cornell University Press, 1997).

The clash between Byfield and Blagrove appears in Hoffer, *Law and People*, 86–87. On the politics of insult in revolutionary and early national America, see Joanne B. Freeman, *Affairs of Honor: National Politics in the New Republic* (New Haven, CT: Yale University Press, 2001); Christopher Grasso, *A Speaking Aristocracy: Transforming Public Discourse in Eighteenth Century Connecticut* (Chapel Hill: University of North Carolina Press, 1999); and Gary B. Nash, *The Unknown American Revolution:*

The Unruly Birth of Democracy and the Struggle to Create America (New York: Viking, 2005).

The *New York Times* case is New York Times v. Sullivan, 376 U.S. 254 (1964). The Sandy Hook parents' defamation case is Heslin v. Jones, District Court of Travis County, Texas, April 17, 2018, D-1-GN-18-001835. Song v. Levine is traced in Beth Landman and Julia Marsh, "Gyno Bad Reviews! Doc Sues Gal for Online Griping," *New York Post*, May 29, 2018, 17, and other online news sites.

CHAPTER 2: LAND-GRABBING AND MONEY-GRUBBING

On land and its value in the eighteenth-century colonies, see Allan Kulikoff, *From British Peasant to Colonial American Farmers* (Chapel Hill: University of North Carolina Press, 2000), 127–37; Claire Priest, "Law and Commerce, 1580–1815," in *The Cambridge History of Law in America*, ed. Michael Grossberg and Christopher Tomlins, vol. 1, *Early America* (New York: Cambridge University Press, 2008), 400–457; Lawrence Friedman, *The History of Law in America*, rev. ed. (New York: Simon and Schuster, 2005), 27–28; and William Cronon, *Changes in the Land, Indians, Colonists, and the Ecology of New England* (New York: Hill and Wang, 1983), 54–82.

On lawyering in early America, see Hoffer, *Law and People*, 44–46, and Anton-Herman Chroust, "The Legal Profession in Colonial America, Part I," *Notre Dame Lawyer*, 33 (1957): 51–91; Part II, ibid., 33 (1958): 51–71; Part III, ibid., 34 (1958): 44–64. Christine Heyrman writes about towns in *Commerce and Culture: The Maritime Communities of Colonial Massachusetts, 1690–1750* (New York: Norton, 1984), 74.

The long-running and sometimes violent Elizabethtown land disputes are the subject of Brendan McConville, *These Daring Disturbers of the Public Peace: The Struggle for Property and Power in Early New Jersey* (Ithaca, NY: Cornell University Press, 1999), 107–201; Thomas L. Purvis, "Origins and Patterns of Agrarian Unrest in New Jersey, 1735 to 1754," *William and Mary Quarterly*, 3rd ser., 39 (1982): 600–627; and Peter O. Wacker, *Land and People: A Cultural Geography of Preindustrial New Jersey Origins and Settlement Patterns* (New Brunswick, NJ: Rutgers University Press, 1975), 331–409.

On the socioeconomic status of the New Jersey colony's assembly, a group reflecting both proprietary and anti-proprietary forces, see Thomas L. Purvis, "'High-Born, Long-Recorded Families': Social Origins of New Jersey Assemblymen, 1703 to 1776," *William and Mary Quarterly*, 3rd ser., 37 (1980): 592–615. On "rough musick," see the essays in William Pencak, Matthew Dennis, and Simon P. Newman, eds., *Riot and Revelry in Early America* (University Park: Pennsylvania State University Press, 2002). For another episode of crowd-enabling jailbreak, see Marjoliene Kars, *Breaking Loose Together: The Regulator Rebellion in Pre-Revolutionary North Carolina* (Chapel Hill: University of North Carolina Press, 2002).

The notion of proto-political parties in the middle colonies is documented in Benjamin H. Newcomb's *Partisanship in the American Middle Colonies, 1700–1776* (Baton Rouge: Louisiana State University Press, 1995).

On the Wyoming Valley land disputes, see Paul Moyer, *Wild Yankees: The Struggle for Independence along Pennsylvania's Revolutionary Frontier* (Ithaca, NY: Cornell University Press, 2007), 175–95, and *Pennsylvania Archives: Documents relating to the Connecticut Settlement in the Wyoming Valley* (Harrisburg: State Printer, 1893), 123–24. On the California lands, see Paul Wallace Gates, "The California Land Act of 1851," *California Historical Quarterly*, 50 (1971): 395–430, and Christian G. Fitz, *Federal Justice in California: The Court of Ogden Hoffman* (Lincoln: University of Nebraska Press, 1991).

The Minnesota mortgage moratorium is the subject of Home Building and Loan Association v. Blaisdell, 290 U.S. 398 (1934). For the 2008 balloon mortgage crisis, see Andrew Ross Sorkin, *Too Big to Fail* (New York: Penguin, 2010), 89–90; for the New Jersey statistics, see State of New Jersey, Department of Banking and Insurance, www20.state.nj.us/DOBI_MRT4 CLSR/ForeclosureReports, and NewJersey.com, http://www.nj.com/data/ 2018/01/foreclosure_rates_in_all_21_counties_rankedddddd.html. Beard v. Ocwen Loan Servicing, Civ. 1-14- cv 1162 (M.D. Pa, 2015) is the case in the text.

CHAPTER 3: SLAVERY AND HONOR

On slavery, see, for example, Edward Baptist, *The Half Has Never Been Told: Slavery and the Making of American Capitalism* (New York: Basic

Books, 2014), 33–34, 125–26; Robert H. Gudmestad, *A Troublesome Commerce: The Transformation of the Interstate Slave Trade* (Baton Rouge: Louisiana State University Press, 2002), figures from p. 9 and appendix on pp. 210–11; Walter Johnson, *Soul by Soul: Life inside the Antebellum Slave Market* (Cambridge, MA: Harvard University Press, 2000); 104–5; Thomas D. Morris, *Southern Slavery and the Law, 1619–1860* (Chapel Hill: University of North Carolina Press, 2004), 65; and Adam Rothman, *Slave Country: American Expansion and the Origins of the Deep South* (Cambridge, MA: Harvard University Press, 2005), 49. Gabriel Thomas to his sister Anna, in 1845, is quoted in Scott Stephen, *Redeeming the Southern Family: Evangelical Women and Domestic Devotion in the Antebellum South* (Athens: University of Georgia Press, 2008), 78. James Oakes, *The Ruling Race: A History of American Slaveholders* (New York: Random House, 1982), 67, and Robert W. Fogel, *Without Consent of Contract: The Rise and Fall of American Slavery* (New York: Norton, 1989), 137, explore the relationship between slavery and law.

On shifty slave sales, see Andrew Fede, "Legal Protection for Slave Buyers in the U.S. South: A Caveat Concerning *Caveat Emptor*," *American Journal of Legal History*, 31 (1987): 322–58; Ariela J. Gross, *Double Character: Slavery and Mastery in the Antebellum Southern Courtroom* (Princeton, NJ: Princeton University Press, 2000), 62–66, and Calvin Schermerhorn, *The Business of Slavery and the Rise of American Capitalism, 1815–1860* (New Haven, CT: Yale University Press, 2015), 40. The concept of the missing slave name is the centerpiece of Diane J. Klein, "Naming and Framing the 'Subject' of Antebellum Slave Contracts: Introducing Julia, 'A Certain Negro Slave,' 'A Man', Joseph, Eliza, and Albert," *Rutgers Race and Law Review*, 9 (2007): 243–83.

Evidence on the stresses growing within slave society can be found in Alabama Reports, *Reports of Cases Argued and Determined in the Supreme Court of Alabama*, vols. 15–35 (Montgomery, various printers, 1849–1861), as explored in Daniell Reese Farnell Jr., "Alabama Courts and the Administration of Slavery" (PhD diss., Auburn University, 2007), 186–202, 223–29, and Jonathan D. Martin, *Divided Mastery: Slave Hiring in the Antebellum South* (Cambridge, MA: Harvard University Press, 2004), 110, 112, 118.

On honor, and the relation between slavery and the coming of the war, see Williamjames Hull Hoffer, *The Caning of Charles Sumner: Honor,*

Idealism, and the Origins of the Civil War (Baltimore, MD: Johns Hopkins University Press, 2010), 85–92; Jon L. Wakelyn, introduction to *Southern Pamphlets on Secession, November 1860–April 1861*, ed. Jon L. Wakelyn (Chapel Hill: University of North Carolina Press, 2000), xxvi; Gary L. Bunker, *From Rail-Splitter to Icon: Lincoln's Image in Illustrated Periodicals, 1860–1865* (Kent, OH: Kent State University Press, 2001), 170; Harold Holzer, "With Malice toward Both: Abraham Lincoln and Jefferson Davis in Caricature," in *Wars within a War: Controversy and Conflict over the American Civil War*, ed. Joan Waugh and Gary W. Gallagher (Chapel Hill: University of North Carolina Press, 2009), 109–36; Armistead L. Robinson, *Bitter Fruits of Bondage: The Demise of Slavery and the Collapse of the Confederacy, 1861–1865* (Charlottesville: University of Virginia Press, 2005), 63.

The slave cases are Atwood's Heirs v. Beck, Administrator, 21 Ala. 590 (1852), and Foster's Heirs v. Foster's Administratrix, *Reports of Cases Argued and Determined in the Supreme Court of the State of Louisiana*, March Term 1837, vol. 6: 253–58 (1854). For reparations, see Alfred Brophy, *Reparations: Pro and Con* (New York: Oxford University Press, 2006). The reparations cases are In Re African-American Descendants Litigation, 272 F. Supp. 2d 755 (N.D. Ill, 2003) (Norgle, J.) and In Re African-American Descendants Litigation, 471 F.3d 754 (7th Cir. 2006) (Posner, J.). On Judge Norgle, see "The Robing Room," www.therobingroom.com/Judge.aspx?ID=1196.

CHAPTER 4: FREE LABOR?

Abraham Lincoln, "Speech at Wisconsin State Fair, September 30, 1859," in *Collected Works of Abraham Lincoln*, ed. Roy P. Basler (New Brunswick, NJ: Rutgers University Press, 1953), 3:478; William Henry Seward, "Irrepressible Conflict" (speech, October 25, 1958, at Rochester, New York), http://www.nyhistory.com/central/conflict.htm. The speech was widely covered in northern newspapers: Walter Stahr, *Seward: Lincoln's Indispensable Man* (New York: Simon and Schuster, 2013), 175–76.

On the shift from servitude to contract labor, see Robert J. Steinfeld, *The Invention of Free Labor: The Employment Relation in English and American Law and Culture, 1350–1870* (Chapel Hill: University of North

Carolina Press, 1991), 172; David Montgomery, *Citizen Worker: The Experience of Workers in the United States with Democracy and the Free Market in the Nineteenth Century* (Cambridge: Cambridge University Press, 1993), 41–42 (the right to quit). For the Sean Wilentz quotation, see Sean Wilentz, *The Rise of American Democracy: Jefferson to Lincoln* (New York: Norton, 2005), 414.

On industrial accidents, see Morton J. Horwitz, *The Transformation of American Law, 1780–1860* (Cambridge, MA: Harvard University Press, 1977), and Peter J. Karsten, *Heart versus Head: Judge-Made Law in Nineteenth-Century America* (Chapel Hill: University of North Carolina Press, 1997). Horwitz believes that the free labor cases demonstrated a shift to conservative principles, while Karsten argues that the judges showed a romantic sentiment when it came to the weak and oppressed. On modern capitalism, see Thomas Piketty, with Arthur Goldhammer, *Capital in the Twenty-First Century* (Cambridge, MA: Harvard University Press, 2017).

The cases are Britton v. Turner, 6 N.H. 481 (1834) (Parker, J.); Commonwealth v. Hunt, 45 Mass. 111 (1842) (Shaw, C.J.); Farwell v. Boston and W.R.R. Corp., 45 Mass 49 (1842) (Shaw, C.J.); Cleveland RR v. Keary, 3 Ohio St. 201 (1854) (Ranney, J) (Warden, J.); and Cruz v. U.S. 219 F. Supp. 2d 1027 (N.D. Cal, 2002) (Breyer, J.); Janus v. American Federation of State, County, and Municipal Workers, Council 31, U.S. Supreme Court, no 16-1466, oral argument, February 26, 2018, p. 27. Parker's decision is critiqued in Clarence D. Ashley, "Britton v. Turner," *Yale Law Journal*, 24 (1914–1915): 544–50, and defended by Herbert D. Laube, "Defaulting Employee—Britton v. Turner Re-viewed," *Pennsylvania Law Review*, 83 (1934–1935): 825–52.

PART II: LITIGATION DEFENDS DEMOCRACY

On African American victories in Jim Crow courts, see Melissa Milewski, *Litigating across the Color Line: Civil Cases between Black and White Southerners from the End of Slavery to Civil Rights* (New York: Oxford University Press, 2018).

Statistics on cases in Reconstruction from Elizabeth Lee Thompson, *The Reconstruction of Southern Debtors: Bankruptcy after the Civil War*

(Athens, GA: University of Georgia Press, 2004), 95, 143; William M. Wiecek, "The Reconstruction of Federal Judicial Power, 1863–1875," *American Journal of Legal History*, 13 (1969): 333–59, quotation from p. 334; Bankruptcy petitions, D.C.N.D. Ga, 1867–1868, National Archives and Records Administration (NARA) Atlanta; Bankruptcy Dockets, D.C.E.D. Mo., June 1867–June 1868, NARA Kansas City; Docket Books, Circuit Court, District of Massachusetts, 1857–1870, NARA Boston. For statistics on state cases, see Peter Charles Hoffer, Williamjames Hull Hoffer, and N. E. H. Hull, *The Federal Courts: An Essential History* (New York: Oxford University Press, 2016), 174–77.

CHAPTER 5: SWINDLES AND SWINDLERS

A defense of railroad insolvency receiverships is James W. Ely Jr., *Railroads and American Law* (Lawrence: University Press of Kansas, 2001), 177–86. Richard White has traced the rise of the railroads in somewhat unsympathetic manner in *Railroaded: The Transcontinentals and the Making of Modern America* (New York: Norton, 2011), 3–5, 80–82, 186–87. See also William G. Thomas, *Lawyering for the Railroad: Business, Law, and Power in the New South* (Baton Rouge: Louisiana State University Press, 1999), 37–38; Andrew B. Arnold, *Fueling the Gilded Age: Railroads, Miners, and Disorder in the Pennsylvania Coal Country* (New York: New York University Press, 2014), 35–62. Jonathan Levy, *Freaks of Fortune: The Emerging World of Risk and Capitalism in America* (Cambridge, MA: Harvard University Press, 2012), 117, 138–39, also focuses on the follies of some of the rail barons. On the Pensy, see Albert J. Churella, *The Pennsylvania Railroad*, vol. 1, *Building an Empire, 1846–1917* (Philadelphia: University of Pennsylvania Press, 2013), 326–28. The strikes are described in Michael Bellesiles, *1877: America's Year of Living Violently* (New York: New Press, 2010), 145–54.

The fraud case is Heath v. Erie Railroad, 11 F. Cas. 976 (1871) (Blatchford, J.). On bankruptcy, the case is Van Siclen v. Bartol, 95 F. 793 (E.D. Pa, 1899) (McPherson, J.). On the judge, see "In Memory of John Bayard McPherson," *Princeton Alumni Weekly*, 19 (1916): 521. Northern Securities Co. v. United States, 193 U.S. 197 (1904), is the foremost antitrust case of the early Sherman Act period. Quotations from Justices White, Harlan, and Holmes appear in the case report. Later cases include Regional Rail Reorganization Act Cases, 419 U.S. 102 (1974).

Bankruptcy law is now almost entirely administrative in nature after the 1898 and 1935 acts provided for separate courts. (Earlier federal acts were of short duration.) In the 1880s and 1890s, it was the subject of various judges' and courts' rulings. A handy guide to bankruptcy law is David Epstein, *Bankruptcy and Related Law* (St. Paul, MN: West, 2005). On Enron, see Bethany McLean and Peter Elkind, *The Smartest Guys in the Room: The Amazing Rise and Scandalous Fall of Enron* (New York: Penguin, 2013).

CHAPTER 6: DIVORCE

On the persistence of states' rights doctrines in divorce law, see In Re Burris, 136 U.S. 586 (1890), and the discussion in Jill Elaine Hasday, *Family Law Reimagined* (Cambridge, MA: Harvard University Press, 2014), 21–25 and after.

On marriage law's transition from coverture to individual rights, see Richard H. Chused, *Private Acts in Public Places: A Social History of Divorce in the Formative Era of American Family Law* (Philadelphia: University of Pennsylvania Press, 1994), 132–58; Hendrik Hartog, *Man and Wife in America: A History* (Cambridge, MA: Harvard University Press, 2000), 287–314; Nancy F. Cott, *Public Vows: A History of Marriage and the Nation* (Cambridge, MA: Harvard University Press, 2000), 132–78; Norma Basch, *Framing American Divorce: From the Revolutionary Generation to the Victorians* (Berkeley: University of California Press, 1999), 187–93; Elaine Tyler May, *Great Expectations: Marriage and Divorce in Post-Victorian America* (Chicago: University of Chicago Press, 1980), 49–50; and William E. Nelson, *The Legalist Reformation: Law, Politics and Ideology in New York, 1920–1980* (Chapel Hill: University of North Carolina Press, 2000), 48–50.

The divorce rates and summaries of the reasons for the Progressive Era shift in values is the subject of S. L. Braver and M. E. Lamb, "Divorce in Historical Perspective," in *Handbook of Marriage and the Family*, ed. Gary W. Peterson and Kevin R. Bush, 3rd ed. (New York: Springer, 2013), 488–92; William O'Neill, *Divorce in the Progressive Era* (New Haven, CT:

Yale University Press, 1967); and Lawrence M. Friedman and Robert C. Percival, "Who Sues for Divorce: From Fault through Fiction to Freedom," *Journal of Legal Studies*, 5 (1976): 61–82.

New York divorce law is treated in William Kuby, *Conjugal Misconduct: Defying Marriage Law in the Twentieth-Century United States* (Cambridge: Cambridge University Press, 2018), 168; Joseph A. Ranney, "Anglicans, Merchants and Feminists: A Comparative Study of the Evolution of Married Women's Rights in Virginia, New York, and Wisconsin," *William and Mary Journal of Women and the Law*, 6 (2000): 493–559, and Isabel Marcus, "Locked In and Locked Out: Reflections on the History of Divorce Reform in New York State," *Buffalo Law Review*, 37 (1988): 375–483.

The featured cases are Haddock v. Haddock, 201 U.S. 562 (1906); Hubbard v. Hubbard, 228 N.Y. 81 (1920); and Rhinelander v. Rhinelander, 219 N.Y. 548 (App. Div. 1927).

Scholars find the Rhinelander-Jones divorce case especially important. See Heidi Ardizzone and Earl Lewis, *Love on Trial: An American Scandal in Black and White* (New York: Norton, 2002); Angela Onwauchi-Willig, "A Beautiful Lie: Exploring *Rhinelander v. Rhinelander* as a Formative Lesson on Race, Identity, Marriage, and Family," *University of California Law Review*, 95 (2007): 2393–458; and Elizabeth M. Smith-Pryor, *Property Rites: The Rhinelander Trial, Passing, and the Protection of Whiteness* (Chapel Hill: University of North Carolina Press, 2009). The case was covered extensively in the *New York Times*, from which many of the quotations above are taken.

For more on Judge Lazansky, see Applegate v. Applegate, 118 Misc. 359 (New York Supreme Court, Special Term, 1922) (Lazansky, J.). For information on interracial marriage law, see Peter Wallenstein, *Tell the Court I Love My Wife: Race, Marriage, and Law—an American History* (New York: Palgrave, 2002).

On no-fault divorce, see Lynn D. Wardle, "No-Fault Divorce and the Divorce Conundrum," *Brigham Young University Law Review*, 1991, 79–142; Peter Nash Swisher, "Reassessing Fault Factors in No-Fault Divorce," *Family Law Quarterly*, 31 (1997): 269–320; and Lenore J. Weitzman, *The Divorce Revolution: The Unexpected Social and Economic Consequences for Women and Children in America* (New York: Free Press, 1985), 323 and after. The statistical analysis at the end of the book is profoundly flawed, but the author's conclusions are still worth considering.

CHAPTER 7: CIVIL RIGHTS AND WRONGS

The literature on civil rights litigation is traced in Peter Charles Hoffer, *The Search for Justice: Lawyers in the Civil Rights Revolution, 1950–1975* (Chicago: University of Chicago Press, 2019), from which some of the materials in this chapter are adapted, and Michael J. Klarman, *From Jim Crow to Civil Rights: The Supreme Court and the Struggle for Racial Equality* (New York: Oxford University Press, 2004).

On *Sweatt*, see Gary M. Lavergne, *Before Brown: Heman Marion Sweatt, Thurgood Marshall, and the Long Road to Justice* (Austin: University of Texas Press, 2010), 125–28, 130, 132, 135, 245–47. On Briggs, see Robert Mickey, *Paths Out of Dixie: The Democratization of Authoritarian Enclaves in America's Deep South, 1944–1972* (Princeton, NJ: Princeton University Press, 2015), 472n4; Richard Kluger, *Simple Justice: The History of Brown v. Board of Education and America's Struggle for Equality* (New York: Knopf, 1975), 9–10, 23, 141–44; John J. Parker, "The Federal Jurisdiction and Recent Attacks upon It" (address to the Georgia Bar Association, June 8, 1932), *American Bar Association Journal*, 18 (1932): 433–79, quote from p. 433. The failed nomination of Parker is discussed in Stephen W. Stathis, *Landmark Debates in Congress* (Washington, DC: CQ Press, 2008), 303–10. On Davis, see William Henry Harbaugh, *Lawyer's Lawyer: John W. Davis* (New York: Oxford University Press, 1973), 221–68, 399–420.

The cases are Sweatt v. Painter, 126 Circuit Court, Travis County No. 74,945, May, 1946, *Herman [i.e. Heman] Marion Sweatt, Petitioners vs. Theophilis Shickel Painter, et al.: [In the] Supreme Court of the United States* (Washington, DC: Judd & Detweiler, printers, 1948–1949), 1:5–8; Sweatt v. Painter, 210 S.W. 2d. 242, 243 (Civ. Div. Ct. of Appeals, Texas) (1948) (McClendon, C.J.); Sweatt v. Painter, 339 U.S. 369 (1950); Briggs v. Elliott, 98 F. Supp. 529, 531, 532 (S.C.E.D., 1951) (Parker, J.); Briggs v. Elliott, 103 F. Supp. 920, 922 (S.C.E.D., 1952) (Parker, J.); and Brown v. Board of Education, 347 U.S. 483 (1954) (Warren, C.J.).

On the public accommodations cases, see Christopher Schmidt, *The Sit-Ins* (Chicago: University of Chicago Press, 2018); Richard C. Cortner, *Civil Rights and Public Accommodations: The Heart of Atlanta Motel and McClung Cases* (Lawrence: University Press of Kansas, 2001), 39–62; and Lizabeth Cohen, *A Consumers' Republic: The Politics of Consumption in Postwar America* (New York: Knopf, 2003), 166–92. The cases are Burton v. Wilmington

Parking Authority, 365 U.S. 715 (1961); Boynton v. Virginia, 364 U.S. 454 (1960); Peterson v. Greenville, 373 U.S. 244 (1963); Bell v. Maryland, 378 U.S. 226 (1964); and Heart of Atlanta v. U.S., 379 U.S. 241 (1964).

Civil rights suits statistics change every year, but see Bureau of Justice Statistics, Department of Justice, "Civil Rights Complaints in U.S. District Courts, 1990–2006," https://www.bjs.gov/content/pub/pdf/crcusdc06.pdf.), *Newsweek*, May 4, 2016, http://www.newsweek.com/department-education-office-civil-rights-report-455752.

CHAPTER 8: TORT LITIGATION

On the ALI's reform mission, see N. E. H. Hull, "Restatement and Reform: A New Perspective on the Origins of the American Law Institute" and "Back to the 'Future of the Institute': William Draper Lewis's Vision of the ALI's Mission during Its First Twenty-Five Years and the Implications for the Institute's Seventy-Fifth Anniversary," in *American Law Institute 75th Anniversary Special Issue* (Philadelphia: American Law Institute, 1998), 49–104, 105–71. On products liability and tort law, see G. Edward White, *Tort Law in America: An Intellectual History*, enlarged ed. (New York: Oxford University Press, 2003), 149.

On the strict liability standard for mass-produced consumer goods injuries, see William Lloyd Prosser, "The Assault on the Citadel," *Yale Law Journal*, 69 (1960): 1099–148, and "The Fall of the Citadel," *Minnesota Law Review*, 50 (1966): 791–848, and ALI, *Restatement of Torts, Second* (Philadelphia: ALI, 1965), 2: sec. 402a.

On class actions, see Martin H. Redish, *Wholesale Justice: Constitutional Democracy and the Problem of the Class Action Lawsuit* (Palo Alto, CA: Stanford University Press, 2009); Robert H. Klonoff, *Class Actions and Other Multi-Party Litigation*, 4th ed. (St. Paul, MN: West, 2012); and Peter H. Schuck, *Agent Orange on Trial: Mass Toxic Disasters in the Courts*, rev. ed. (Cambridge, MA: Harvard University Press, 1987).

The IUD cases are the focus of Richard B. Sobol, *Bending the Law: The Story of the Dalkon Shield Bankruptcy* (Chicago: University of Chicago Press, 1993), 15–45 and after. Similar problems of proving individuals belonged in the class, that an individual's malady was caused by the product, and that the fund was sufficient to pay off the damages plagued the Agent Orange cases: Schuck, *Agent Orange*, 7 (Agent Orange first mass toxic suit certified as class action), 46 (novelty of the trust fund relief idea), 300–301 (problems on appeal with proximate cause).

The products liability cases are MacPherson v. Buick Motor Co., 217 N.Y. 382, 111 N.E. 1050 (1916) (Cardozo, J.); Escola v. Coca-Cola Bottling Co., 24 Cal. 2d 453, 462 (1948) (Traynor, J.); Henningsen v. Bloomfield Motors, Inc., 32 N.J. 358 (1960) (Francis, J.); and Greenman v. Yuba Power Company, 59 C2d 57 (1963) (Traynor, C.J.). The IUD cases are In Re A.H. Robins Co., 880 F. 2d. 709, 711, 712, 724, 740 (4th Cir. 1989) (Russell, J.). The Dalkon Shield case was certified in 1981 and decertified in 1982, and finally certified, tried, and settled in In Re A.H. Robins Co, 880 F. 2d. 709 (4th Cir. 1989). For more on tort law, see Thomas F. Burke, *Lawyers, Lawsuits, and Legal Rights: The Battle over Litigation in American Society* (Berkeley: University of California Press, 2002), and Virginia Nolan, *Understanding Enterprise Liability: Rethinking Tort Liability for the Twenty-First Century* (Philadelphia: Temple University Press, 2011).

The Federal Rules of Civil Procedure, with Forms, December 1, 2014, printed for the use of the Judiciary Committee of the House of Representatives (Washington, DC: U.S. Printing Office, 2014), is a 170-page document, in which pp. 26–29 trace the evolution of Rule 23 for class actions. On modern rules of procedure for federal courts, see, for example, Federal Judicial Center, *Manual for Complex Litigation*, 4th ed. (St. Paul, MN: Thompson, West, 2004). Class action law does not provide for the "opt-in"—that would be joinder or interpleader. Class Action Fairness Act of 2005, 119 Stat 4. Still, the absence of the opt-in, along with the difficulties of opt-out, concern some students of class action. See, for example, Redish, *Wholesale Justice*, 126, 218–19, 231, and Emery G. Lee and Thomas E. Willging, "The Impact of the Class Action Fairness Act of 2005 on the Federal Courts" (Fourth Interim Report to the Judicial Conference Advisory Committee on Civil Rules, Federal Judicial Center, April 2008), figures 1–3, pp. 18–20.

CONCLUSION: THE VALUE OF LITIGATION IN AMERICA

On lumping it, see David M. Engel, *The Myth of the Litigious Society: Why We Don't Sue* (Chicago: University of Chicago Press, 2016), 23, as long as one is insured and one's insurance company pays immediate costs. Policyholders "cede" control of litigation to their insurers' lawyers, and insurers pay out over 90 percent of all liability claims. Richard Lewis, "Insurance and the Tort System," *Legal Studies*, 25 (2006): 85–116, quotation at p. 89.

On James Dale's fight to be a scout leader, see Richard J. Ellis, *Judging the Boy Scouts of America: Gay Rights, Freedom of Association, and the Dale Case* (Lawrence: University Press of Kansas, 2014). Chief Justice Rehnquist's and Justice Stevens's opinions can be found in Boy Scouts of America v. Dale, 530 U.S. 640 (2000).

Index